JLA ★ EARTH ★ 2

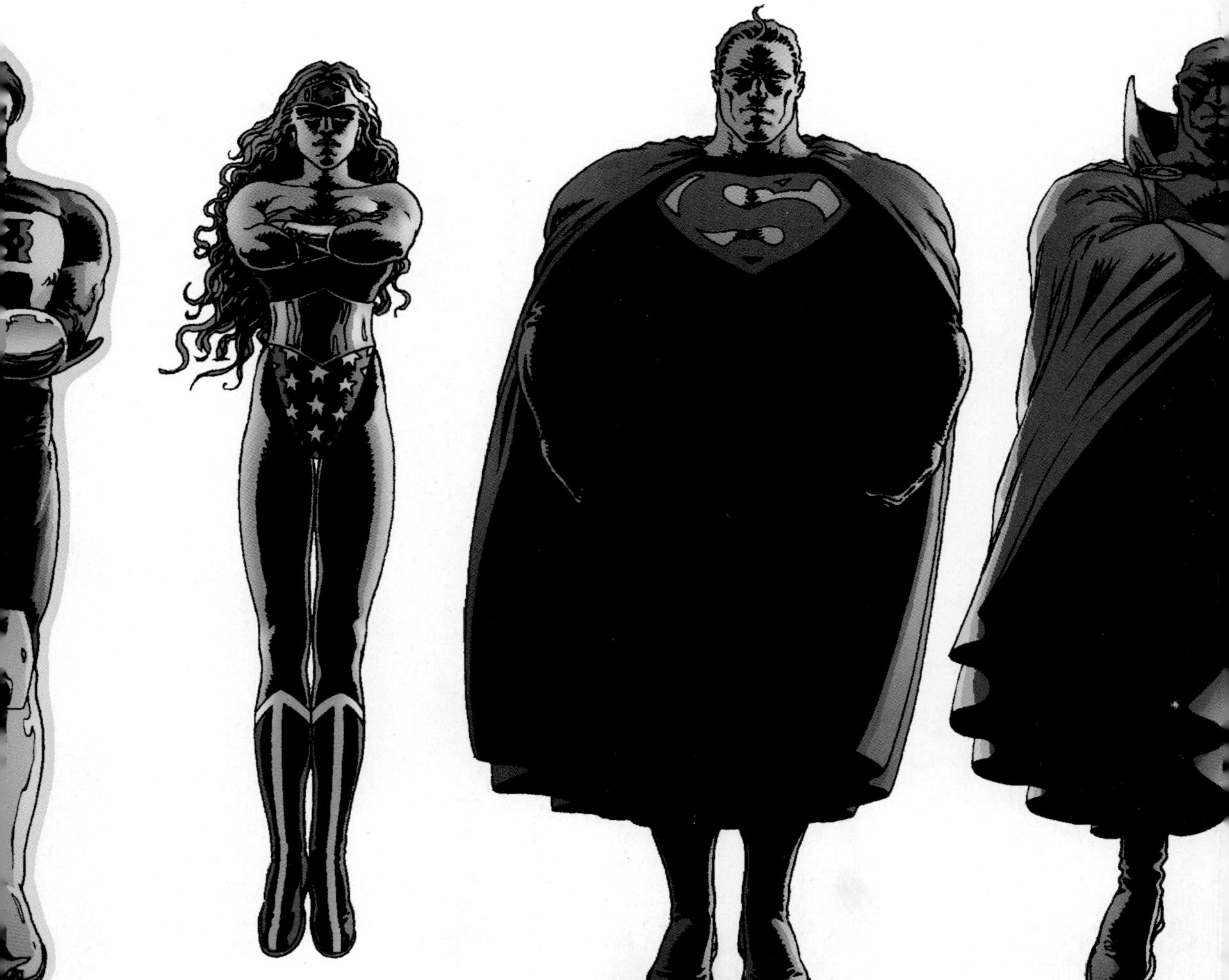

WRITER
Grant Morrison

ARTIST
Frank Quitely

LETTERER
Kenny Lopez

COLOR AND SEPARATIONS
Laura Martin
WildStorm FX

Superman created by Jerry Siegel and Joe Shuster.
By special arrangement with the Jerry Siegel family.

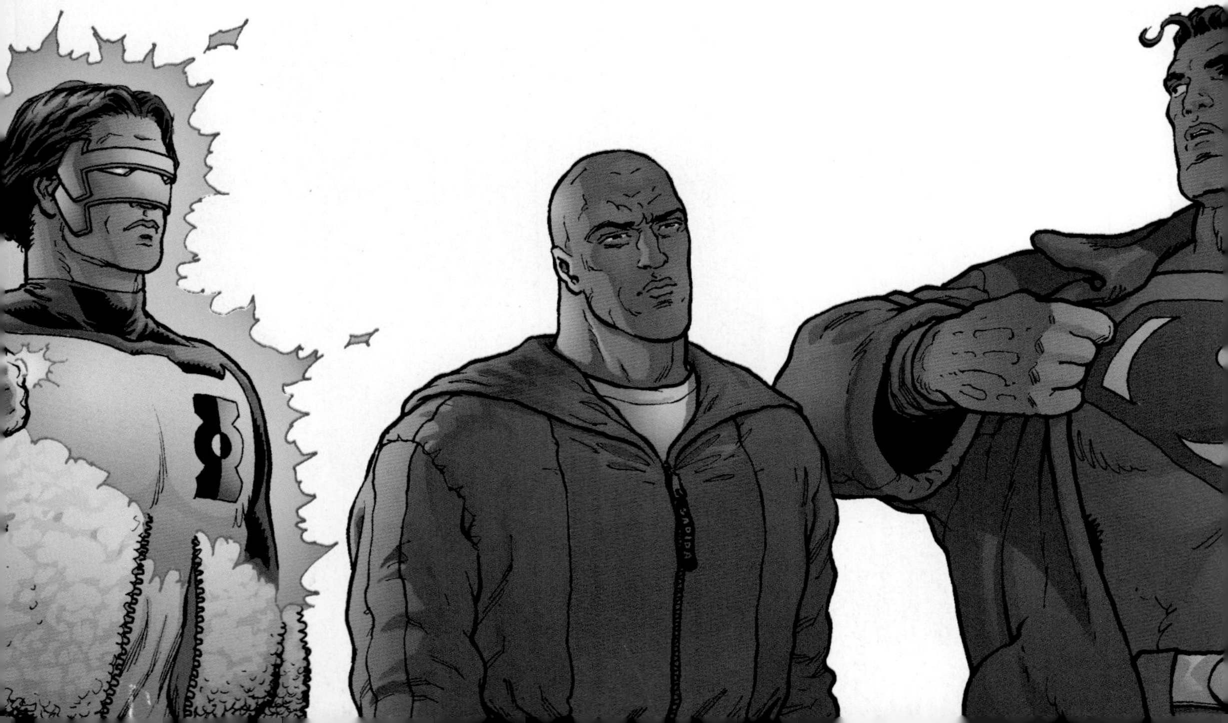

JLA ★ EARTH ★ 2

DAN RASPLER EDITOR – ORIGINAL SERIES

TONY BEDARD ASSOCIATE EDITOR – ORIGINAL SERIES

PETER HAMBOUSSI EDITOR

ROBBIN BROSTERMAN DESIGN DIRECTOR – BOOKS

DAMIAN RYLAND PUBLICATION DESIGN

BOB HARRAS SENIOR VP – EDITOR-IN-CHIEF, DC COMICS

DIANE NELSON PRESIDENT

DAN DIDIO AND JIM LEE CO-PUBLISHERS

GEOFF JOHNS CHIEF CREATIVE OFFICER

AMIT DESAI SENIOR VP – MARKETING AND FRANCHISE MANAGEMENT

AMY GENKINS SENIOR VP – BUSINESS AND LEGAL AFFAIRS

NAIRI GARDINER SENIOR VP – FINANCE

JEFF BOISON VP – PUBLISHING PLANNING

MARK CHIARELLO VP – ART DIRECTION AND DESIGN

JOHN CUNNINGHAM VP – MARKETING

TERRI CUNNINGHAM VP – EDITORIAL ADMINISTRATION

LARRY GANEM VP – TALENT RELATIONS AND SERVICES

ALISON GILL SENIOR VP – MANUFACTURING AND OPERATIONS

HANK KANALZ SENIOR VP – VERTIGO AND INTEGRATED PUBLISHING

JAY KOGAN VP – BUSINESS AND LEGAL AFFAIRS, PUBLISHING

JACK MAHAN VP – BUSINESS AFFAIRS, TALENT

NICK NAPOLITANO VP – MANUFACTURING ADMINISTRATION

SUE POHJA VP – BOOK SALES

FRED RUIZ VP – MANUFACTURING OPERATIONS

COURTNEY SIMMONS SENIOR VP – PUBLICITY

BOB WAYNE SENIOR VP – SALES

JLA EARTH 2

Published by DC Comics. Copyright © 2013 DC Comics. All Rights Reserved.

Originally published as JLA EARTH 2 Copyright © 2000 DC Comics.
All Rights Reserved. All characters, their distinctive likenesses and related elements
featured in this publication are trademarks of DC Comics. The stories, characters
and incidents featured in this publication are entirely fictional. DC Comics does not
read or accept unsolicited ideas, stories or artwork.

DC Comics, 1700 Broadway, New York, NY 10019
A Warner Bros. Entertainment Company.
Printed by RR Donnelley, Salem, VA, USA. 8/1/14. First Printing.
ISBN: 978-1-4012-5135-2

Library of Congress Cataloging-in-Publication Data

Morrison, Grant, author.
JLA Earth 2, the deluxe edition / Grant Morrison, Frank Quitely.
pages cm
"Originally published JLA Earth 2."
ISBN 978-1-4012-5135-2
1. Graphic novels. I. Quitely, Frank, 1968- illustrator. II. Title.
PN6728.J87M6733 2013
741.5'973—dc23
                                    2013020540

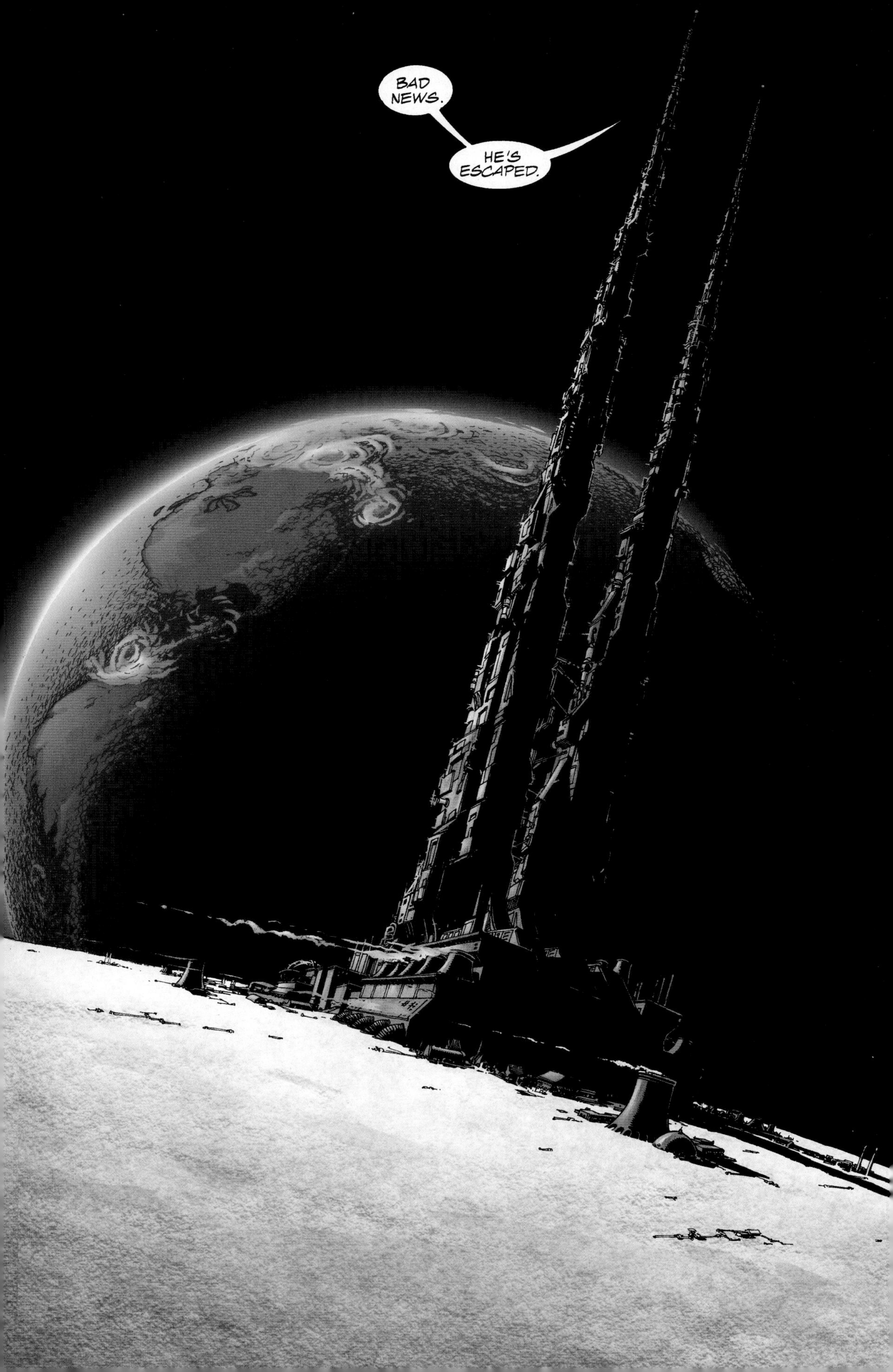
BAD NEWS.
HE'S ESCAPED.

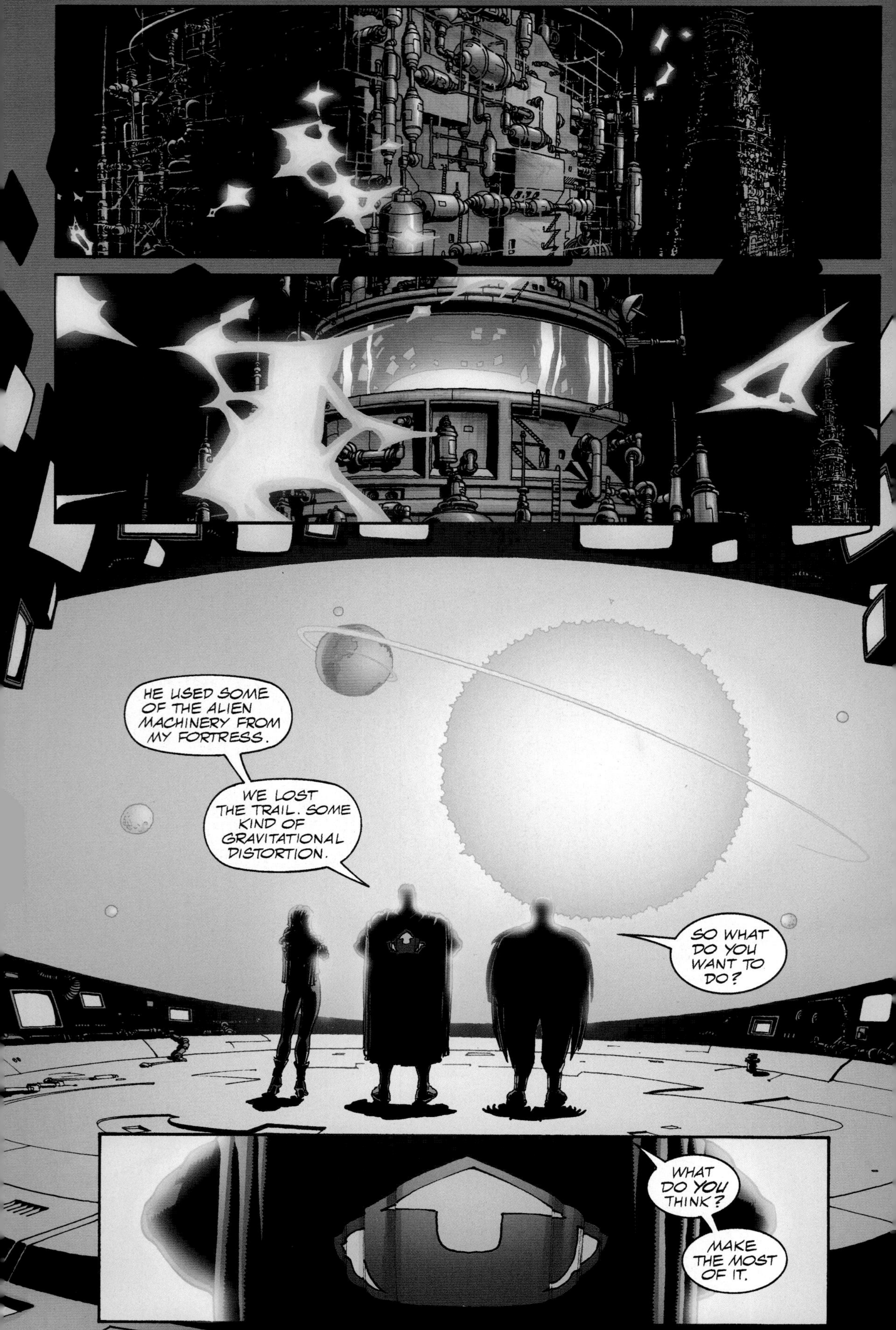

HE USED SOME OF THE ALIEN MACHINERY FROM MY FORTRESS.
WE LOST THE TRAIL. SOME KIND OF GRAVITATIONAL DISTORTION.
SO WHAT DO YOU WANT TO DO?
WHAT DO YOU THINK?
MAKE THE MOST OF IT.

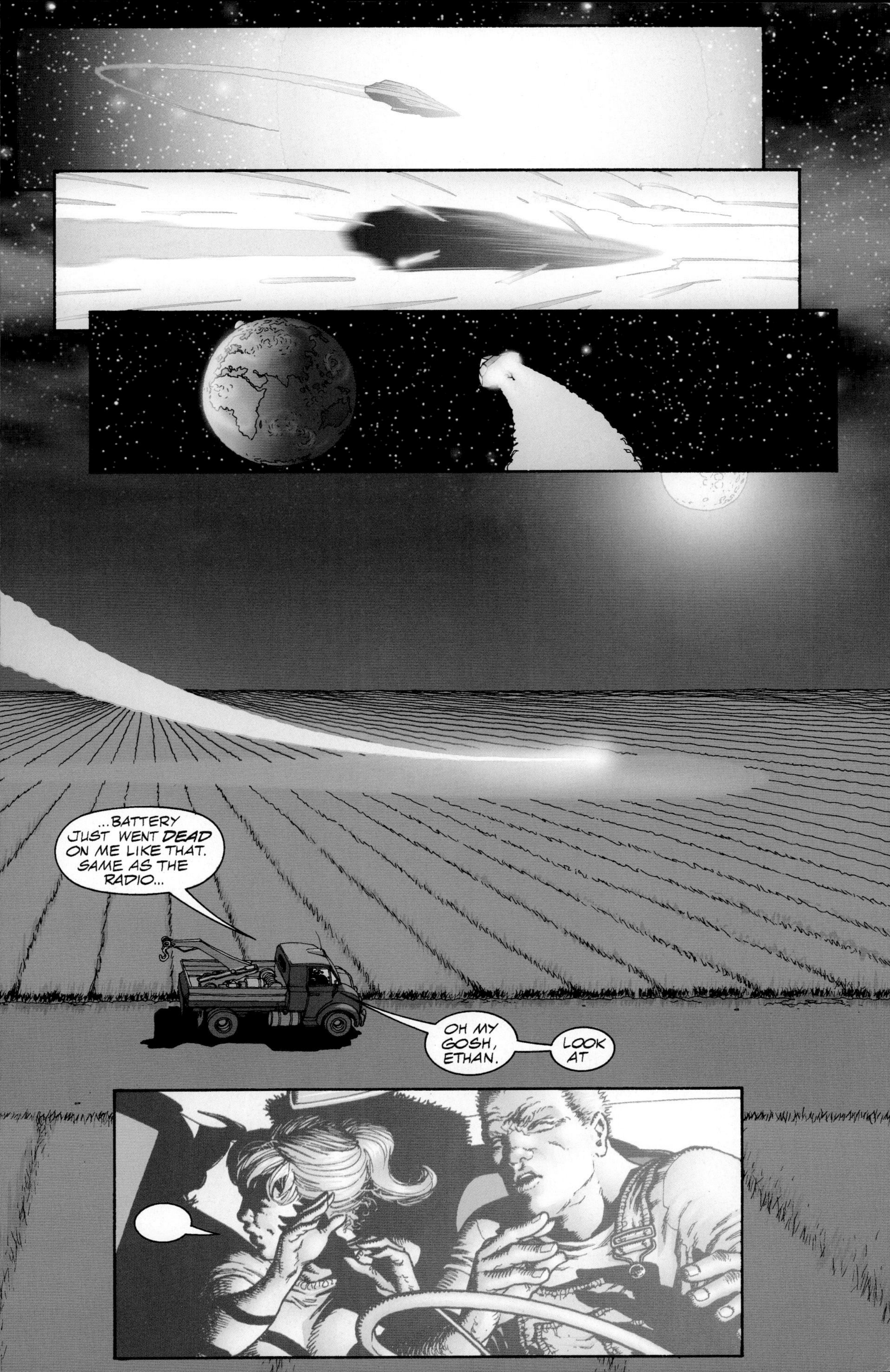
...BATTERY JUST WENT DEAD ON ME LIKE THAT. SAME AS THE RADIO...
OH MY GOSH, ETHAN.
LOOK AT

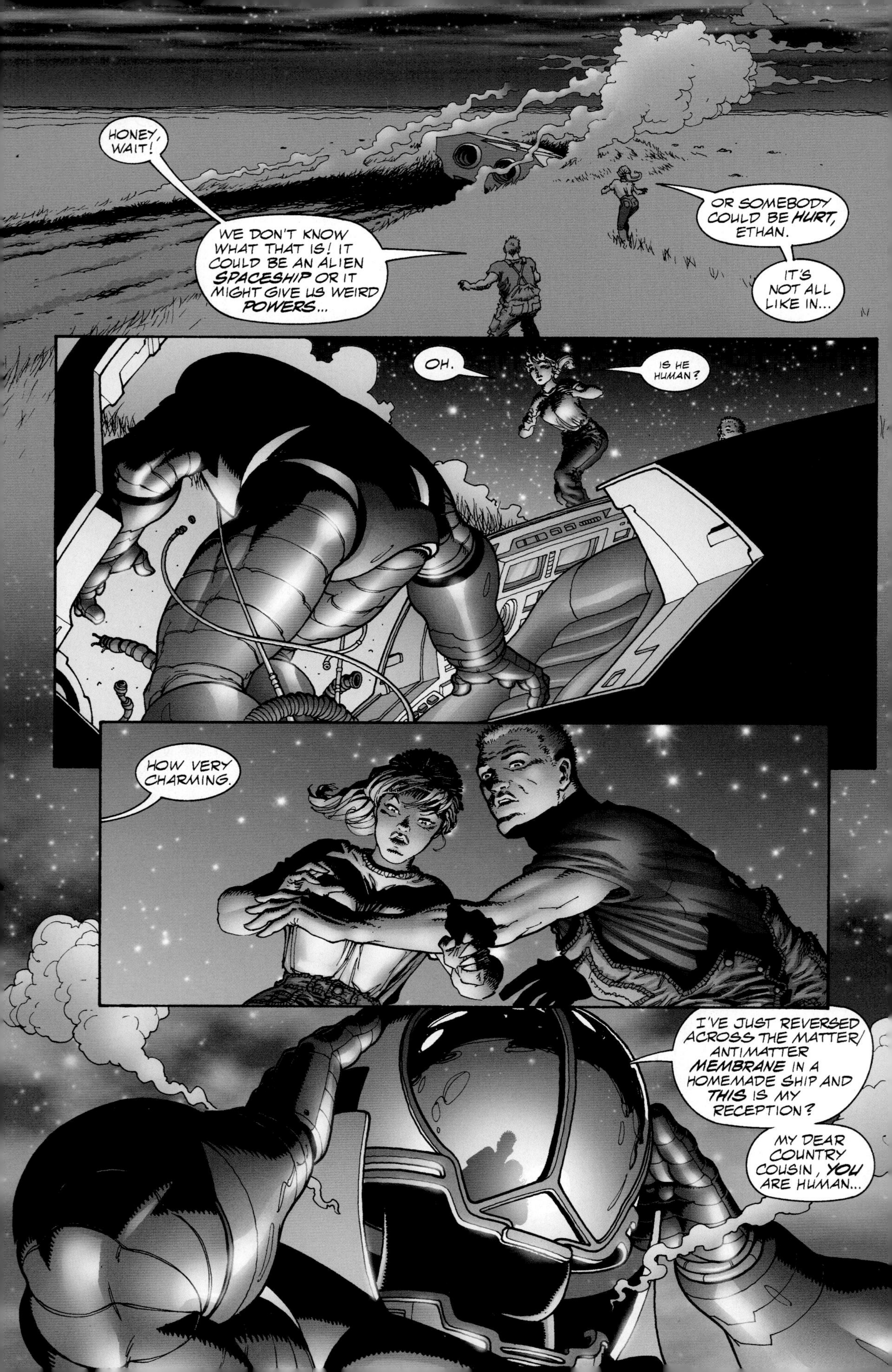
HONEY, WAIT!
WE DON'T KNOW WHAT THAT IS! IT COULD BE AN ALIEN SPACESHIP OR IT MIGHT GIVE US WEIRD POWERS...
OR SOMEBODY COULD BE HURT, ETHAN.
IT'S NOT ALL LIKE IN...
OH.
IS HE HUMAN?
HOW VERY CHARMING.
I'VE JUST REVERSED ACROSS THE MATTER/ ANTIMATTER MEMBRANE IN A HOMEMADE SHIP AND THIS IS MY RECEPTION?
MY DEAR COUNTRY COUSIN, YOU ARE HUMAN...

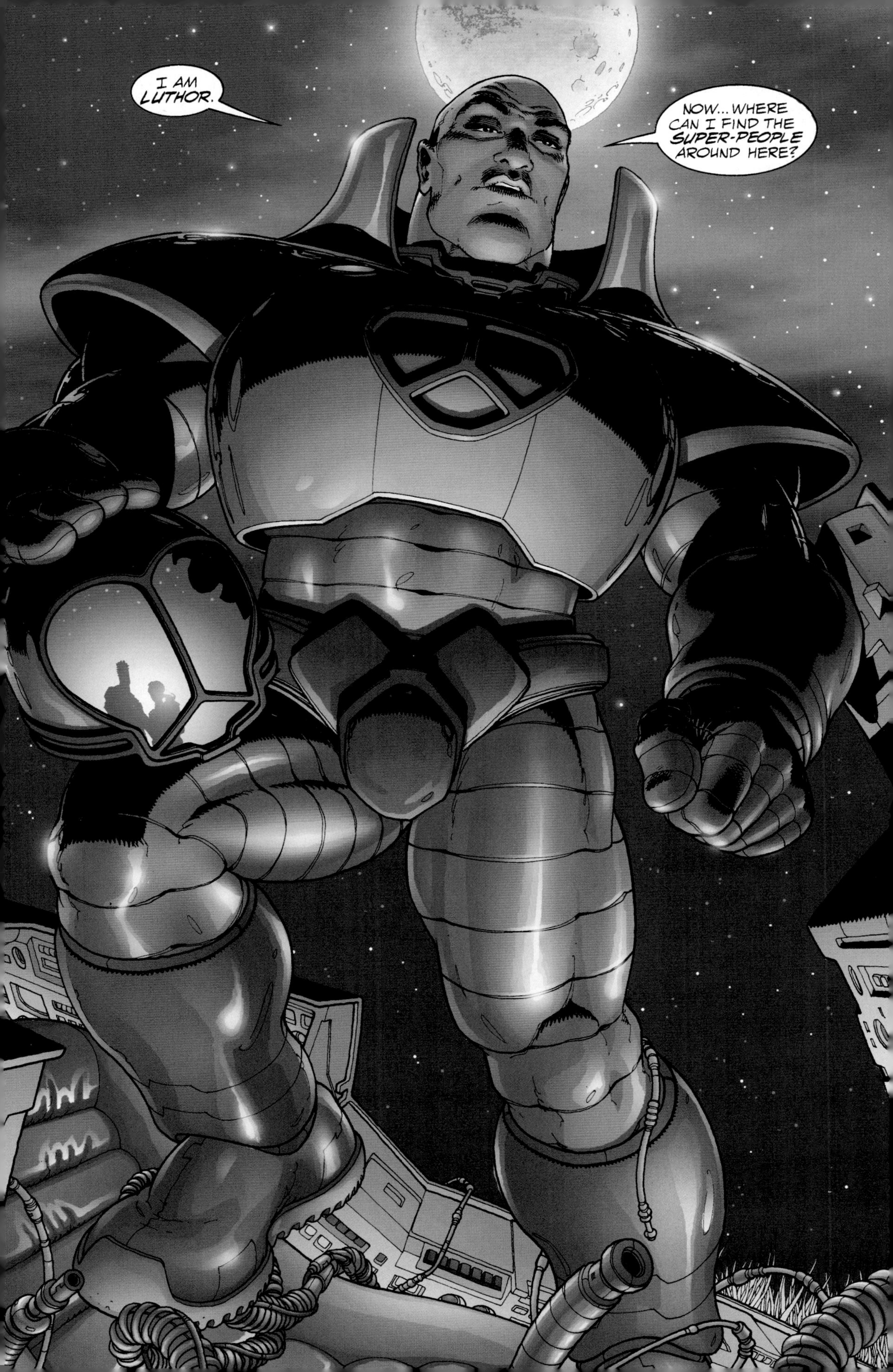
I AM LUTHOR.
NOW... WHERE CAN I FIND THE SUPER-PEOPLE AROUND HERE?

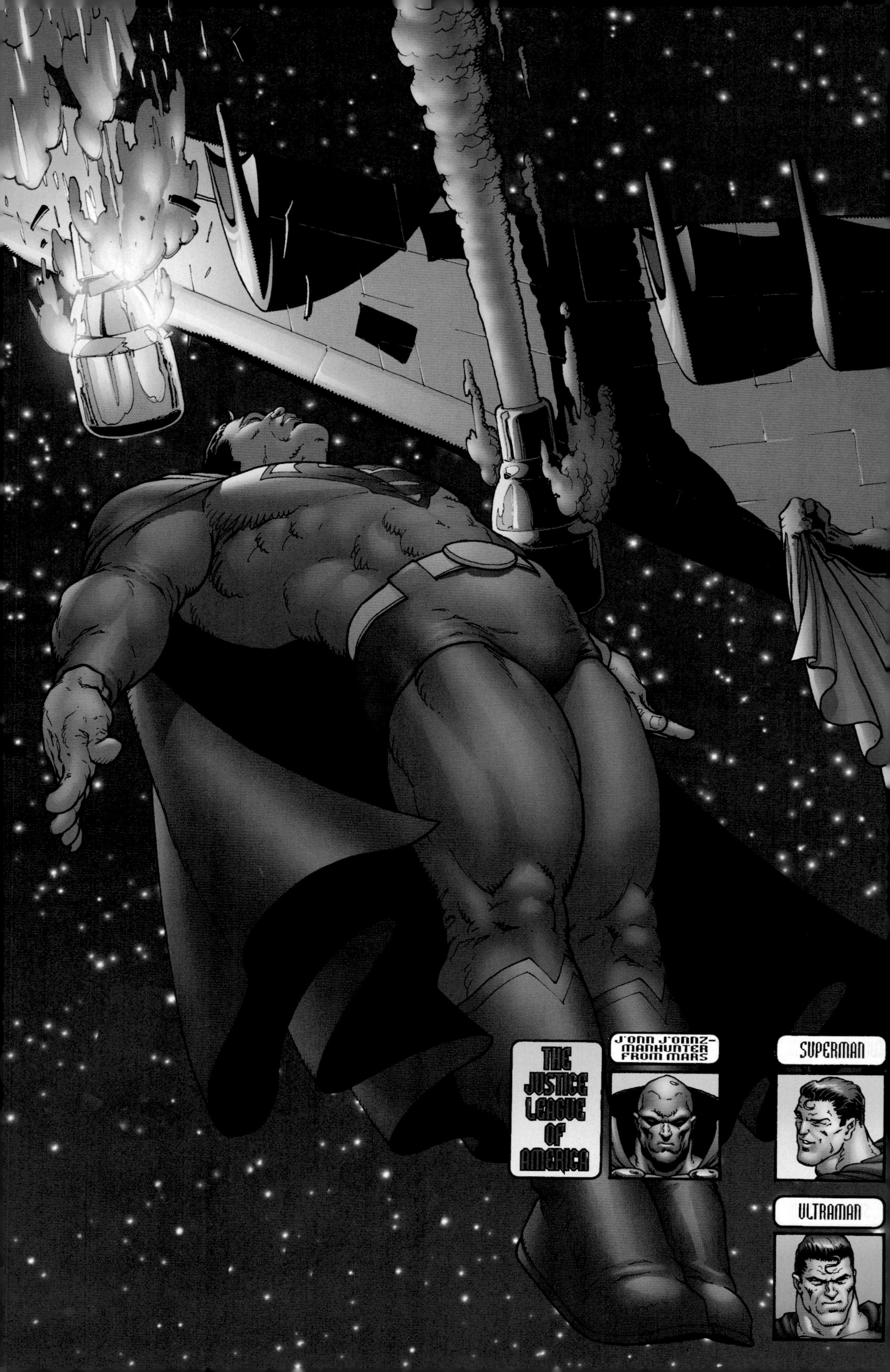

THE JUSTICE LEAGUE OF AMERICA
J'ONN J'ONZZ–MANHUNTER FROM MARS
SUPERMAN
ULTRAMAN

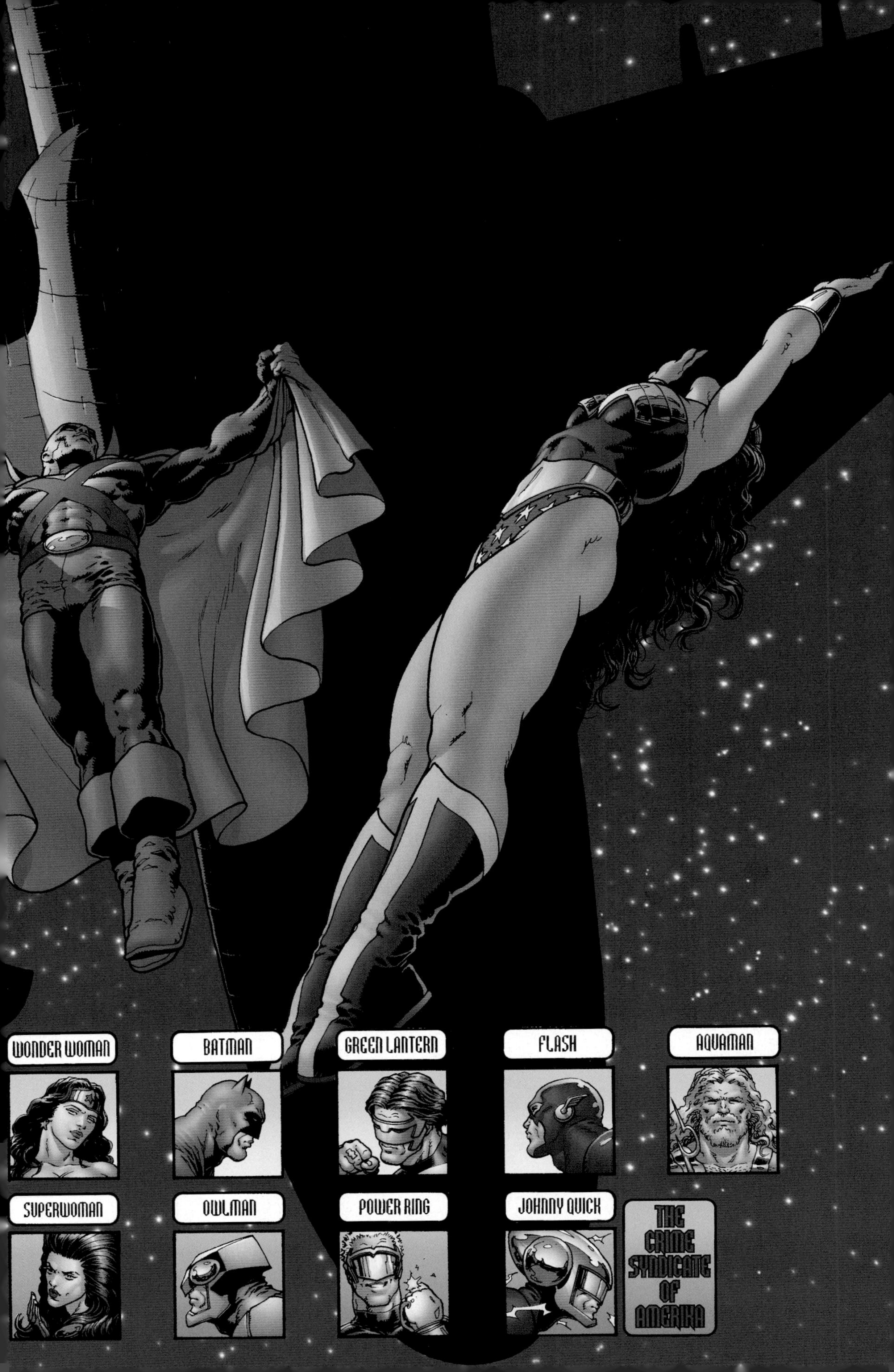
WONDER WOMAN
BATMAN
GREEN LANTERN
FLASH
AQUAMAN
SUPERWOMAN
OWLMAN
POWER RING
JOHNNY QUICK
THE CRIME SYNDICATE OF AMERIKA

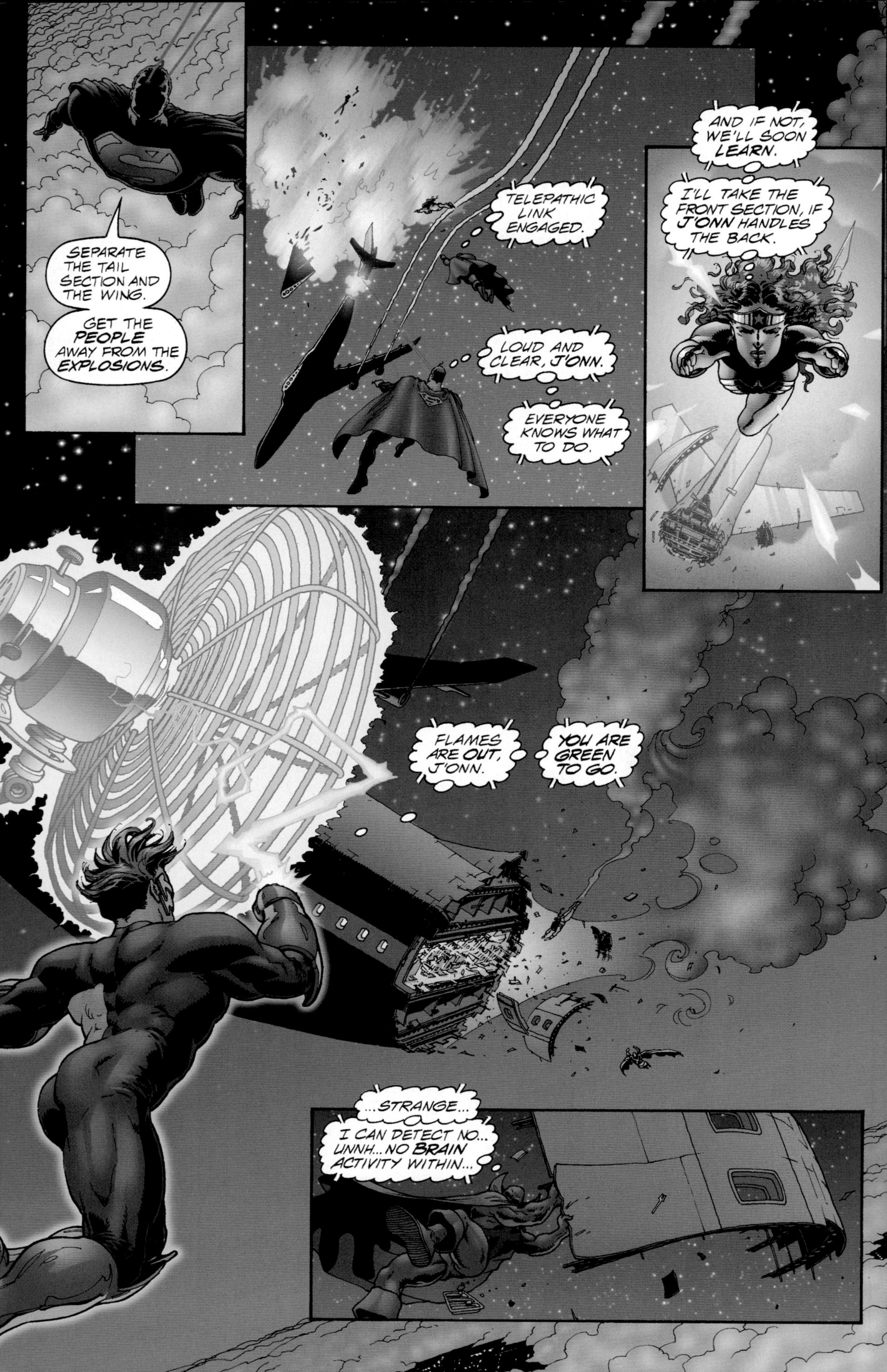
SEPARATE THE TAIL SECTION AND THE WING.
GET THE PEOPLE AWAY FROM THE EXPLOSIONS.
TELEPATHIC LINK ENGAGED.
LOUD AND CLEAR, J'ONN.
EVERYONE KNOWS WHAT TO DO.
AND IF NOT, WE'LL SOON LEARN.
I'LL TAKE THE FRONT SECTION, IF J'ONN HANDLES THE BACK.
FLAMES ARE OUT, J'ONN.
YOU ARE GREEN TO GO.
...STRANGE...
I CAN DETECT NO... UNNH... NO BRAIN ACTIVITY WITHIN...

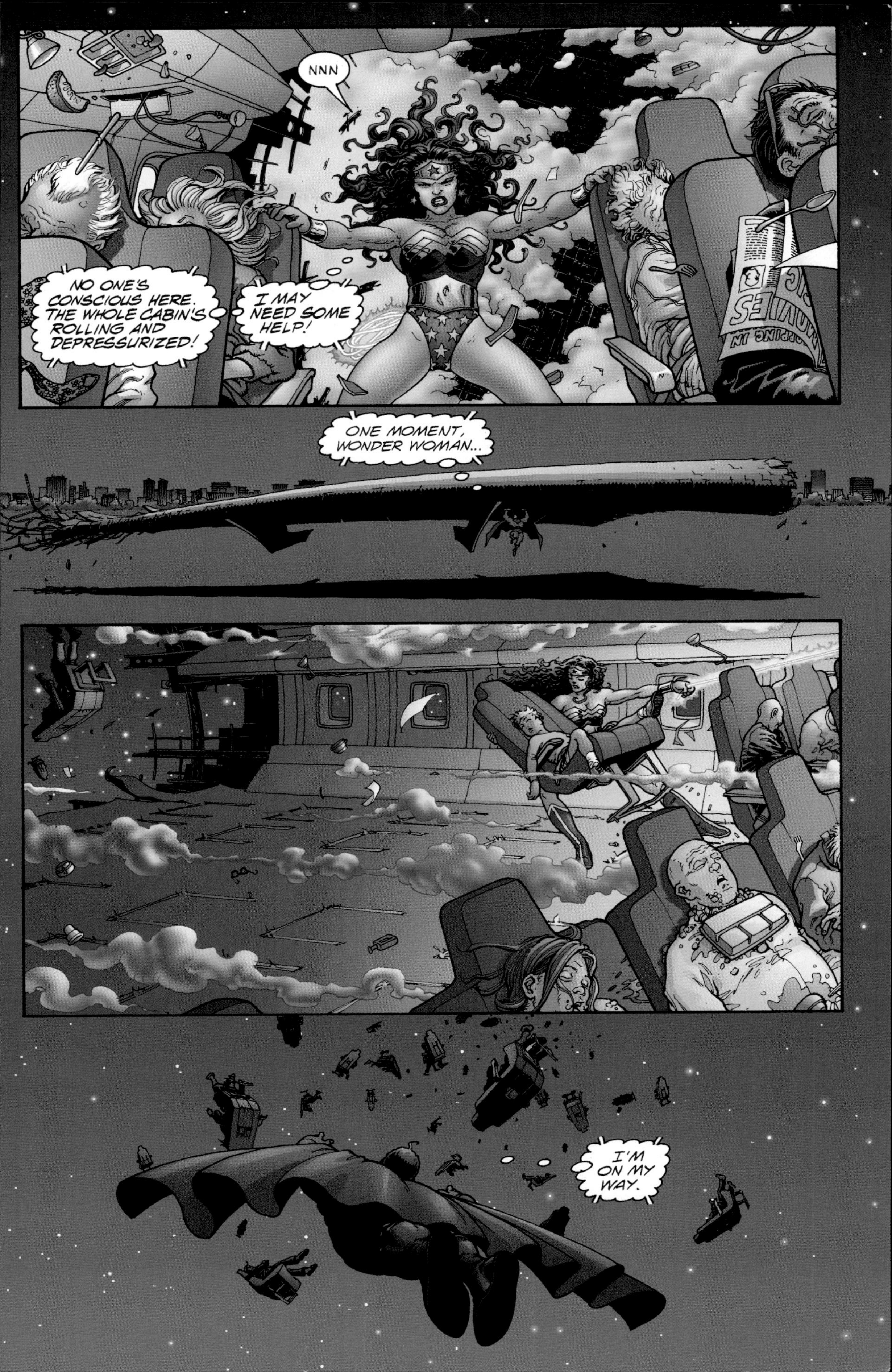
NNN
NO ONE'S CONSCIOUS HERE. THE WHOLE CABIN'S ROLLING AND DEPRESSURIZED!
I MAY NEED SOME HELP!
ONE MOMENT, WONDER WOMAN...
I'M ON MY WAY.

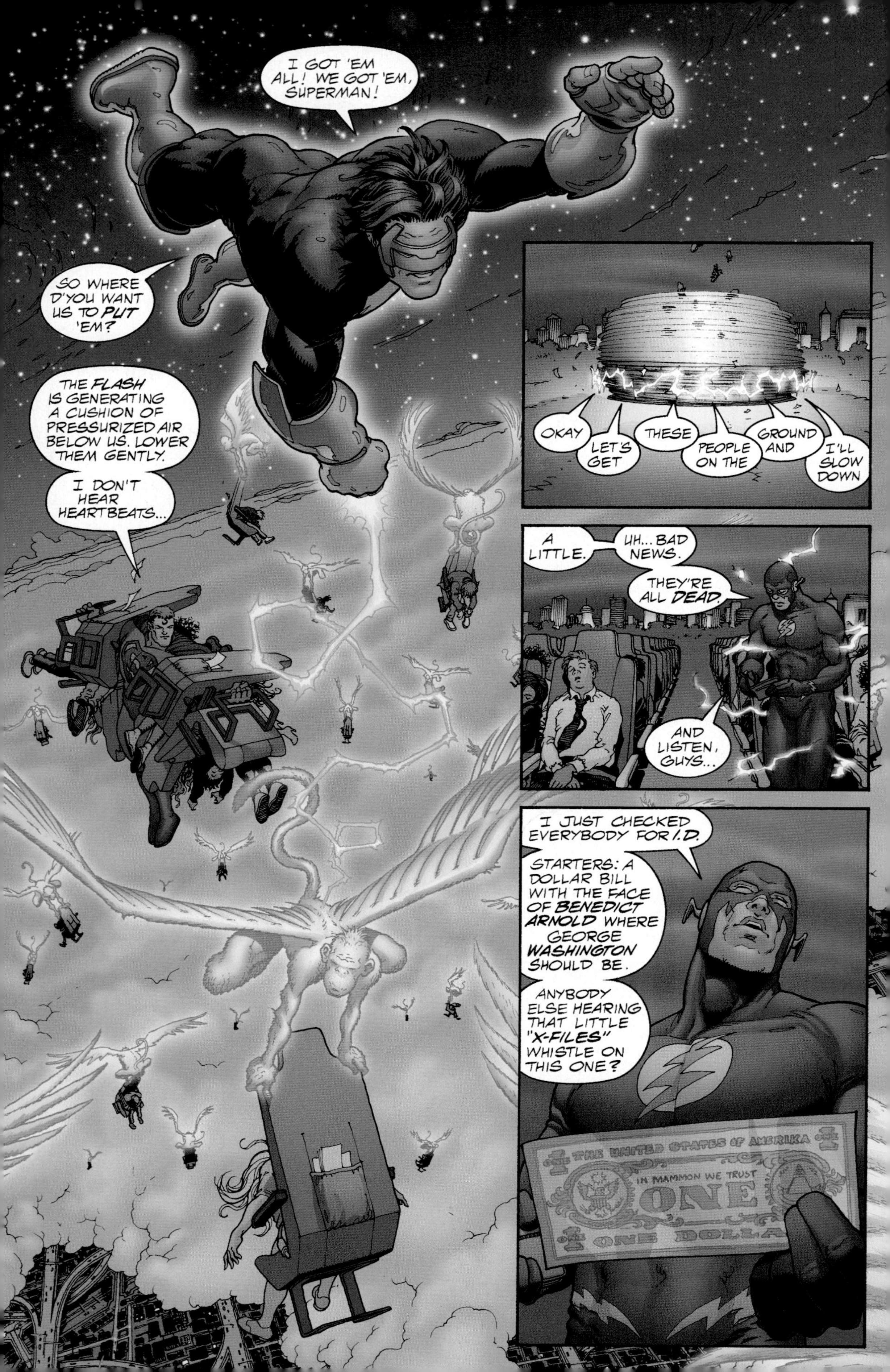

I GOT 'EM ALL! WE GOT 'EM, SUPERMAN!
SO WHERE D'YOU WANT US TO PUT 'EM?
THE FLASH IS GENERATING A CUSHION OF PRESSURIZED AIR BELOW US. LOWER THEM GENTLY.
I DON'T HEAR HEARTBEATS...
OKAY
LET'S GET
THESE
PEOPLE ON THE
GROUND AND
I'LL SLOW DOWN
A LITTLE.
UH... BAD NEWS.
THEY'RE ALL DEAD.
AND LISTEN, GUYS...
I JUST CHECKED EVERYBODY FOR I.D.
STARTERS: A DOLLAR BILL WITH THE FACE OF BENEDICT ARNOLD WHERE GEORGE WASHINGTON SHOULD BE.
ANYBODY ELSE HEARING THAT LITTLE "X-FILES" WHISTLE ON THIS ONE?
THE UNITED STATES OF AMERIKA
IN MAMMON WE TRUST
ONE
ONE DOLLA

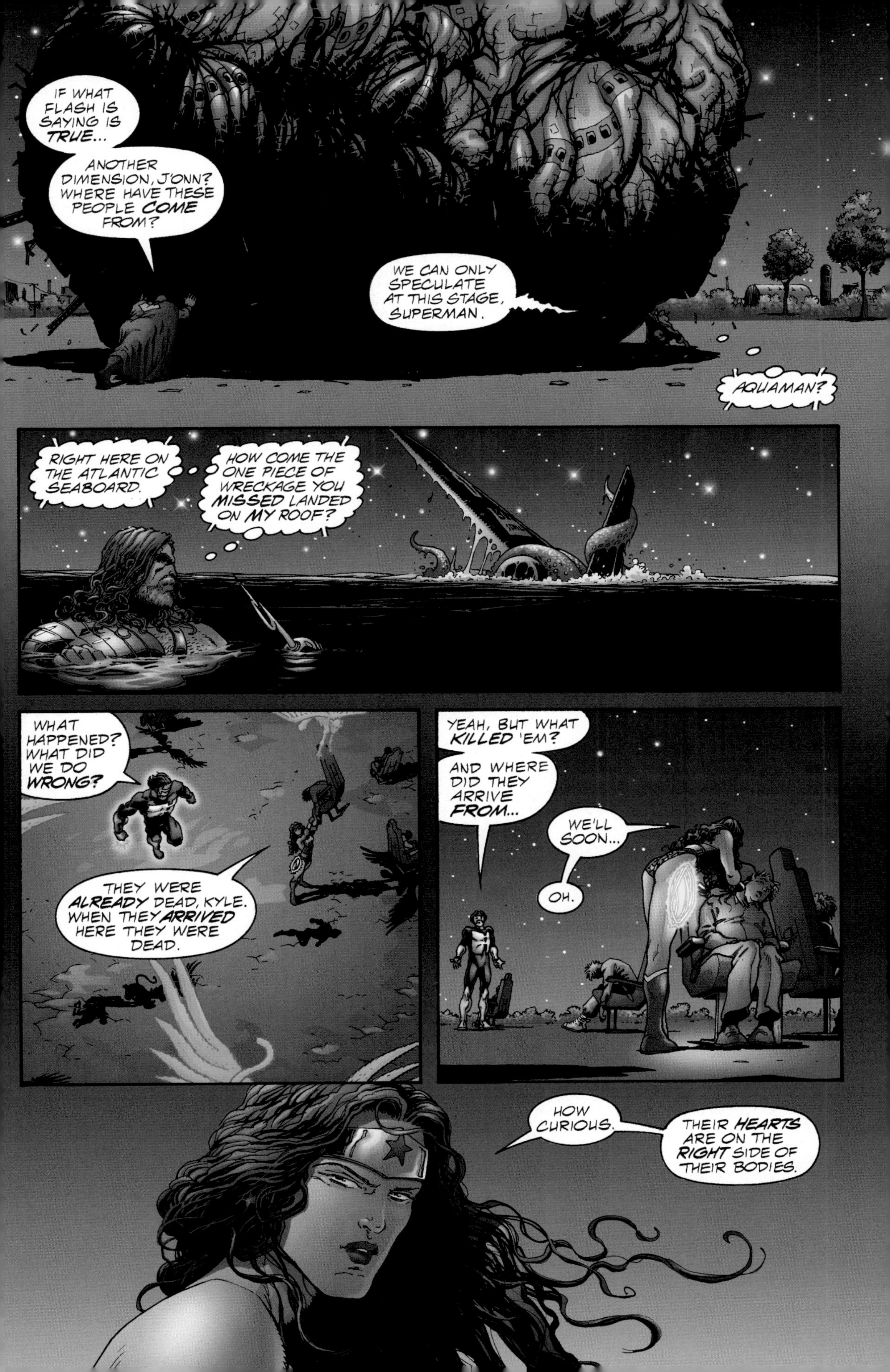

IF WHAT FLASH IS SAYING IS TRUE...
ANOTHER DIMENSION, J'ONN? WHERE HAVE THESE PEOPLE COME FROM?
WE CAN ONLY SPECULATE AT THIS STAGE, SUPERMAN.
AQUAMAN?
RIGHT HERE ON THE ATLANTIC SEABOARD.
HOW COME THE ONE PIECE OF WRECKAGE YOU MISSED LANDED ON MY ROOF?
WHAT HAPPENED? WHAT DID WE DO WRONG?
THEY WERE ALREADY DEAD, KYLE. WHEN THEY ARRIVED HERE THEY WERE DEAD.
YEAH, BUT WHAT KILLED 'EM?
AND WHERE DID THEY ARRIVE FROM...
WE'LL SOON...
OH.
HOW CURIOUS.
THEIR HEARTS ARE ON THE RIGHT SIDE OF THEIR BODIES.

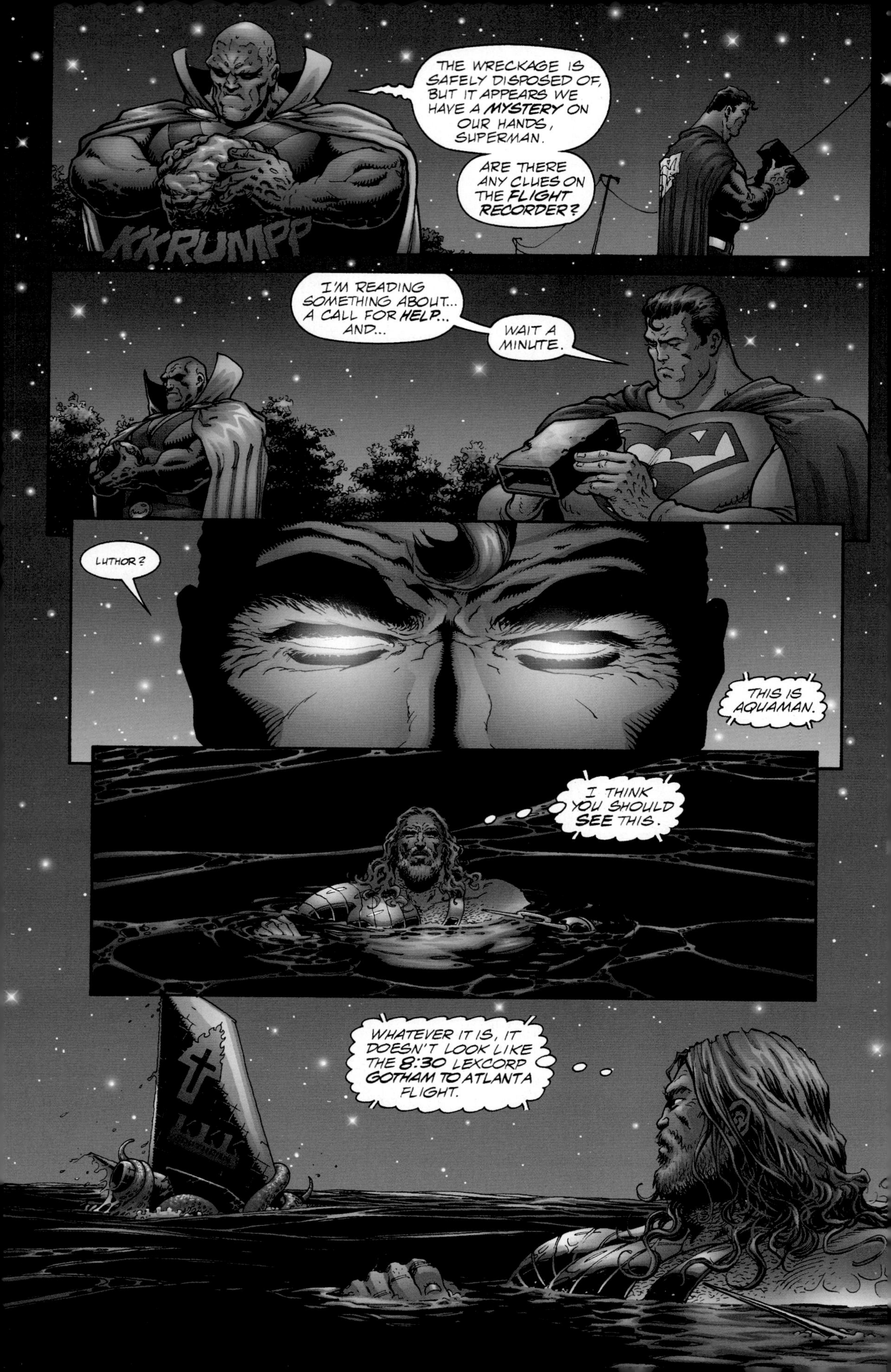
THE WRECKAGE IS SAFELY DISPOSED OF, BUT IT APPEARS WE HAVE A MYSTERY ON OUR HANDS, SUPERMAN.
ARE THERE ANY CLUES ON THE FLIGHT RECORDER?
KKRUMPP
I'M READING SOMETHING ABOUT... A CALL FOR HELP... AND...
WAIT A MINUTE.
LUTHOR?
THIS IS AQUAMAN.
I THINK YOU SHOULD SEE THIS.
WHATEVER IT IS, IT DOESN'T LOOK LIKE THE 8:30 LEXCORP GOTHAM TO ATLANTA FLIGHT.

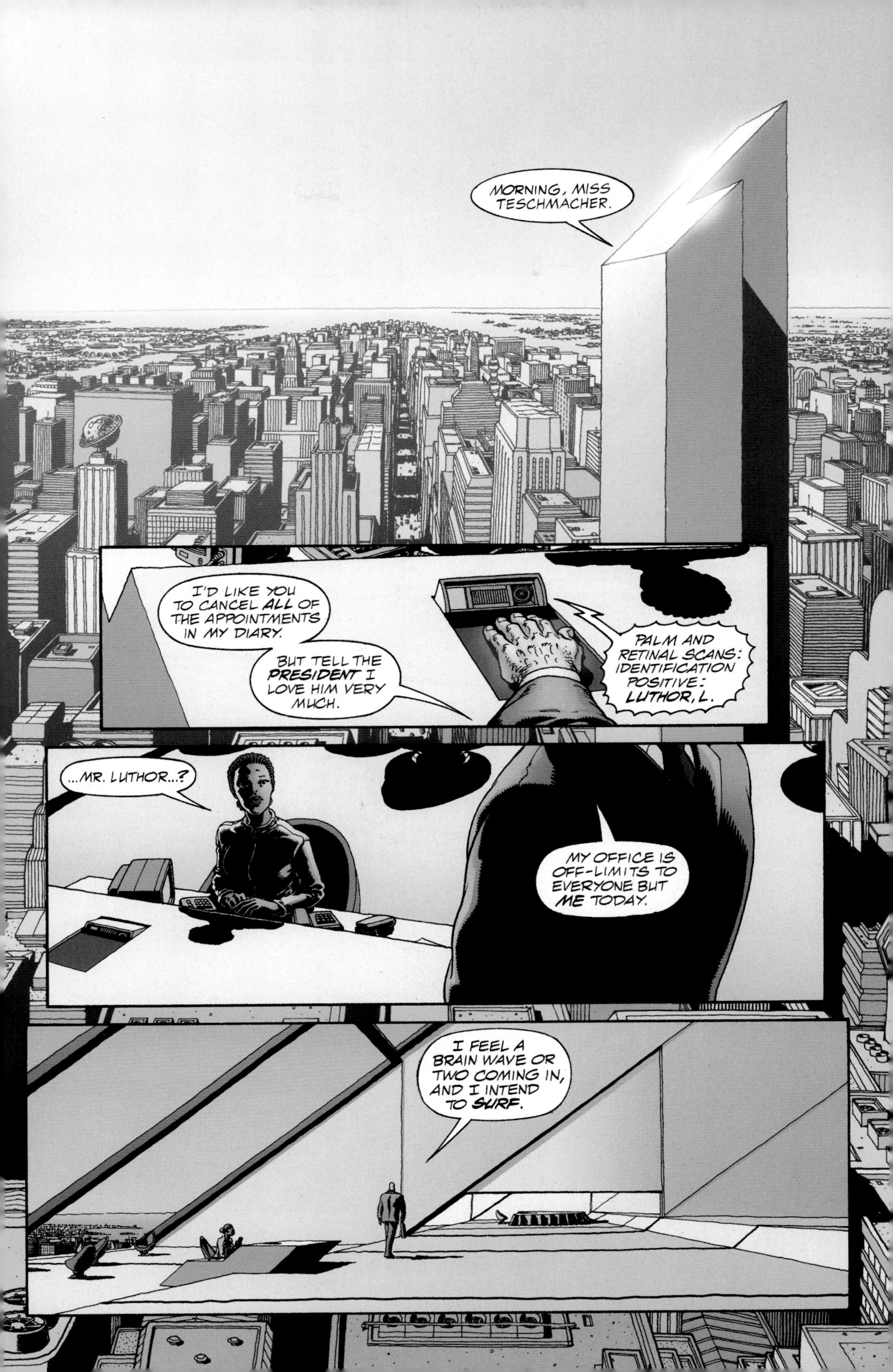
MORNING, MISS TESCHMACHER.
I'D LIKE YOU TO CANCEL ALL OF THE APPOINTMENTS IN MY DIARY.
BUT TELL THE PRESIDENT I LOVE HIM VERY MUCH.
PALM AND RETINAL SCANS: IDENTIFICATION POSITIVE: LUTHOR, L.
...MR. LUTHOR...?
MY OFFICE IS OFF-LIMITS TO EVERYONE BUT ME TODAY.
I FEEL A BRAIN WAVE OR TWO COMING IN, AND I INTEND TO SURF.

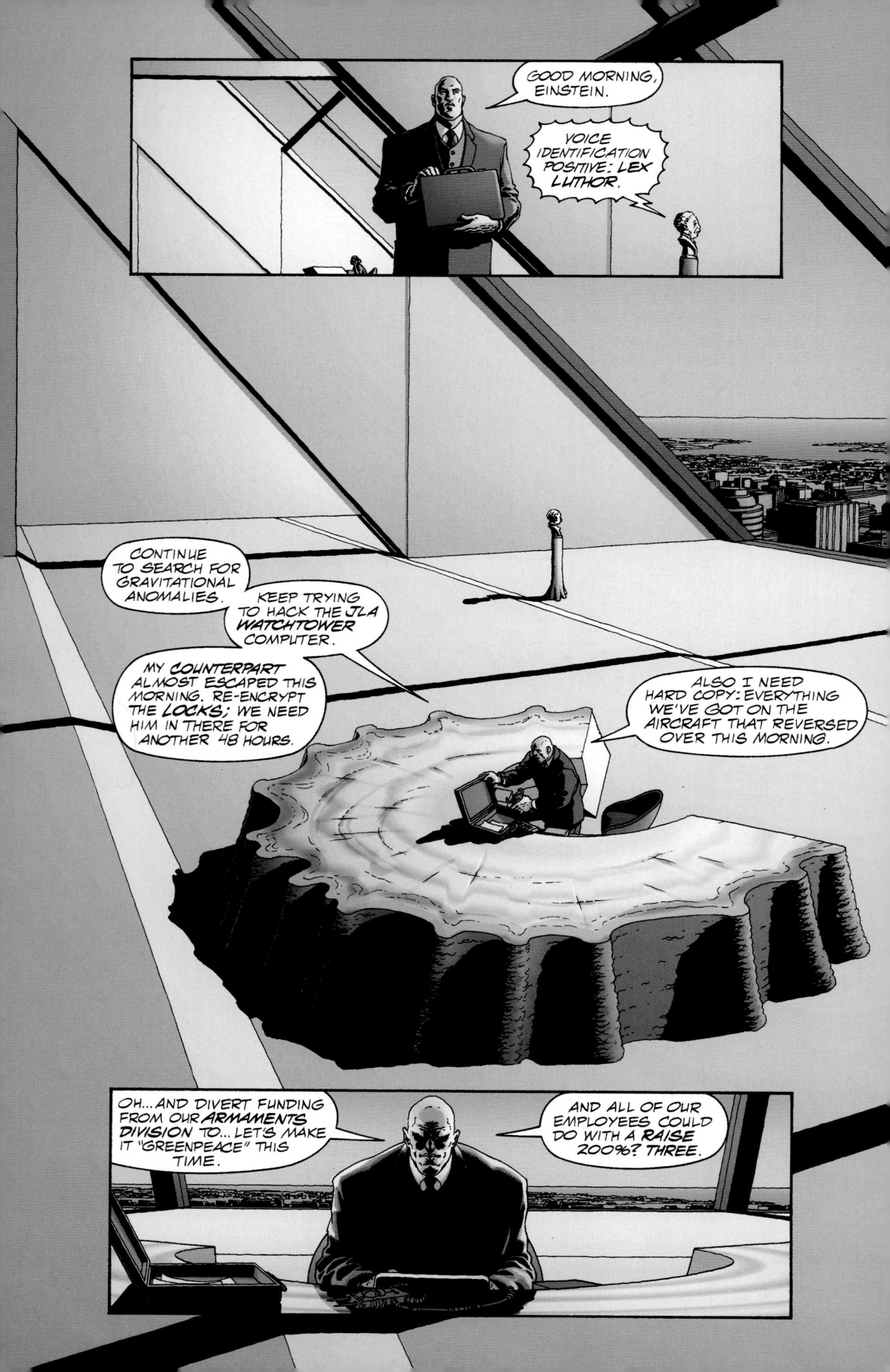
GOOD MORNING, EINSTEIN.
VOICE IDENTIFICATION POSITIVE: LEX LUTHOR.
CONTINUE TO SEARCH FOR GRAVITATIONAL ANOMALIES.
KEEP TRYING TO HACK THE JLA WATCHTOWER COMPUTER.
MY COUNTERPART ALMOST ESCAPED THIS MORNING. RE-ENCRYPT THE LOCKS; WE NEED HIM IN THERE FOR ANOTHER 48 HOURS.
ALSO I NEED HARD COPY: EVERYTHING WE'VE GOT ON THE AIRCRAFT THAT REVERSED OVER THIS MORNING.
OH...AND DIVERT FUNDING FROM OUR ARMAMENTS DIVISION TO... LET'S MAKE IT "GREENPEACE" THIS TIME.
AND ALL OF OUR EMPLOYEES COULD DO WITH A RAISE 200%? THREE.

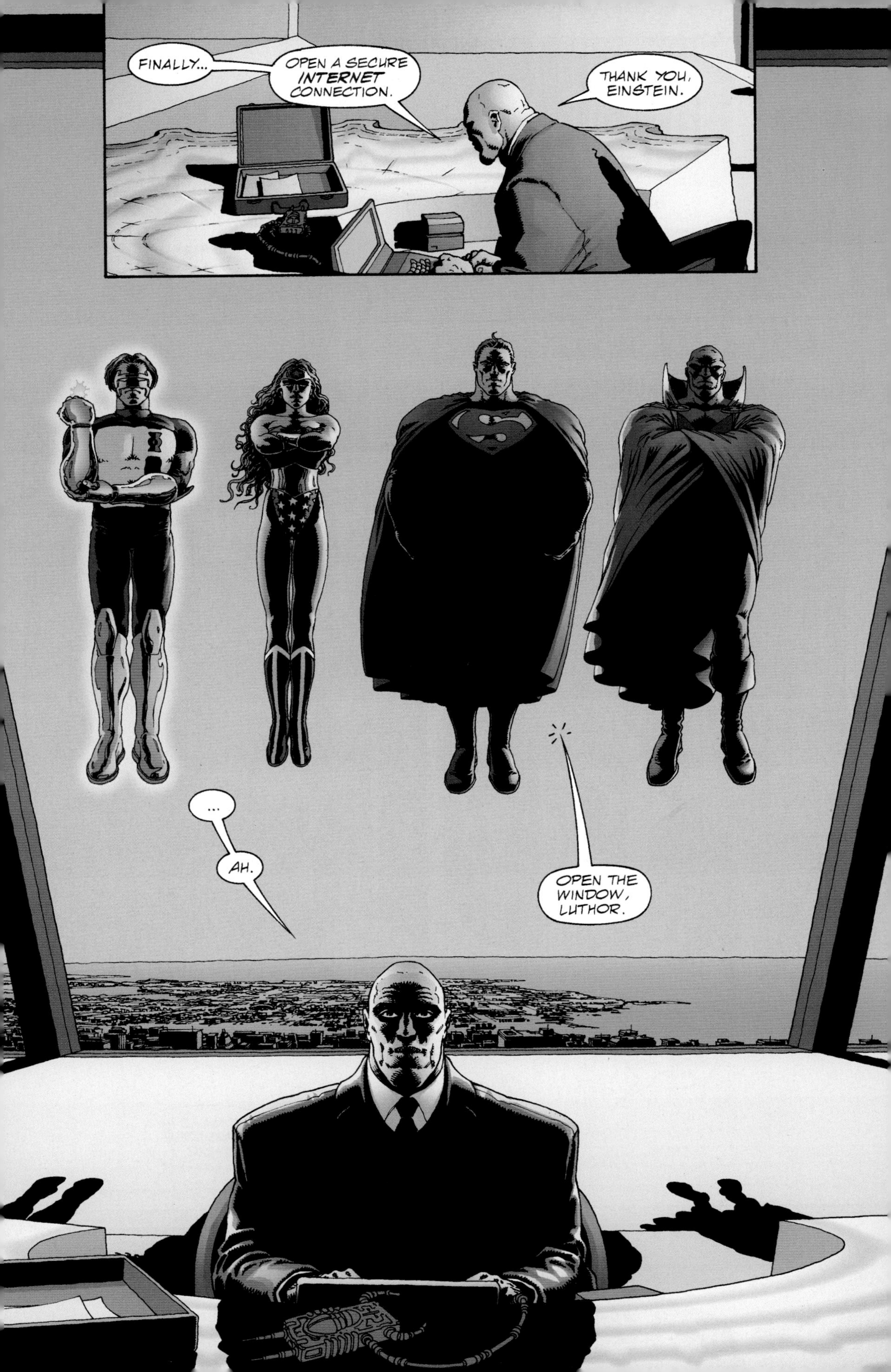
FINALLY...
OPEN A SECURE INTERNET CONNECTION.
THANK YOU, EINSTEIN.
...
AH.
OPEN THE WINDOW, LUTHOR.

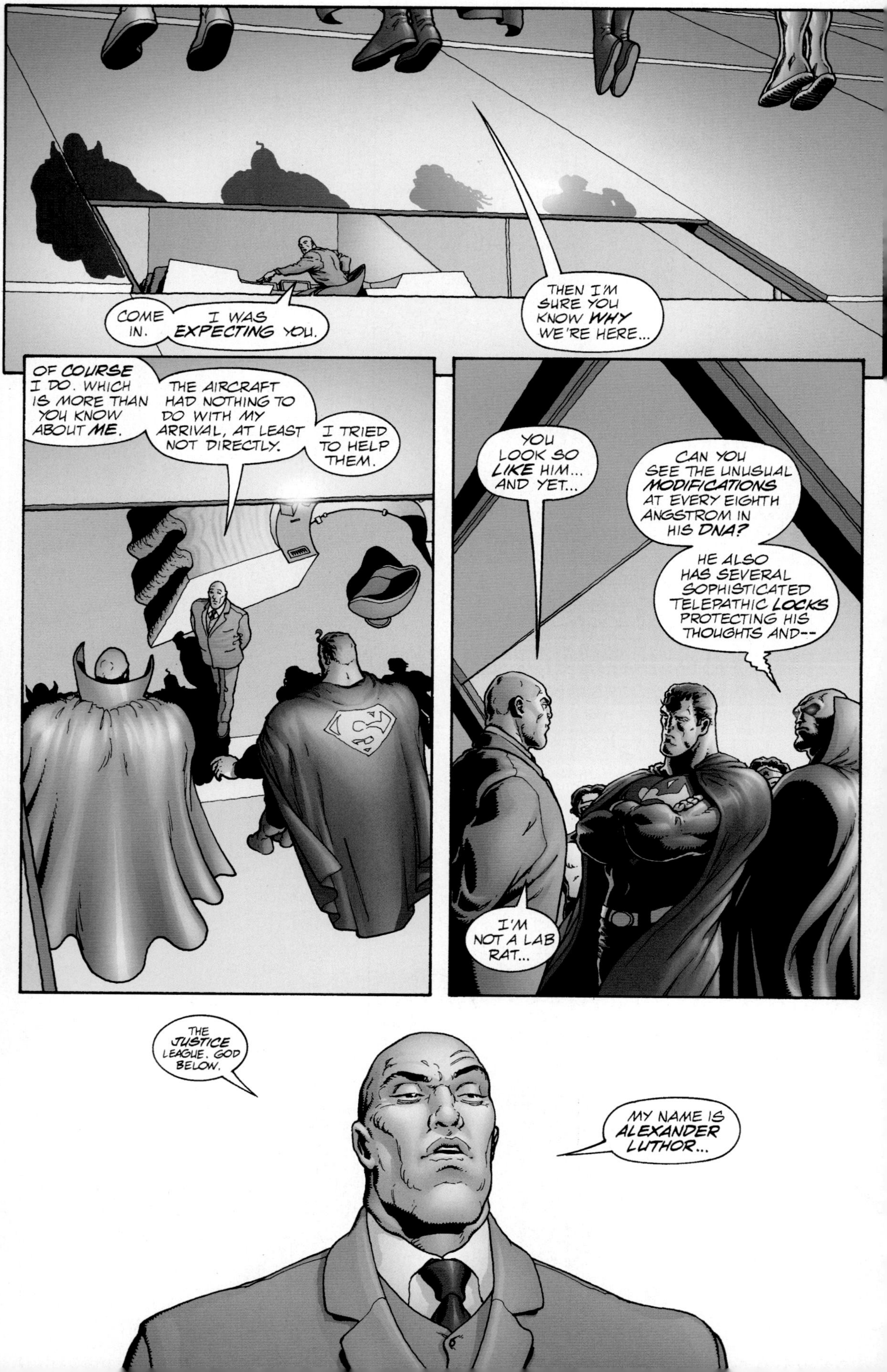
COME IN.
I WAS EXPECTING YOU.
THEN I'M SURE YOU KNOW WHY WE'RE HERE...
OF COURSE I DO. WHICH IS MORE THAN YOU KNOW ABOUT ME.
THE AIRCRAFT HAD NOTHING TO DO WITH MY ARRIVAL, AT LEAST NOT DIRECTLY.
I TRIED TO HELP THEM.
YOU LOOK SO LIKE HIM... AND YET...
CAN YOU SEE THE UNUSUAL MODIFICATIONS AT EVERY EIGHTH ANGSTROM IN HIS DNA?
HE ALSO HAS SEVERAL SOPHISTICATED TELEPATHIC LOCKS PROTECTING HIS THOUGHTS AND--
I'M NOT A LAB RAT...
THE JUSTICE LEAGUE. GOD BELOW.
MY NAME IS ALEXANDER LUTHOR...

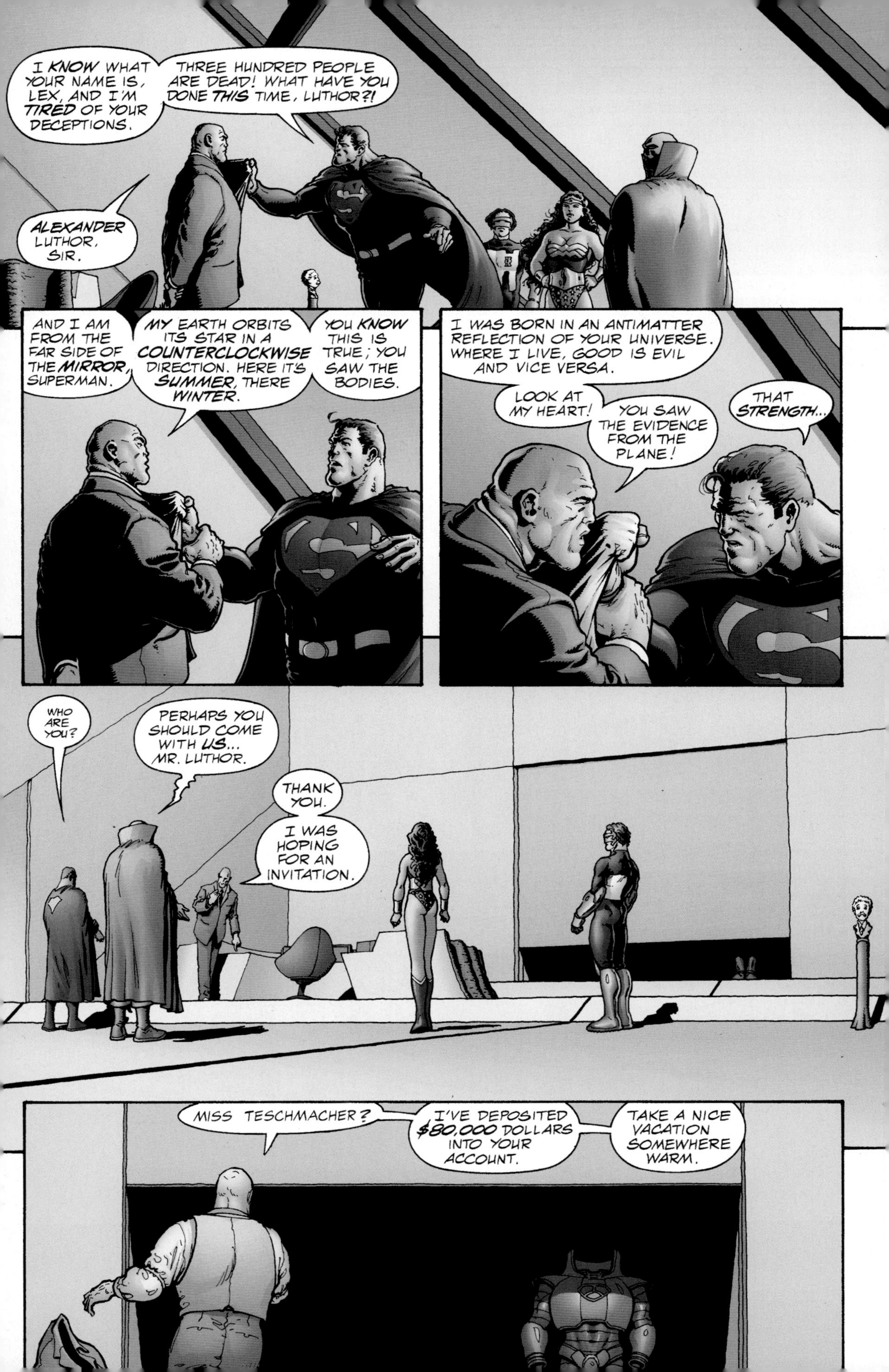
I KNOW WHAT YOUR NAME IS, LEX, AND I'M TIRED OF YOUR DECEPTIONS.
THREE HUNDRED PEOPLE ARE DEAD! WHAT HAVE YOU DONE THIS TIME, LUTHOR?!
ALEXANDER LUTHOR, SIR.
AND I AM FROM THE FAR SIDE OF THE MIRROR, SUPERMAN.
MY EARTH ORBITS ITS STAR IN A COUNTERCLOCKWISE DIRECTION. HERE IT'S SUMMER, THERE WINTER.
YOU KNOW THIS IS TRUE; YOU SAW THE BODIES.
I WAS BORN IN AN ANTIMATTER REFLECTION OF YOUR UNIVERSE. WHERE I LIVE, GOOD IS EVIL AND VICE VERSA.
LOOK AT MY HEART!
YOU SAW THE EVIDENCE FROM THE PLANE!
THAT STRENGTH...
WHO ARE YOU?
PERHAPS YOU SHOULD COME WITH US... MR. LUTHOR.
THANK YOU.
I WAS HOPING FOR AN INVITATION.
MISS TESCHMACHER?
I'VE DEPOSITED $80,000 DOLLARS INTO YOUR ACCOUNT.
TAKE A NICE VACATION SOMEWHERE WARM.

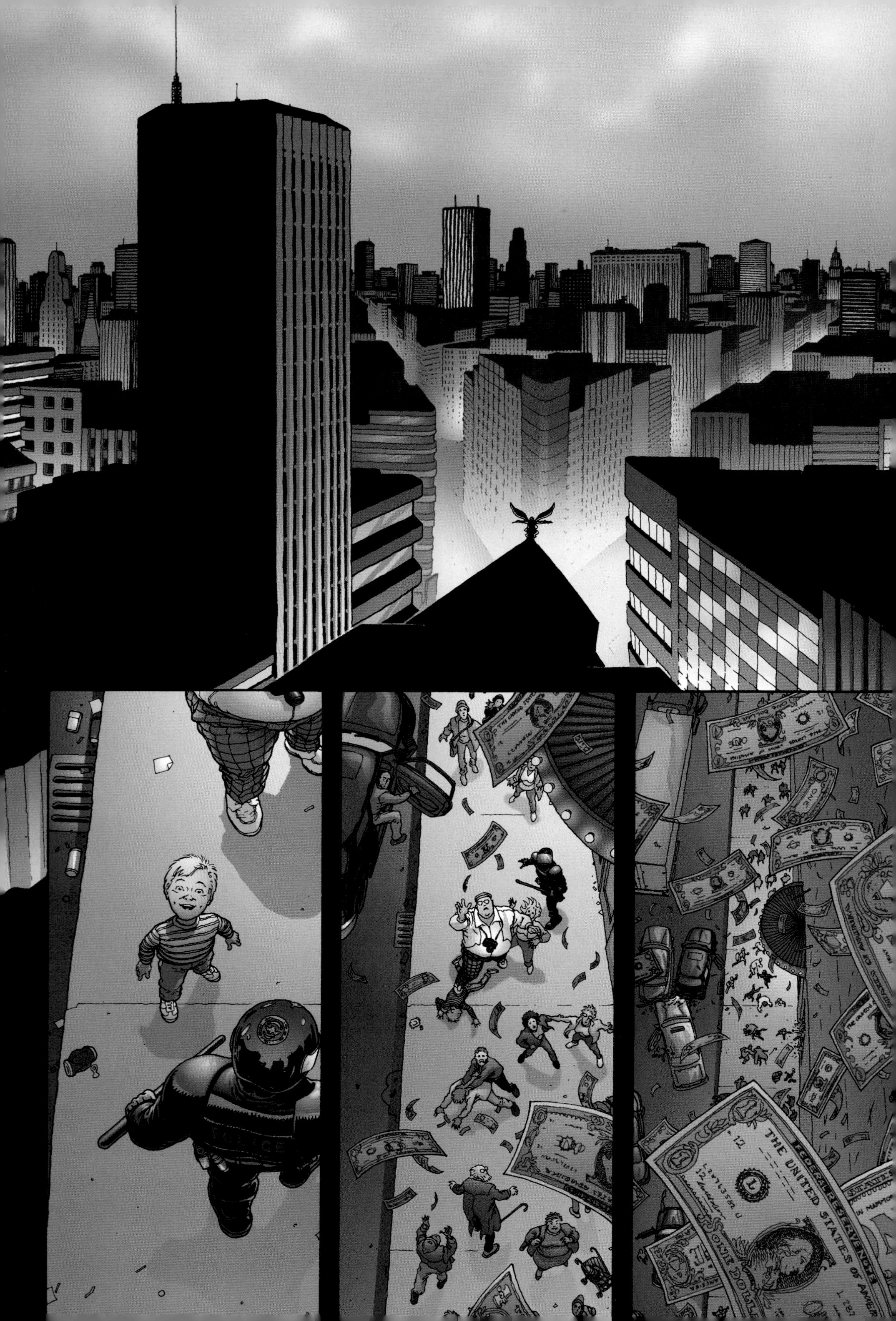

FEDERAL RESERVE NOTE
THE UNITED STATES

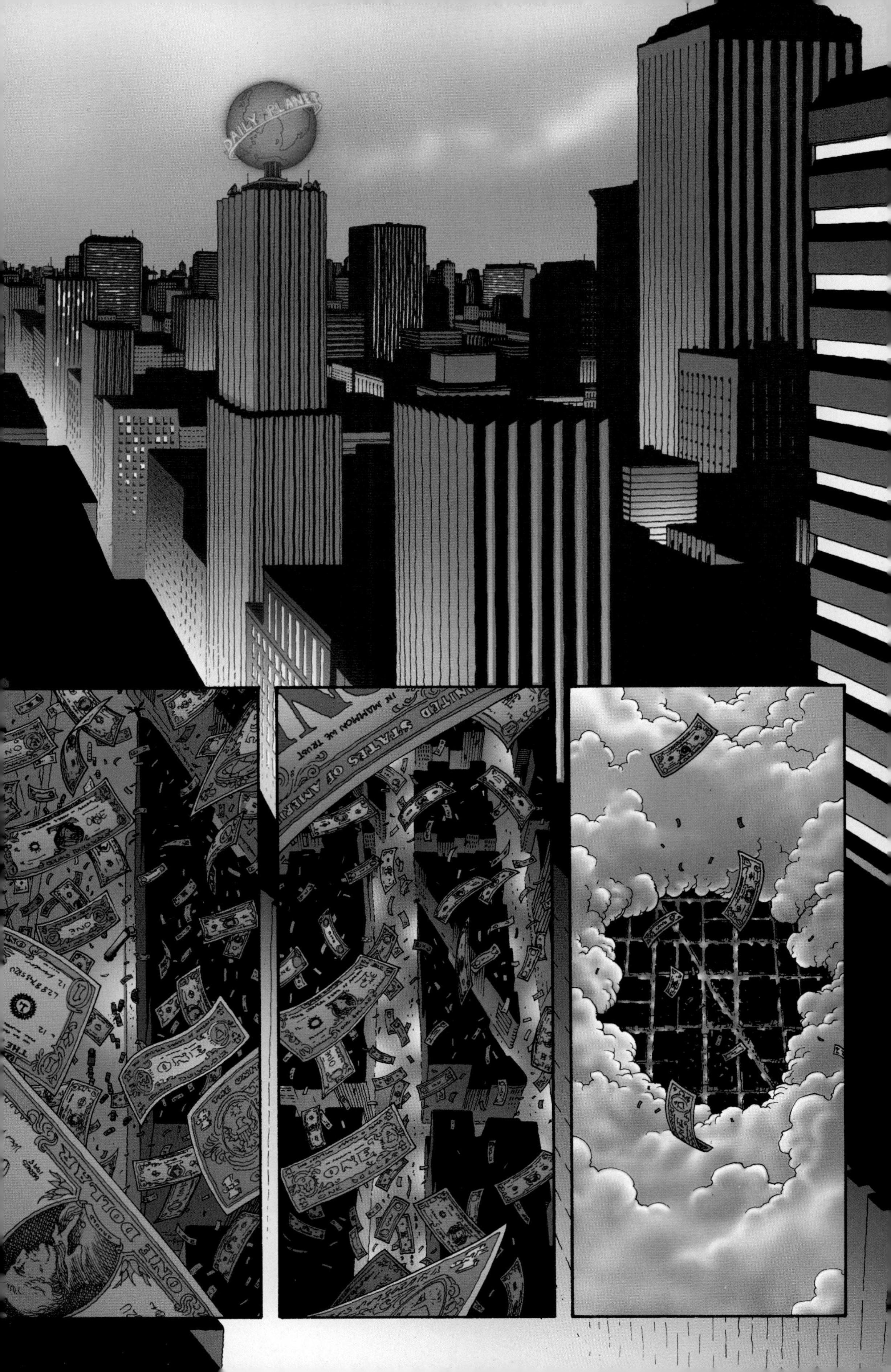
DAILY PLANET
IN MAMMON WE TRUST

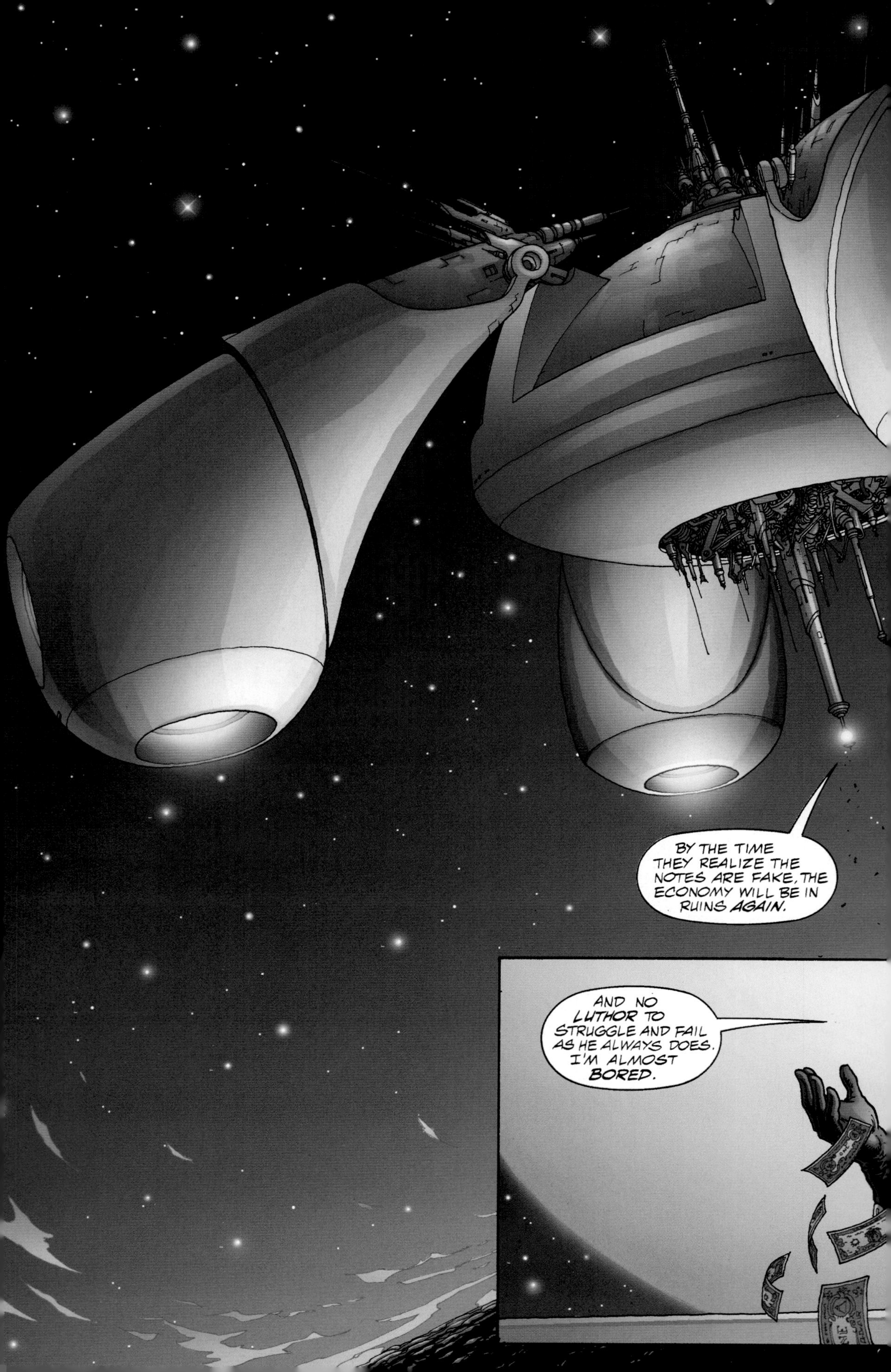
BY THE TIME THEY REALIZE THE NOTES ARE FAKE, THE ECONOMY WILL BE IN RUINS AGAIN.
AND NO LUTHOR TO STRUGGLE AND FAIL AS HE ALWAYS DOES. I'M ALMOST BORED.

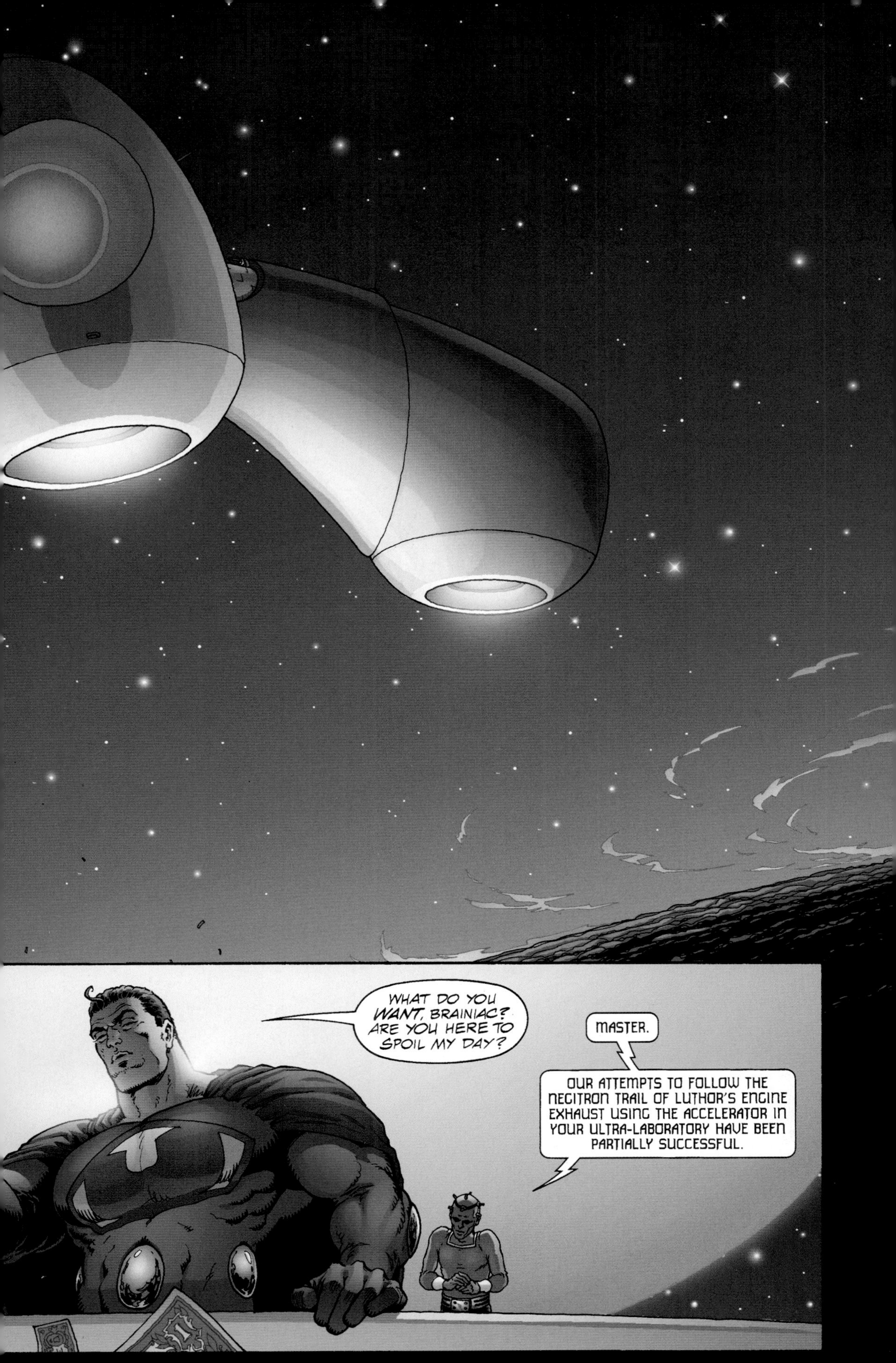
WHAT DO YOU *WANT,* BRAINIAC? ARE YOU HERE TO SPOIL MY DAY?
MASTER.
OUR ATTEMPTS TO FOLLOW THE NEGITRON TRAIL OF LUTHOR'S ENGINE EXHAUST USING THE ACCELERATOR IN YOUR ULTRA-LABORATORY HAVE BEEN PARTIALLY SUCCESSFUL.

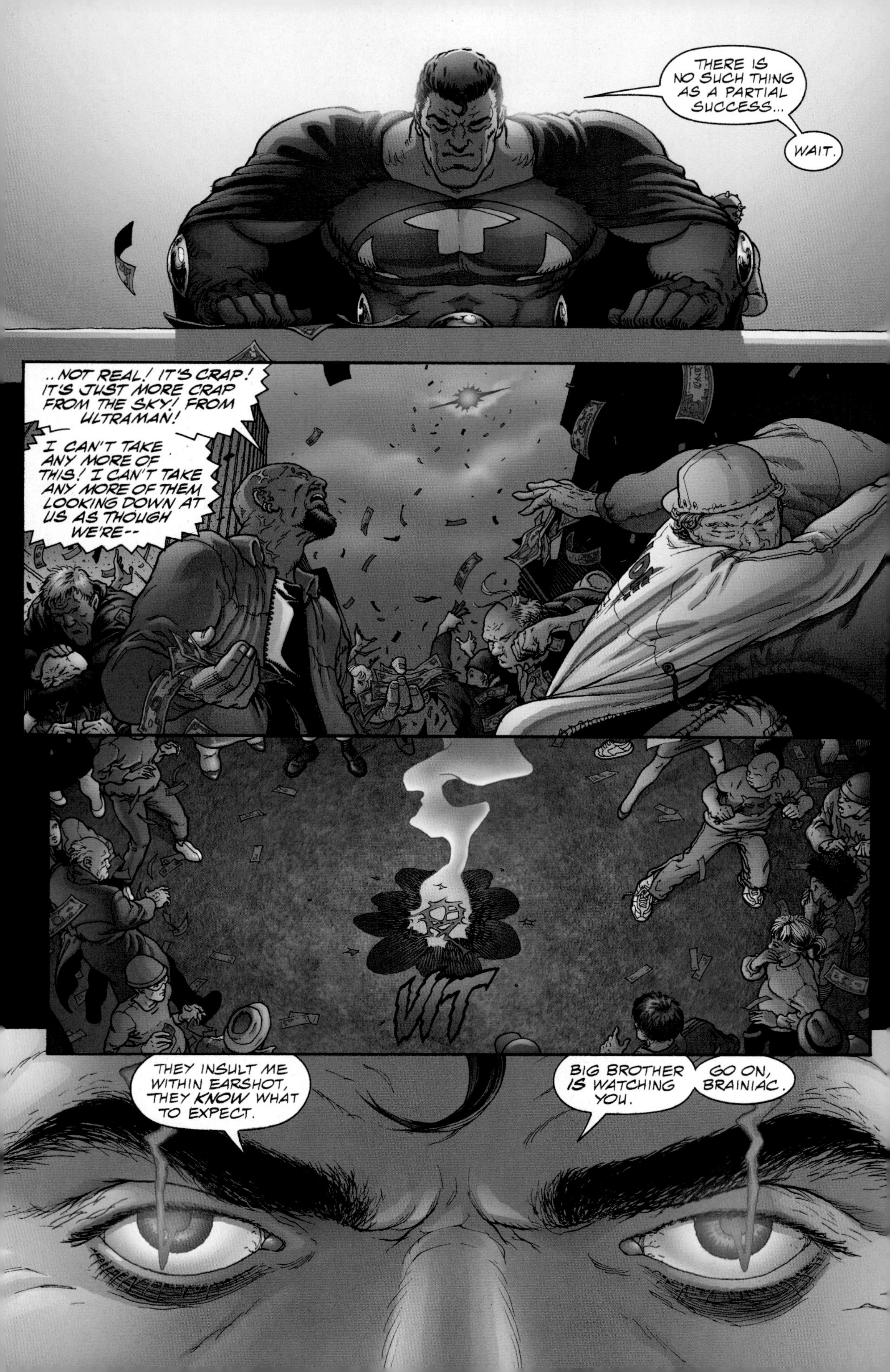
THERE IS NO SUCH THING AS A PARTIAL SUCCESS...
WAIT.
..NOT REAL! IT'S CRAP! IT'S JUST MORE CRAP FROM THE SKY! FROM ULTRAMAN!
I CAN'T TAKE ANY MORE OF THIS! I CAN'T TAKE ANY MORE OF THEM LOOKING DOWN AT US AS THOUGH WE'RE--
VIT
THEY INSULT ME WITHIN EARSHOT, THEY KNOW WHAT TO EXPECT.
BIG BROTHER IS WATCHING YOU.
GO ON, BRAINIAC.

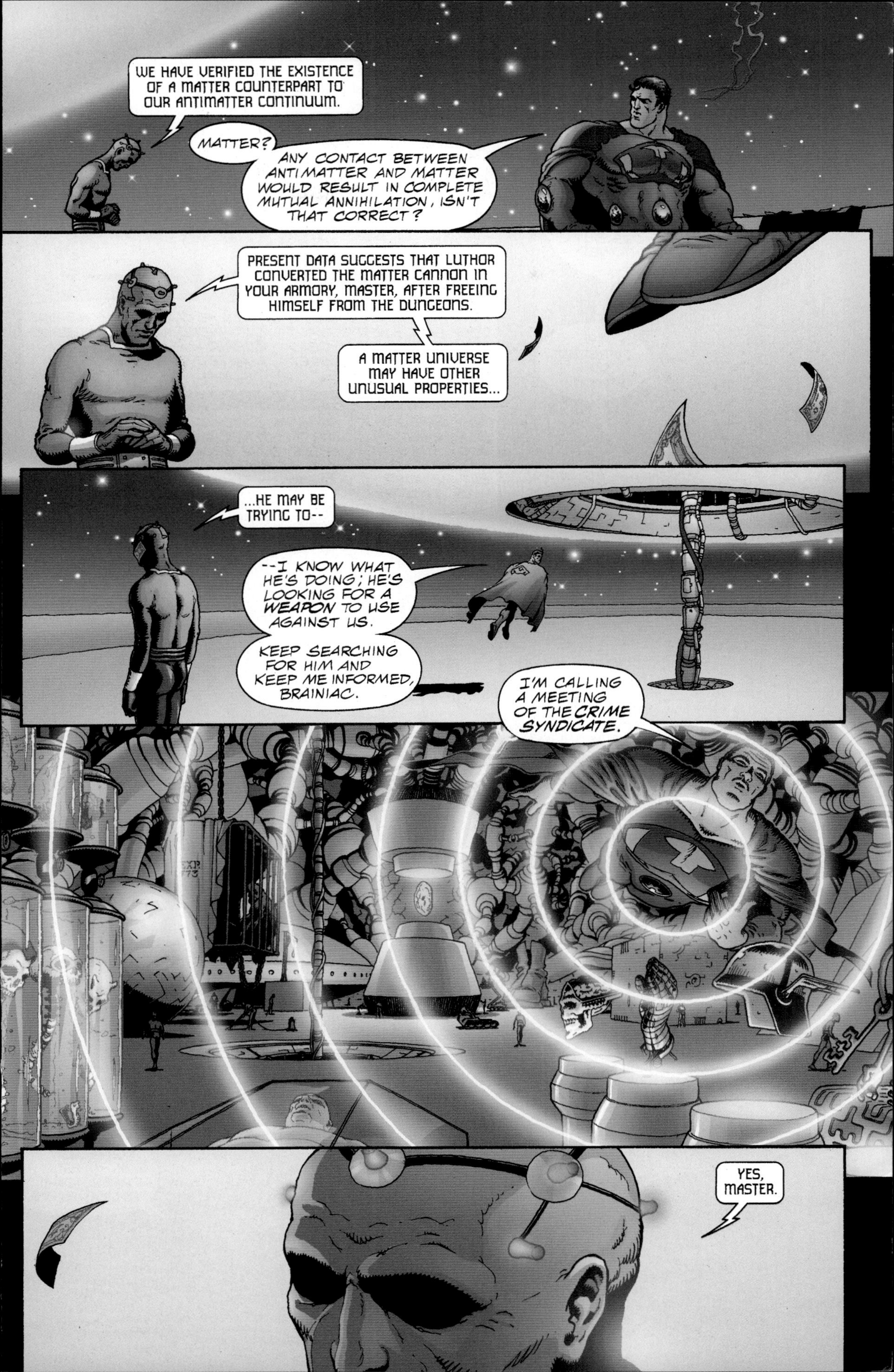
WE HAVE VERIFIED THE EXISTENCE OF A MATTER COUNTERPART TO OUR ANTIMATTER CONTINUUM.
MATTER?
ANY CONTACT BETWEEN ANTIMATTER AND MATTER WOULD RESULT IN COMPLETE MUTUAL ANNIHILATION, ISN'T THAT CORRECT?
PRESENT DATA SUGGESTS THAT LUTHOR CONVERTED THE MATTER CANNON IN YOUR ARMORY, MASTER, AFTER FREEING HIMSELF FROM THE DUNGEONS.
A MATTER UNIVERSE MAY HAVE OTHER UNUSUAL PROPERTIES...
...HE MAY BE TRYING TO--
--I KNOW WHAT HE'S DOING; HE'S LOOKING FOR A WEAPON TO USE AGAINST US.
KEEP SEARCHING FOR HIM AND KEEP ME INFORMED, BRAINIAC.
I'M CALLING A MEETING OF THE CRIME SYNDICATE.
EXP 773
YES, MASTER.

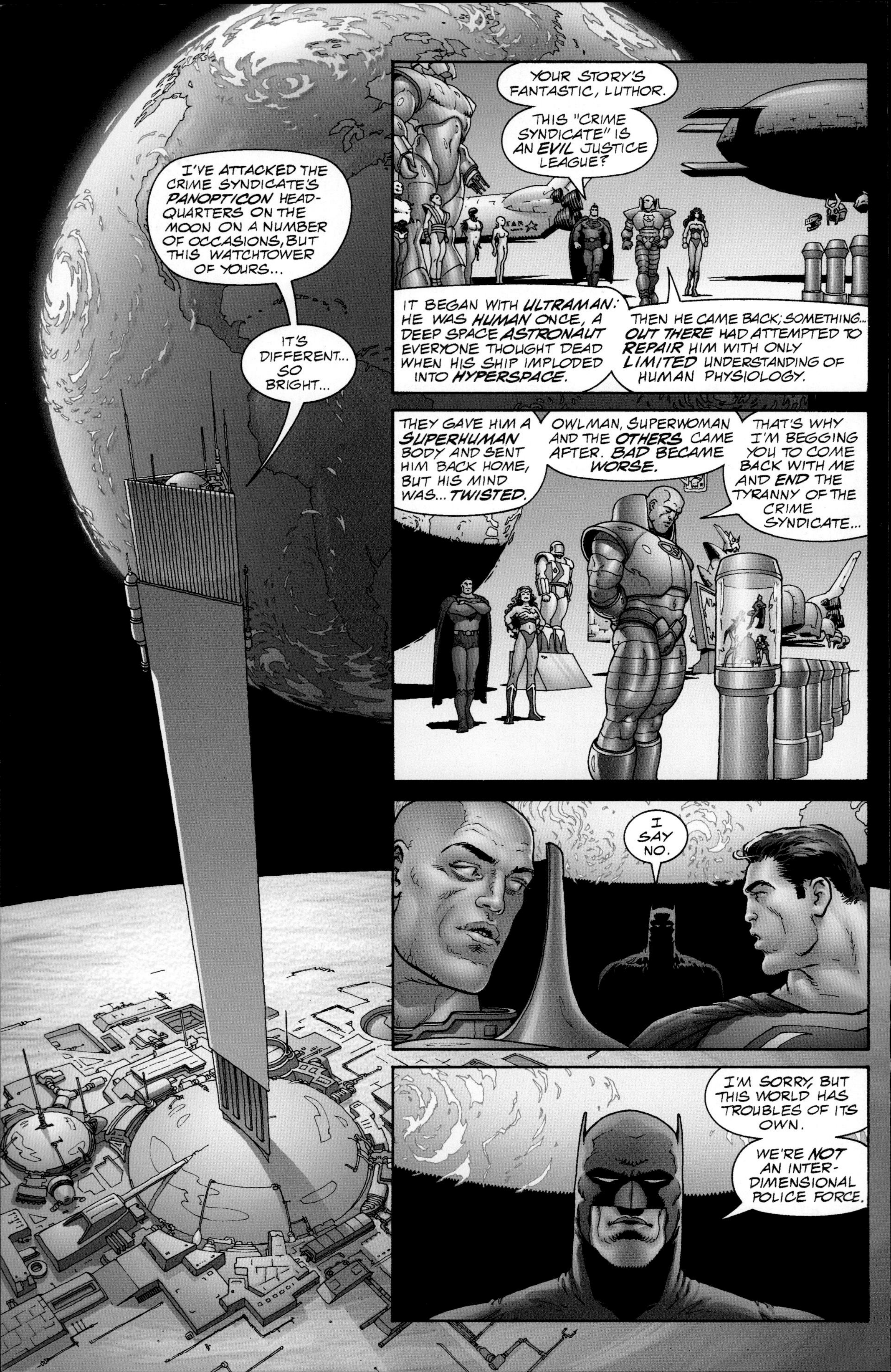
I'VE ATTACKED THE CRIME SYNDICATE'S PANOPTICON HEAD-QUARTERS ON THE MOON ON A NUMBER OF OCCASIONS, BUT THIS WATCHTOWER OF YOURS...
IT'S DIFFERENT... SO BRIGHT...
YOUR STORY'S FANTASTIC, LUTHOR.
THIS "CRIME SYNDICATE" IS AN EVIL JUSTICE LEAGUE?
IT BEGAN WITH ULTRAMAN: HE WAS HUMAN ONCE, A DEEP SPACE ASTRONAUT EVERYONE THOUGHT DEAD WHEN HIS SHIP IMPLODED INTO HYPERSPACE.
THEN HE CAME BACK; SOMETHING... OUT THERE HAD ATTEMPTED TO REPAIR HIM WITH ONLY LIMITED UNDERSTANDING OF HUMAN PHYSIOLOGY.
THEY GAVE HIM A SUPERHUMAN BODY AND SENT HIM BACK HOME, BUT HIS MIND WAS... TWISTED.
OWLMAN, SUPERWOMAN AND THE OTHERS CAME AFTER. BAD BECAME WORSE.
THAT'S WHY I'M BEGGING YOU TO COME BACK WITH ME AND END THE TYRANNY OF THE CRIME SYNDICATE...
I SAY NO.
I'M SORRY, BUT THIS WORLD HAS TROUBLES OF ITS OWN.
WE'RE NOT AN INTER-DIMENSIONAL POLICE FORCE.

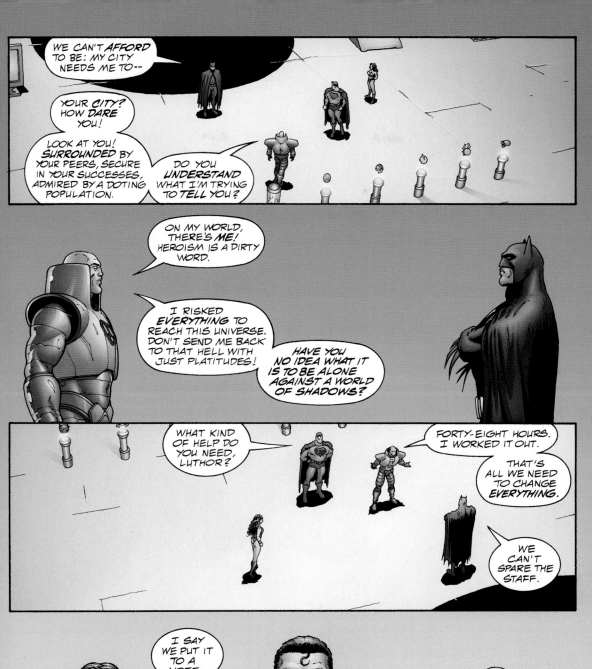

WE CAN'T *AFFORD* TO BE: MY CITY NEEDS ME TO--

YOUR CITY? HOW *DARE* YOU!

LOOK AT YOU! *SURROUNDED* BY YOUR PEERS, SECURE IN YOUR SUCCESSES, ADMIRED BY A DOTING POPULATION.

DO YOU *UNDERSTAND* WHAT I'M TRYING TO *TELL* YOU?

ON MY WORLD, THERE'S *ME!* HEROISM IS A DIRTY WORD.

I RISKED *EVERYTHING* TO REACH THIS UNIVERSE. DON'T SEND ME BACK TO THAT HELL WITH JUST PLATITUDES!

HAVE YOU *NO IDEA* WHAT IT IS TO BE ALONE AGAINST A WORLD OF SHADOWS?

WHAT KIND OF HELP DO YOU NEED, LUTHOR?

FORTY-EIGHT HOURS. I WORKED IT OUT.

THAT'S ALL WE NEED TO CHANGE *EVERYTHING.*

WE CAN'T SPARE THE STAFF.

I SAY WE PUT IT TO A VOTE.

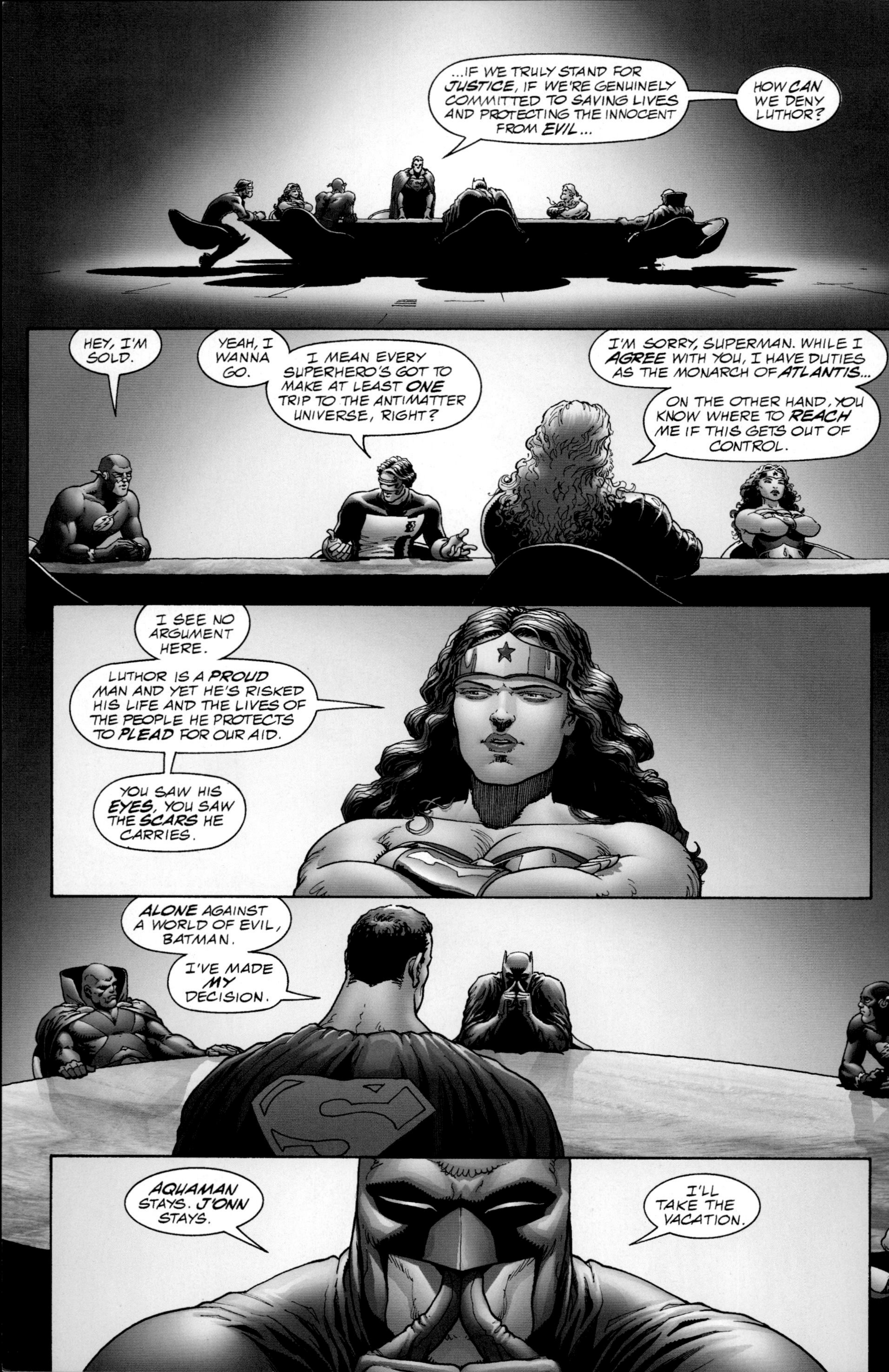
...IF WE TRULY STAND FOR JUSTICE, IF WE'RE GENUINELY COMMITTED TO SAVING LIVES AND PROTECTING THE INNOCENT FROM EVIL...
HOW CAN WE DENY LUTHOR?
HEY, I'M SOLD.
YEAH, I WANNA GO.
I MEAN EVERY SUPERHERO'S GOT TO MAKE AT LEAST ONE TRIP TO THE ANTIMATTER UNIVERSE, RIGHT?
I'M SORRY, SUPERMAN. WHILE I AGREE WITH YOU, I HAVE DUTIES AS THE MONARCH OF ATLANTIS...
ON THE OTHER HAND, YOU KNOW WHERE TO REACH ME IF THIS GETS OUT OF CONTROL.
I SEE NO ARGUMENT HERE.
LUTHOR IS A PROUD MAN AND YET HE'S RISKED HIS LIFE AND THE LIVES OF THE PEOPLE HE PROTECTS TO PLEAD FOR OUR AID.
YOU SAW HIS EYES, YOU SAW THE SCARS HE CARRIES.
ALONE AGAINST A WORLD OF EVIL, BATMAN.
I'VE MADE MY DECISION.
AQUAMAN STAYS. J'ONN STAYS.
I'LL TAKE THE VACATION.

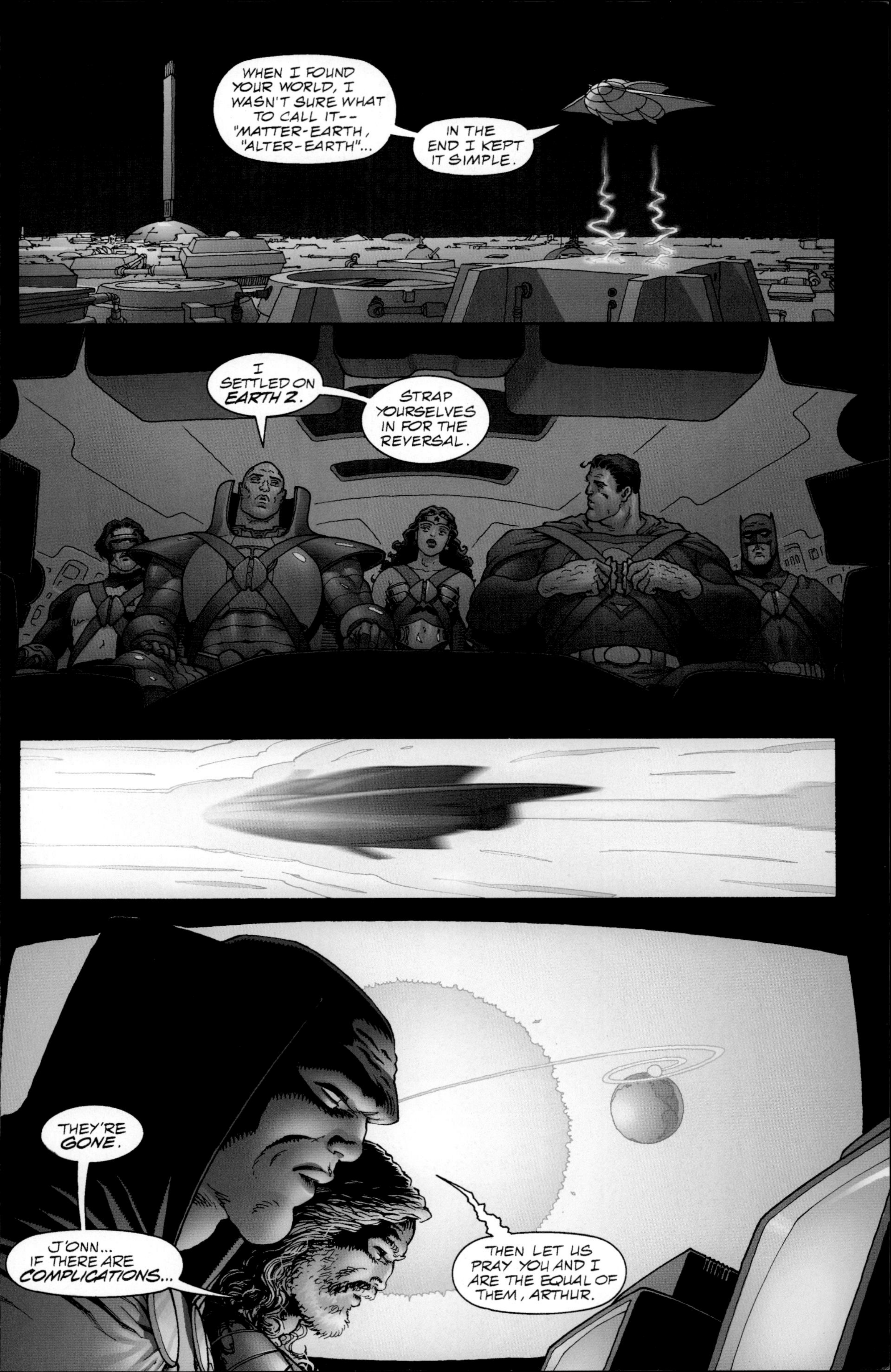
WHEN I FOUND YOUR WORLD, I WASN'T SURE WHAT TO CALL IT-- "MATTER-EARTH, "ALTER-EARTH"...
IN THE END I KEPT IT SIMPLE.
I SETTLED ON EARTH 2.
STRAP YOURSELVES IN FOR THE REVERSAL.
THEY'RE GONE.
J'ONN... IF THERE ARE COMPLICATIONS...
THEN LET US PRAY YOU AND I ARE THE EQUAL OF THEM, ARTHUR.

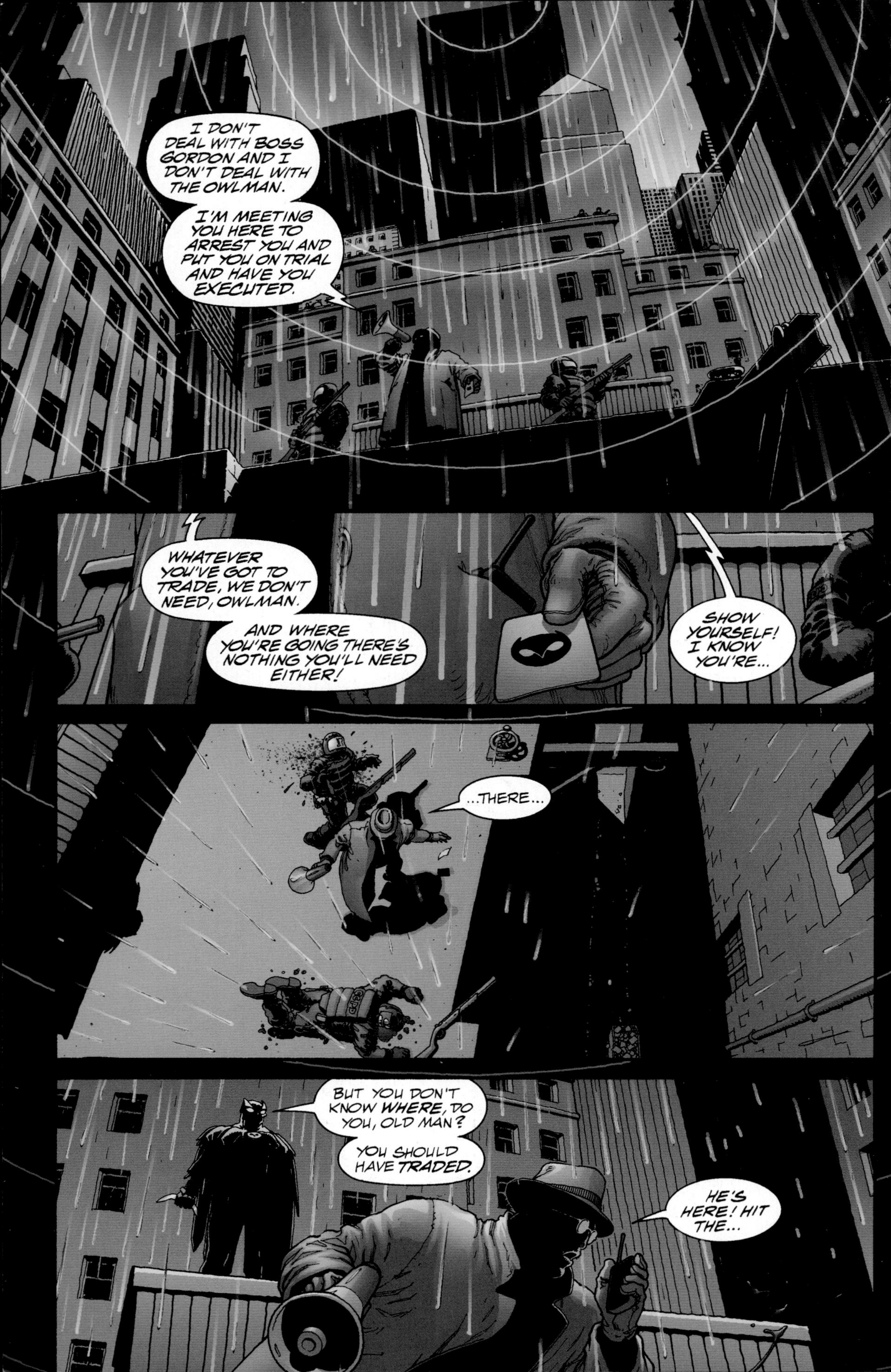
I DON'T DEAL WITH BOSS GORDON AND I DON'T DEAL WITH THE OWLMAN.
I'M MEETING YOU HERE TO ARREST YOU AND PUT YOU ON TRIAL AND HAVE YOU EXECUTED.
WHATEVER YOU'VE GOT TO TRADE, WE DON'T NEED, OWLMAN.
AND WHERE YOU'RE GOING THERE'S NOTHING YOU'LL NEED EITHER!
SHOW YOURSELF! I KNOW YOU'RE...
...THERE...
BUT YOU DON'T KNOW WHERE, DO YOU, OLD MAN?
YOU SHOULD HAVE TRADED.
HE'S HERE! HIT THE...

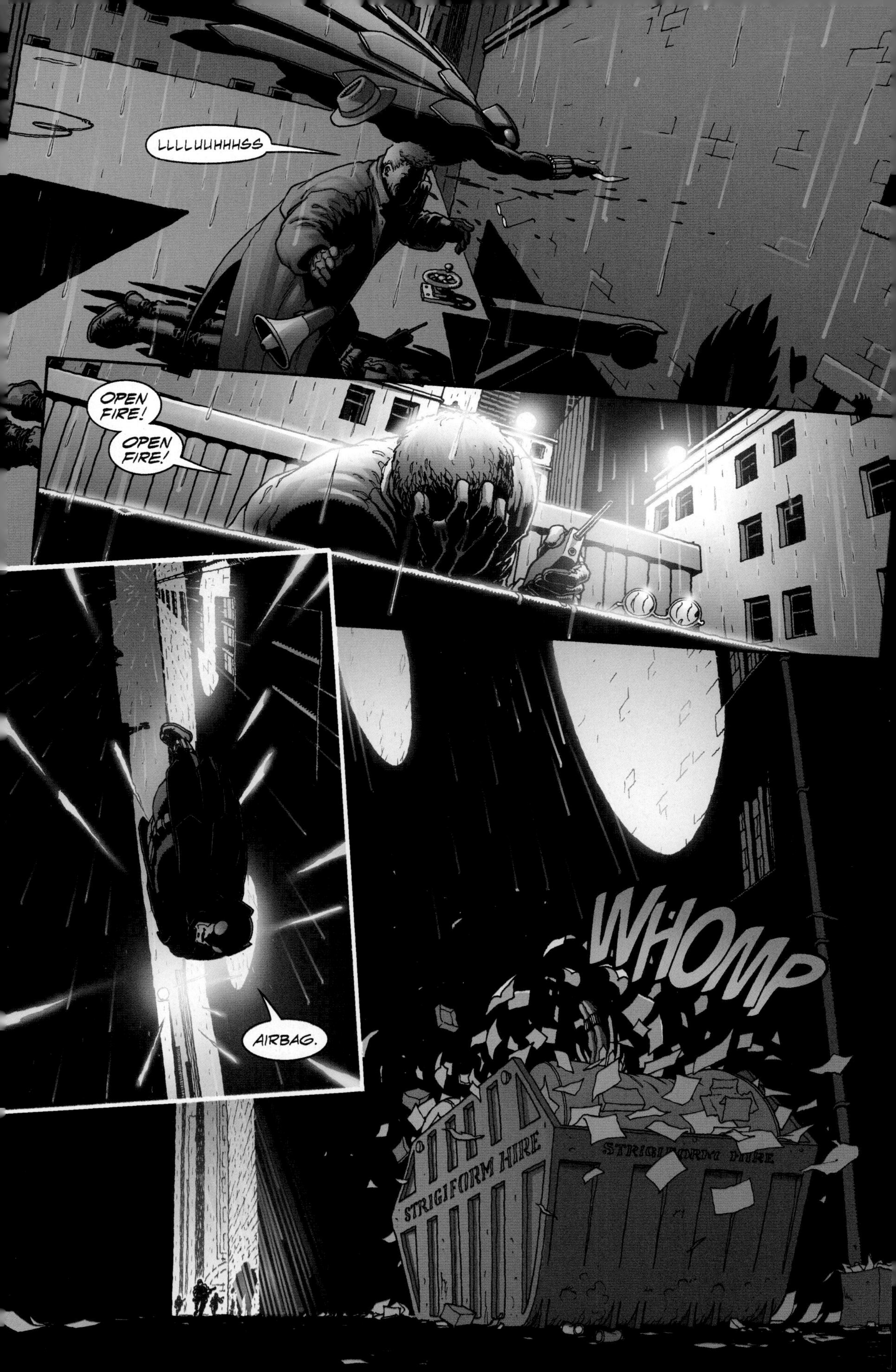
LLLLUUHHHSS
OPEN FIRE!
OPEN FIRE!
AIRBAG.
WHOMP
STRIGIFORM HIRE
STRIGIFORM HIRE

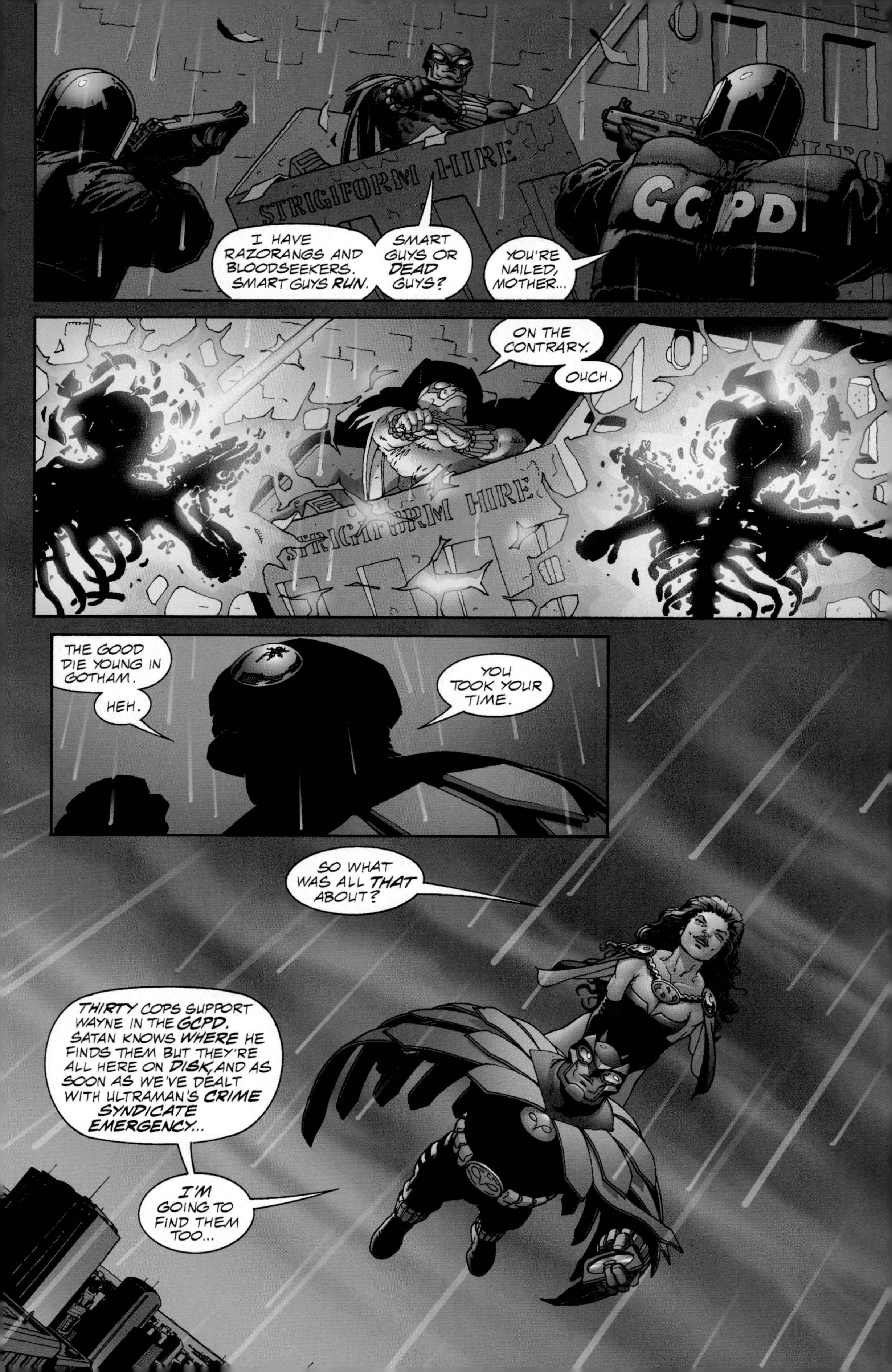
STRIGIFORM HIRE
GCPD
I HAVE RAZORANGS AND BLOODSEEKERS. SMART GUYS RUN.
SMART GUYS OR DEAD GUYS?
YOU'RE NAILED, MOTHER...
ON THE CONTRARY.
OUCH.
STRIGIFORM HIRE
THE GOOD DIE YOUNG IN GOTHAM.
HEH.
YOU TOOK YOUR TIME.
SO WHAT WAS ALL THAT ABOUT?
THIRTY COPS SUPPORT WAYNE IN THE GCPD. SATAN KNOWS WHERE HE FINDS THEM BUT THEY'RE ALL HERE ON DISK, AND AS SOON AS WE'VE DEALT WITH ULTRAMAN'S CRIME SYNDICATE EMERGENCY...
I'M GOING TO FIND THEM TOO...

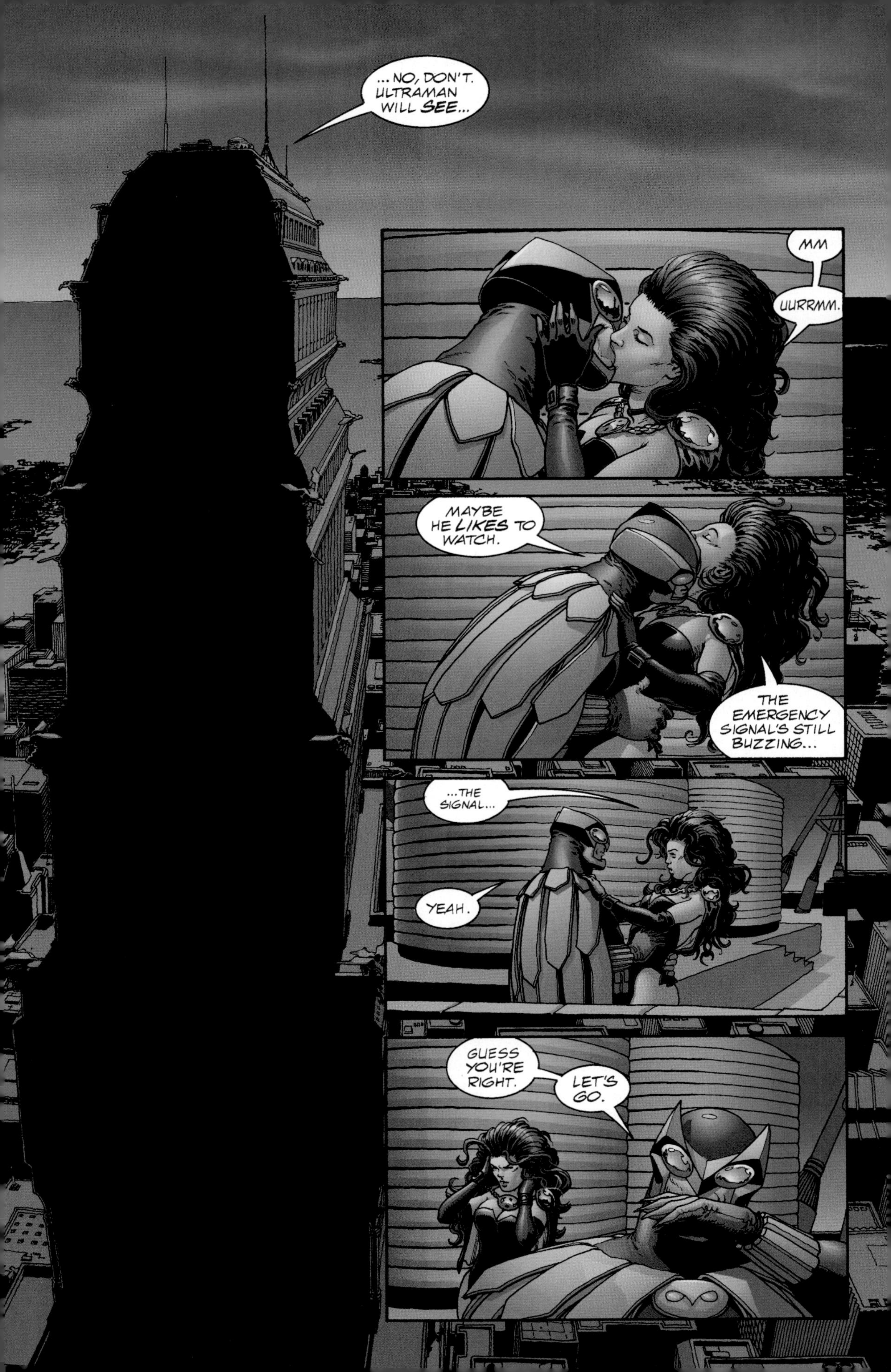

... NO, DON'T. ULTRAMAN WILL SEE...
MM
UURRMM.
MAYBE HE LIKES TO WATCH.
THE EMERGENCY SIGNAL'S STILL BUZZING...
...THE SIGNAL...
YEAH.
GUESS YOU'RE RIGHT.
LET'S GO.

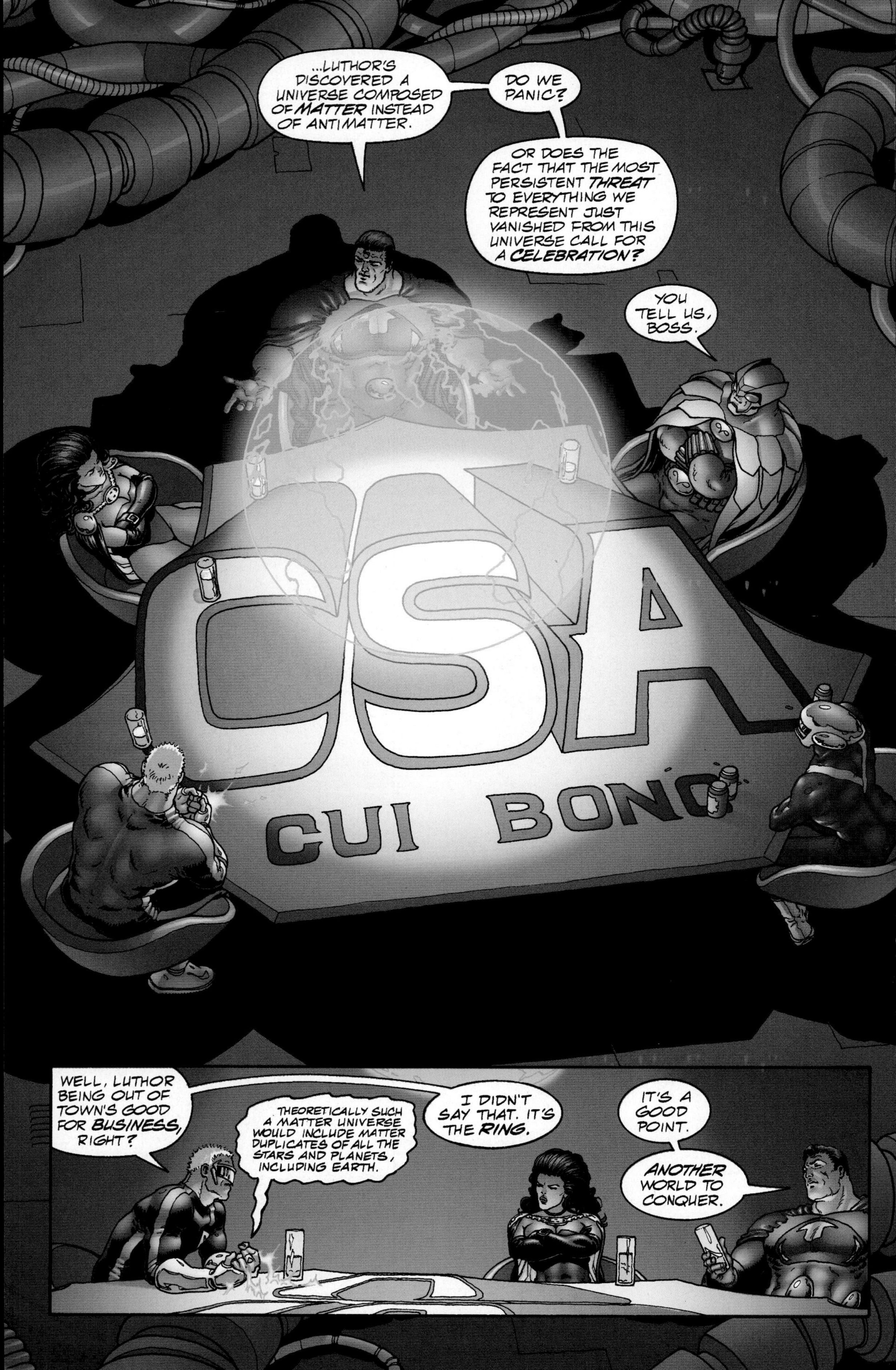
...LUTHOR'S DISCOVERED A UNIVERSE COMPOSED OF *MATTER* INSTEAD OF ANTIMATTER.
DO WE PANIC?
OR DOES THE FACT THAT THE MOST PERSISTENT *THREAT* TO EVERYTHING WE REPRESENT JUST VANISHED FROM THIS UNIVERSE CALL FOR A *CELEBRATION?*
YOU TELL US, BOSS.
CSA
CUI BONO
WELL, LUTHOR BEING OUT OF TOWN'S GOOD FOR *BUSINESS,* RIGHT?
THEORETICALLY SUCH A MATTER UNIVERSE WOULD INCLUDE MATTER DUPLICATES OF ALL THE STARS AND PLANETS, INCLUDING EARTH.
I DIDN'T SAY THAT. IT'S THE *RING.*
IT'S A GOOD POINT.
ANOTHER WORLD TO CONQUER.

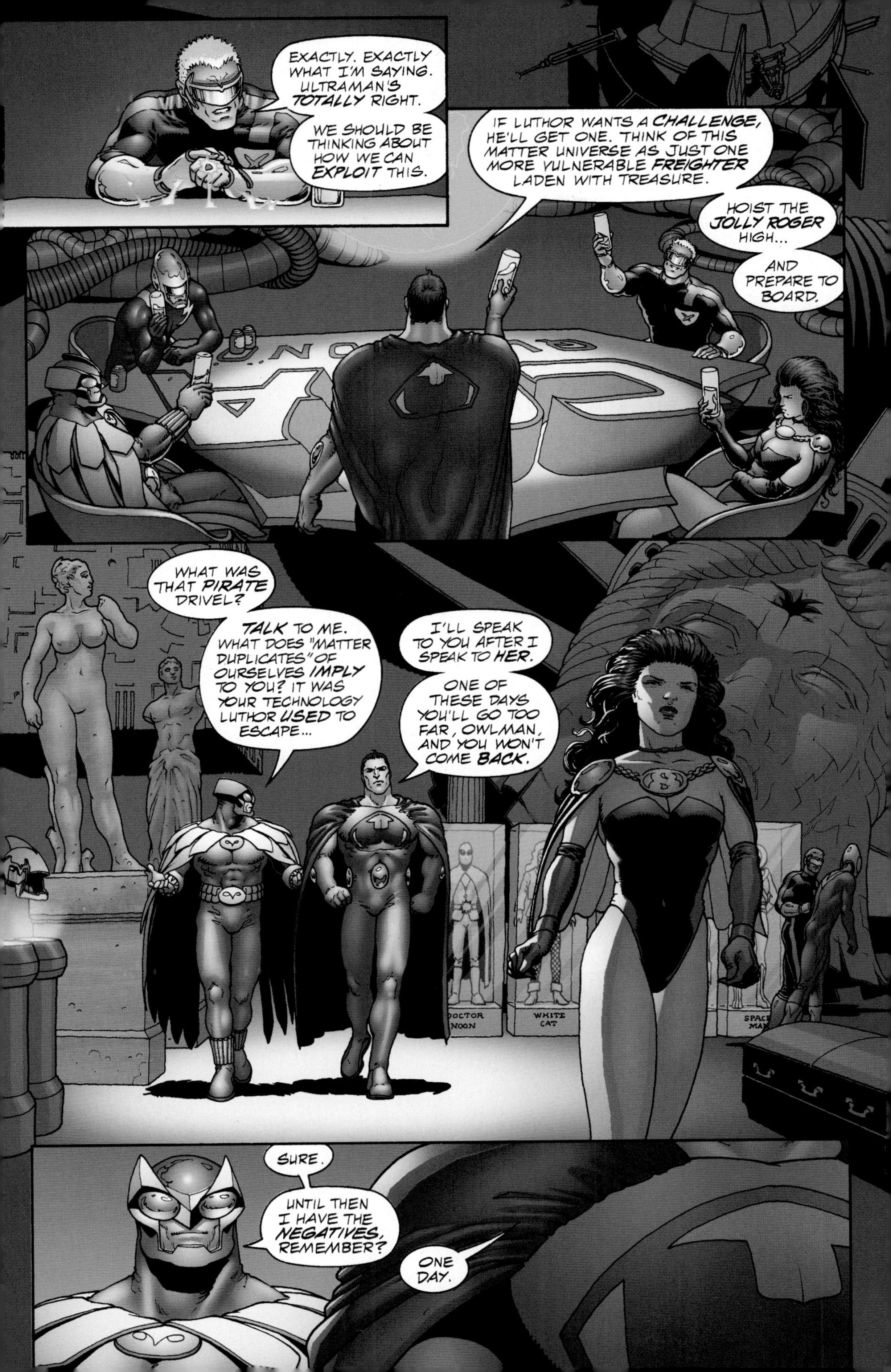
EXACTLY. EXACTLY WHAT I'M SAYING. ULTRAMAN'S **TOTALLY** RIGHT.
WE SHOULD BE THINKING ABOUT HOW WE CAN **EXPLOIT** THIS.
IF LUTHOR WANTS A **CHALLENGE**, HE'LL GET ONE. THINK OF THIS MATTER UNIVERSE AS JUST ONE MORE VULNERABLE **FREIGHTER** LADEN WITH TREASURE.
HOIST THE **JOLLY ROGER** HIGH...
AND PREPARE TO BOARD.
WHAT WAS THAT **PIRATE** DRIVEL?
TALK TO ME. WHAT DOES "MATTER DUPLICATES" OF OURSELVES **IMPLY** TO YOU? IT WAS **YOUR** TECHNOLOGY LUTHOR **USED** TO ESCAPE...
I'LL SPEAK TO YOU AFTER I SPEAK TO **HER**.
ONE OF THESE DAYS YOU'LL GO TOO FAR, OWLMAN, AND YOU WON'T COME **BACK**.
DOCTOR NOON
WHITE CAT
SURE.
UNTIL THEN I HAVE THE **NEGATIVES**, REMEMBER?
ONE DAY.

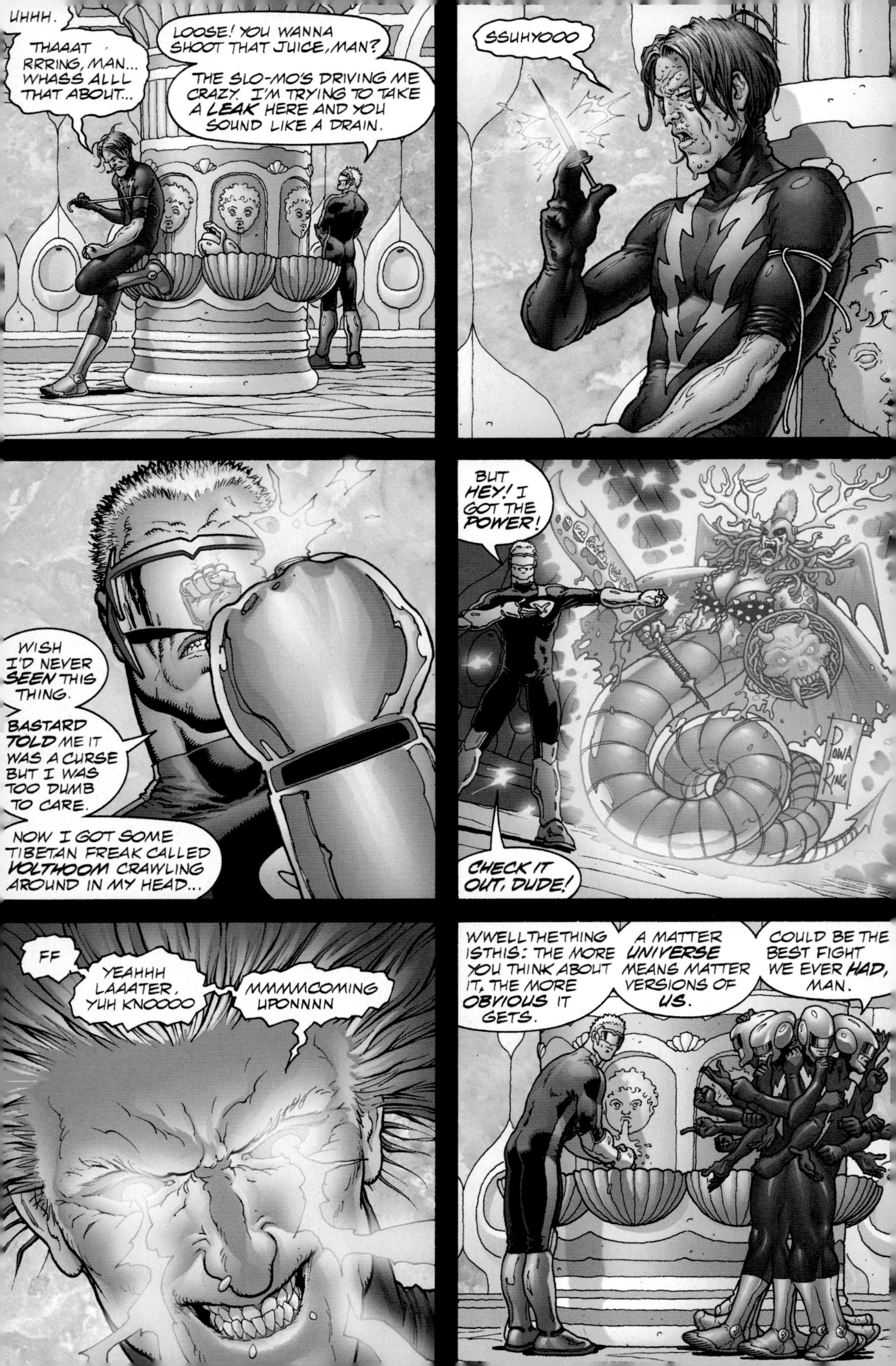

UHHH.
THAAAT RRRING, MAN... WHASS ALLL THAT ABOUT...
LOOSE! YOU WANNA SHOOT THAT JUICE, MAN?
THE SLO-MO'S DRIVING ME CRAZY. I'M TRYING TO TAKE A **LEAK** HERE AND YOU SOUND LIKE A DRAIN.
SSUHYOOO
WISH I'D NEVER **SEEN** THIS THING.
BASTARD **TOLD** ME IT WAS A CURSE BUT I WAS TOO DUMB TO CARE.
NOW I GOT SOME TIBETAN FREAK CALLED **VOLTHOOM** CRAWLING AROUND IN MY HEAD...
BUT **HEY!** I GOT THE **POWER!**
POWA RING
CHECK IT OUT, DUDE!
FF
YEAHHH LAAATER, YUH KNOOOO
MMMMCOMING UPONNNN
WWELLTHETHING ISTHIS: THE MORE YOU THINK ABOUT IT, THE MORE **OBVIOUS** IT GETS.
A MATTER **UNIVERSE** MEANS MATTER VERSIONS OF **US**.
COULD BE THE BEST FIGHT WE EVER **HAD**, MAN.

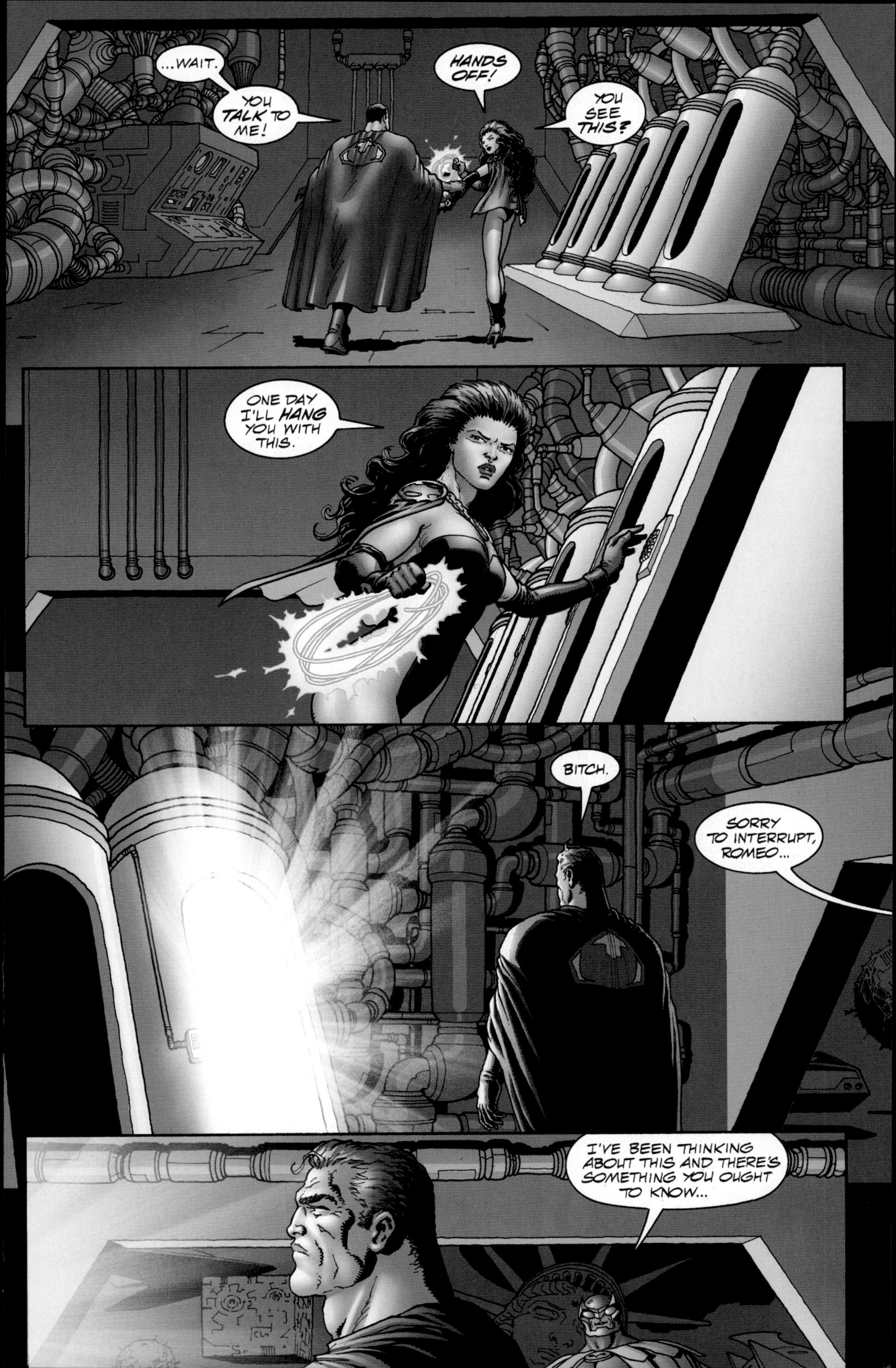
...WAIT.
YOU TALK TO ME!
HANDS OFF!
YOU SEE THIS?
ONE DAY I'LL HANG YOU WITH THIS.
BITCH.
SORRY TO INTERRUPT, ROMEO...
I'VE BEEN THINKING ABOUT THIS AND THERE'S SOMETHING YOU OUGHT TO KNOW...

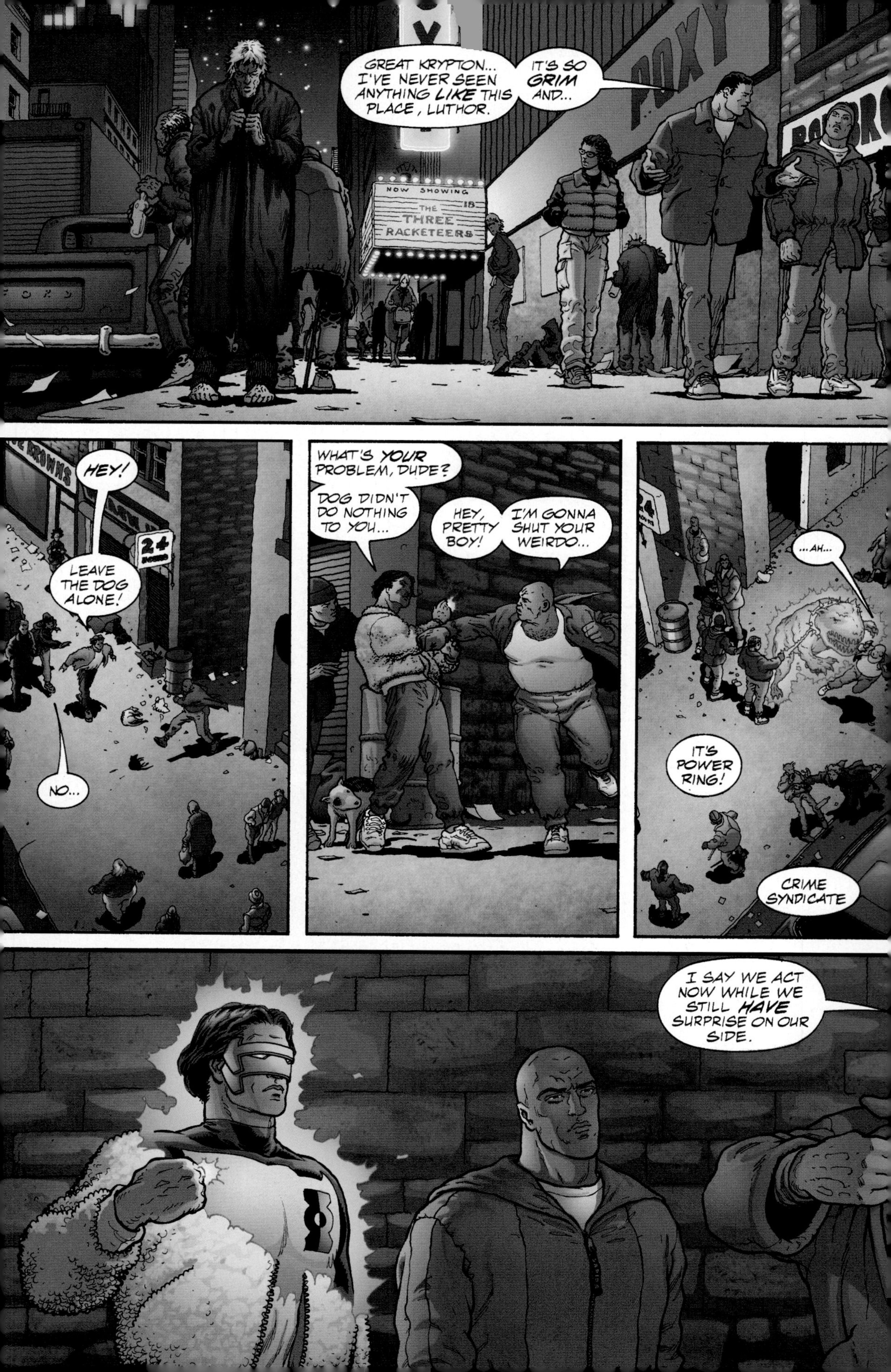

GREAT KRYPTON... I'VE NEVER SEEN ANYTHING LIKE THIS PLACE, LUTHOR.
IT'S SO GRIM AND...
POXY
NOW SHOWING
THE THREE RACKETEERS
18
HEY!
LEAVE THE DOG ALONE!
NO...
24 HOURS
WHAT'S YOUR PROBLEM, DUDE?
DOG DIDN'T DO NOTHING TO YOU...
HEY, PRETTY BOY!
I'M GONNA SHUT YOUR WEIRDO...
...AH...
IT'S POWER RING!
CRIME SYNDICATE
I SAY WE ACT NOW WHILE WE STILL HAVE SURPRISE ON OUR SIDE.

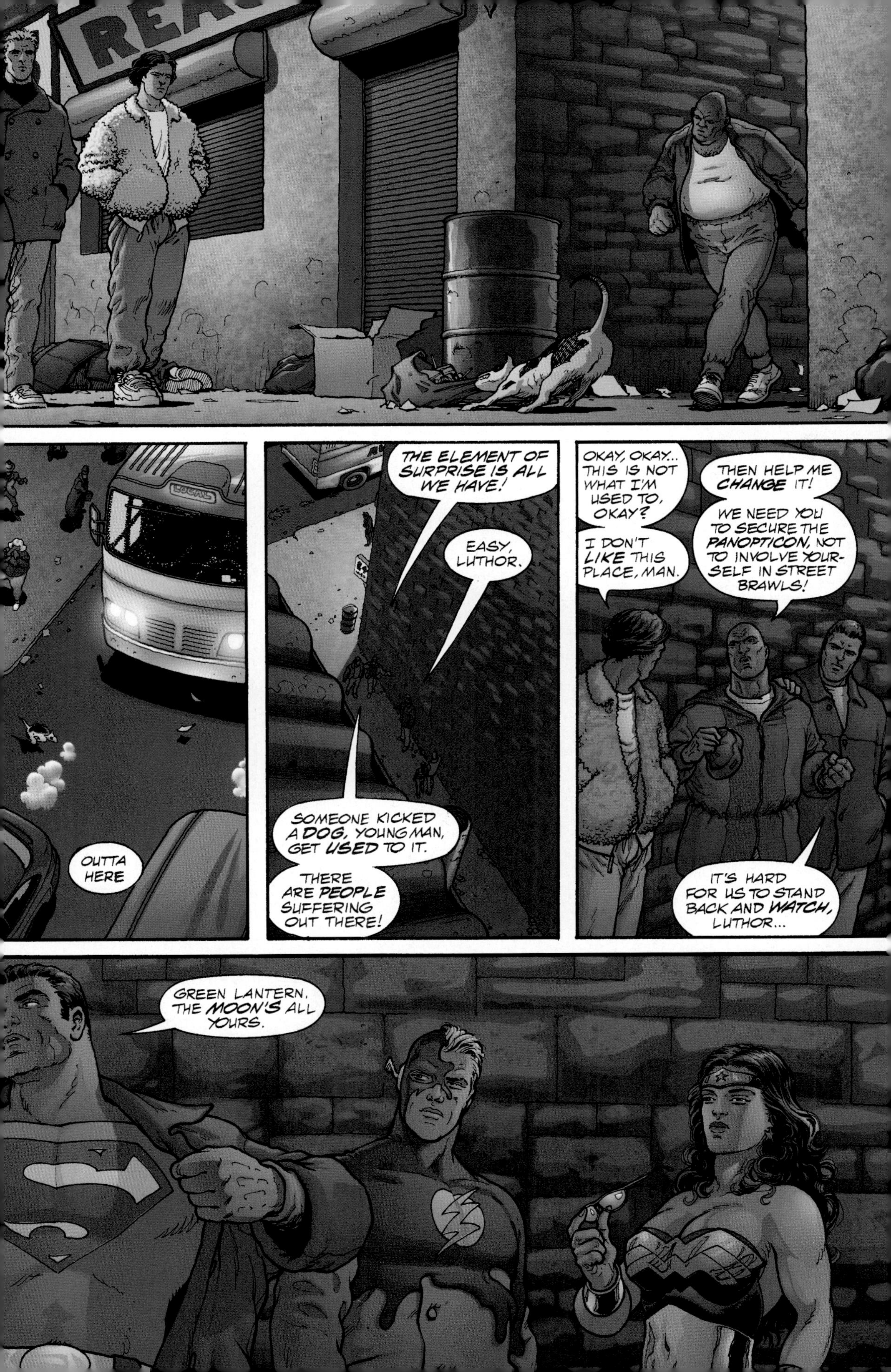

OUTTA HERE
THE ELEMENT OF SURPRISE IS ALL WE HAVE!
EASY, LUTHOR.
SOMEONE KICKED A DOG, YOUNG MAN, GET USED TO IT.
THERE ARE PEOPLE SUFFERING OUT THERE!
OKAY, OKAY... THIS IS NOT WHAT I'M USED TO, OKAY?
I DON'T LIKE THIS PLACE, MAN.
THEN HELP ME CHANGE IT!
WE NEED YOU TO SECURE THE PANOPTICON, NOT TO INVOLVE YOURSELF IN STREET BRAWLS!
IT'S HARD FOR US TO STAND BACK AND WATCH, LUTHOR...
GREEN LANTERN, THE MOON'S ALL YOURS.

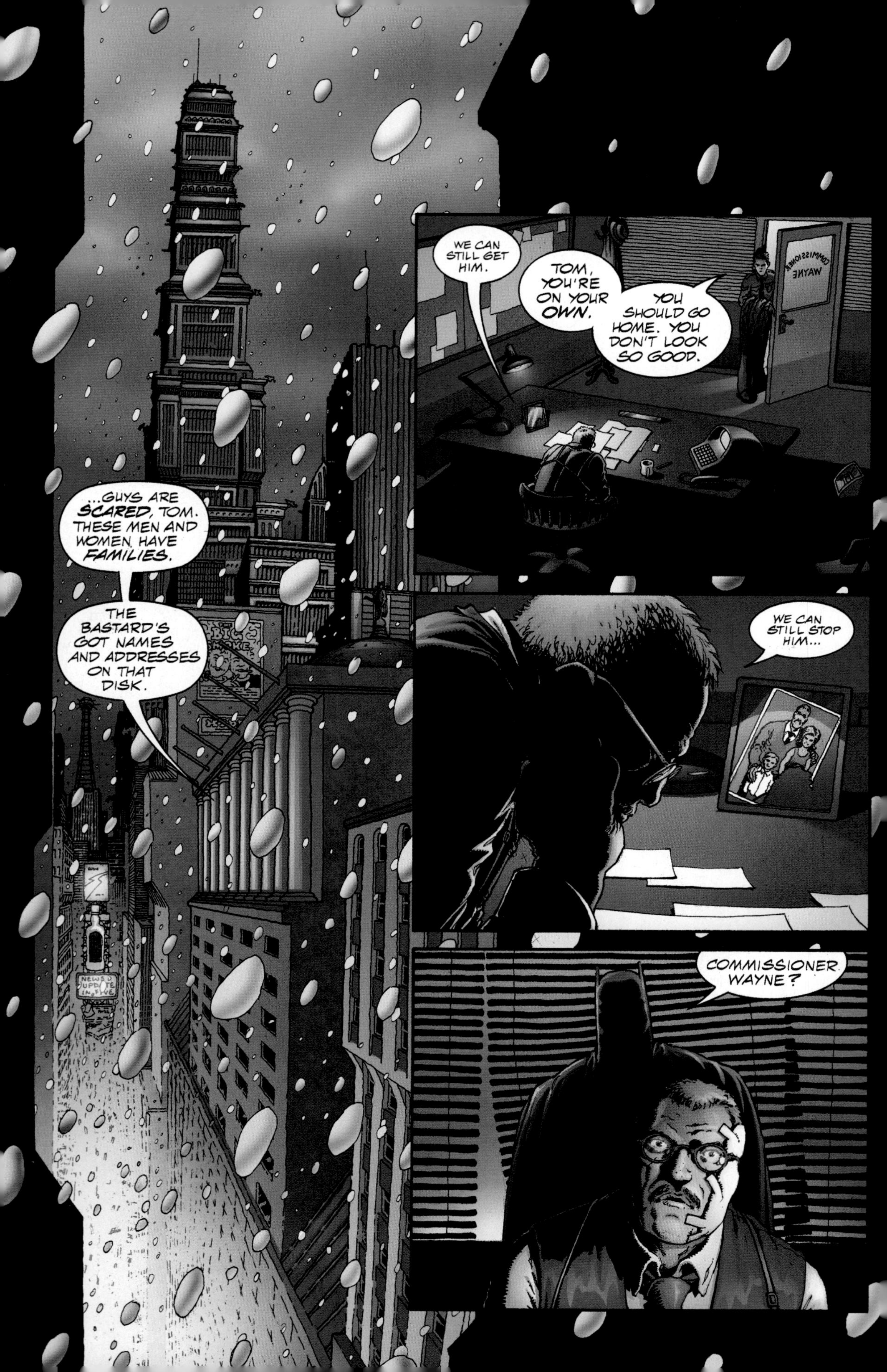

...GUYS ARE SCARED, TOM. THESE MEN AND WOMEN HAVE FAMILIES.
THE BASTARD'S GOT NAMES AND ADDRESSES ON THAT DISK.
COMMISSIONER WAYNE
WE CAN STILL GET HIM.
TOM, YOU'RE ON YOUR OWN.
YOU SHOULD GO HOME. YOU DON'T LOOK SO GOOD.
WE CAN STILL STOP HIM...
COMMISSIONER WAYNE?

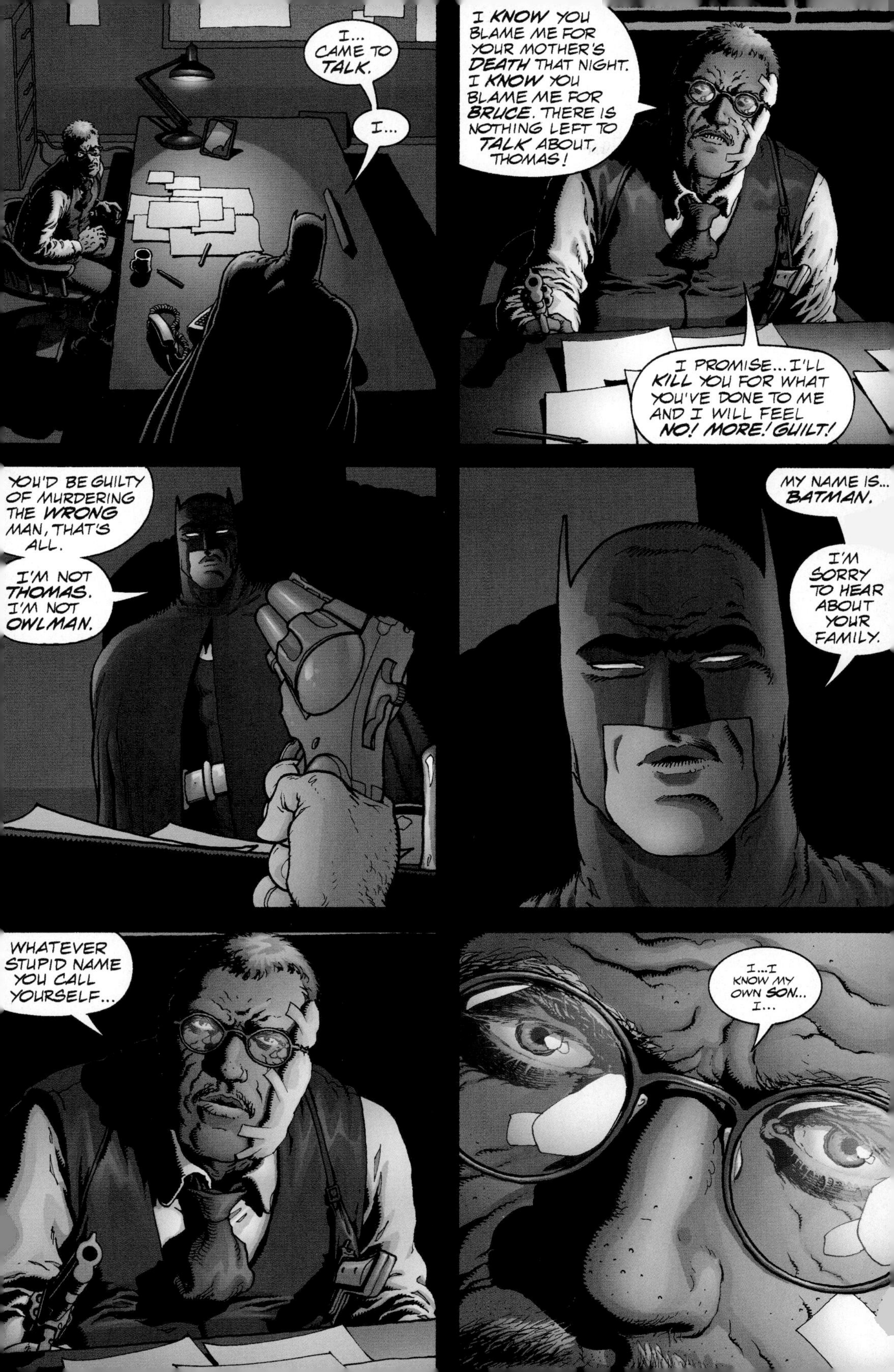

I... CAME TO TALK.
I...
I KNOW YOU BLAME ME FOR YOUR MOTHER'S DEATH THAT NIGHT. I KNOW YOU BLAME ME FOR BRUCE. THERE IS NOTHING LEFT TO TALK ABOUT, THOMAS!
I PROMISE... I'LL KILL YOU FOR WHAT YOU'VE DONE TO ME AND I WILL FEEL NO! MORE! GUILT!
YOU'D BE GUILTY OF MURDERING THE WRONG MAN, THAT'S ALL.
I'M NOT THOMAS. I'M NOT OWLMAN.
MY NAME IS... BATMAN.
I'M SORRY TO HEAR ABOUT YOUR FAMILY.
WHATEVER STUPID NAME YOU CALL YOURSELF...
I...I KNOW MY OWN SON... I...

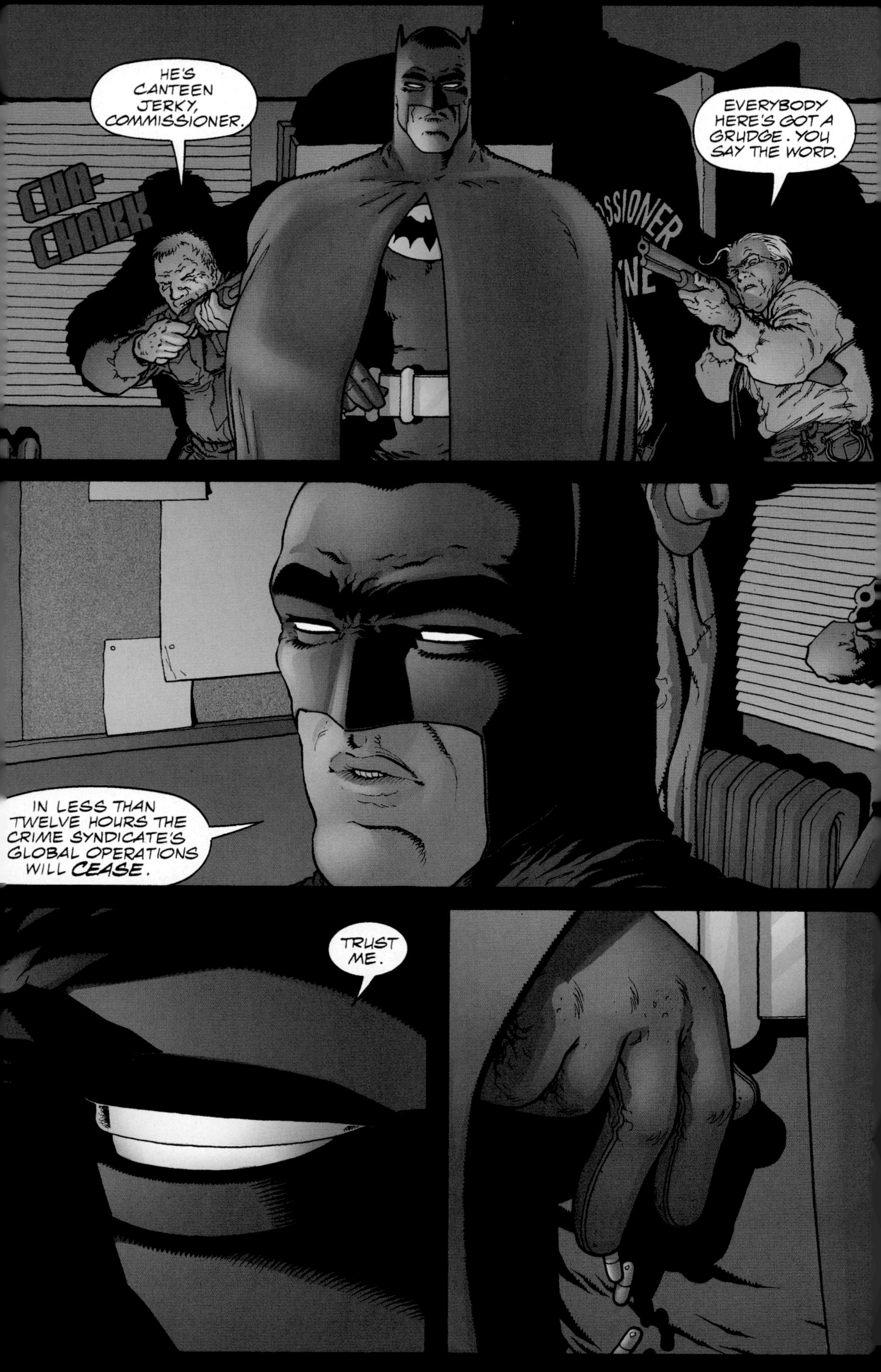
HE'S CANTEEN JERKY, COMMISSIONER.
CHA-CHAKK
EVERYBODY HERE'S GOT A GRUDGE. YOU SAY THE WORD.
IN LESS THAN TWELVE HOURS THE CRIME SYNDICATE'S GLOBAL OPERATIONS WILL CEASE.
TRUST ME.

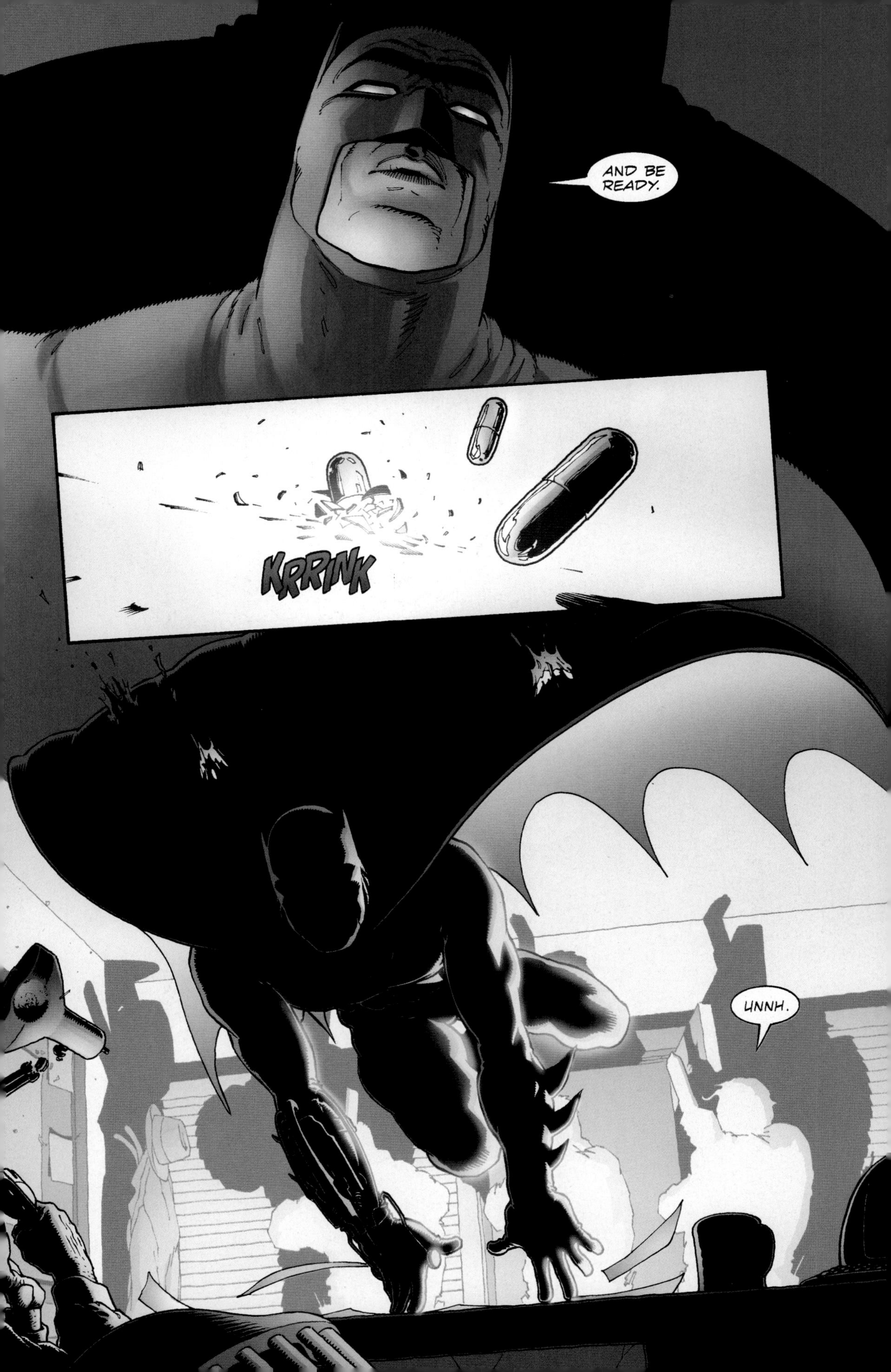
AND BE READY.
KRRINK
UNNH.

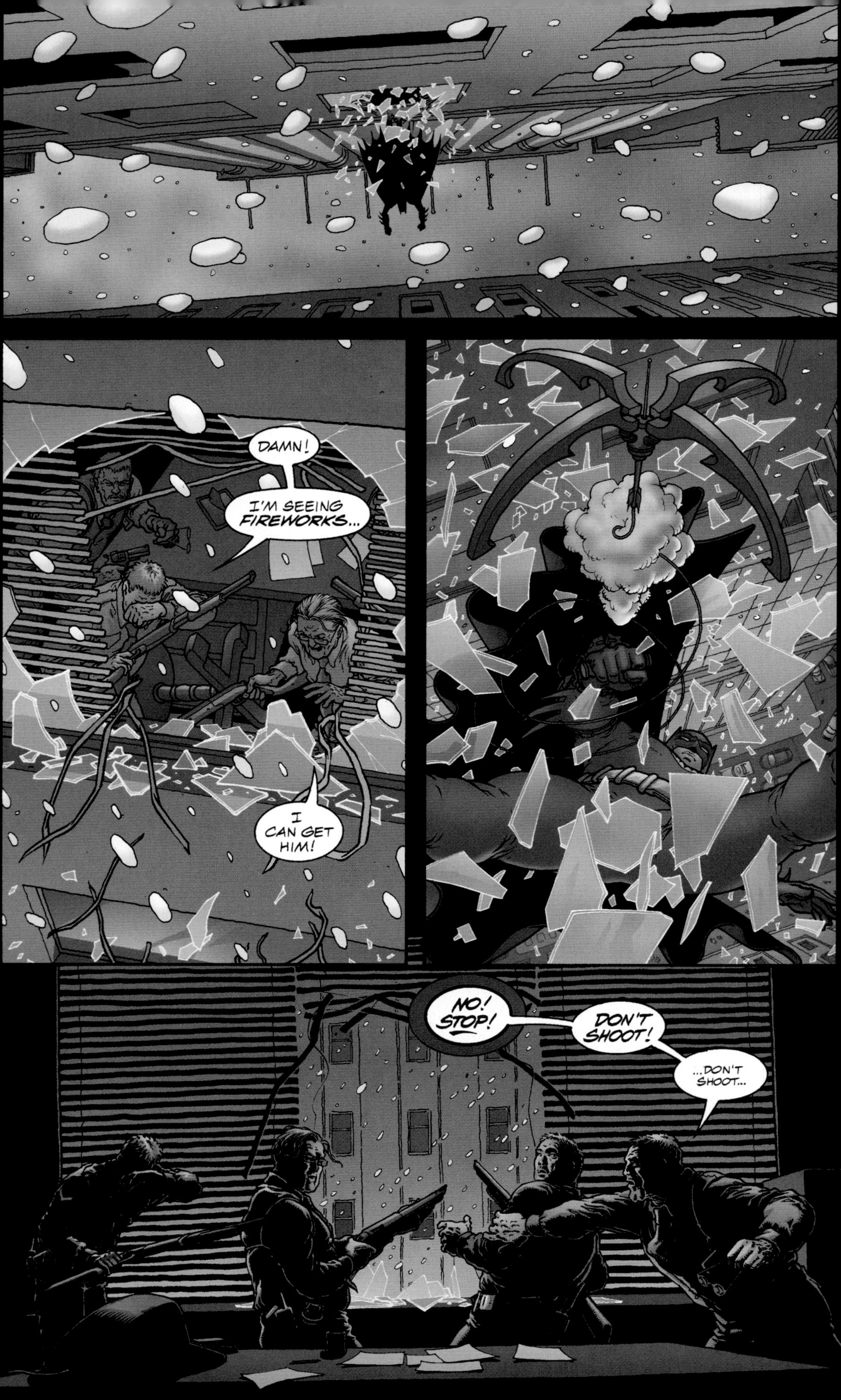
DAMN!
I'M SEEING FIREWORKS...
I CAN GET HIM!
NO! STOP!
DON'T SHOOT!
...DON'T SHOOT...

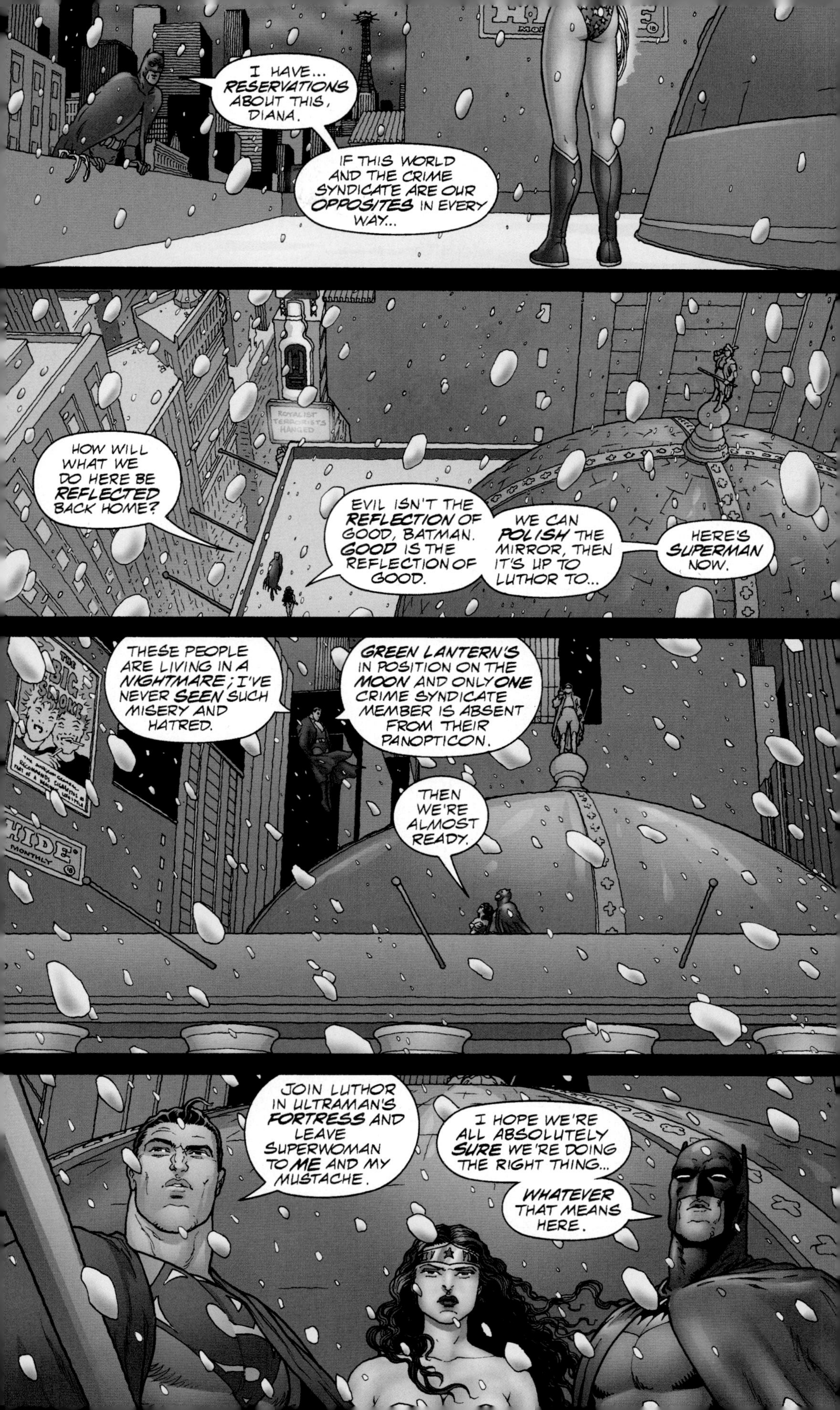

I HAVE... RESERVATIONS ABOUT THIS, DIANA.
IF THIS WORLD AND THE CRIME SYNDICATE ARE OUR OPPOSITES IN EVERY WAY...
ROYALIST TERRORISTS HANGED
HOW WILL WHAT WE DO HERE BE REFLECTED BACK HOME?
EVIL ISN'T THE REFLECTION OF GOOD, BATMAN. GOOD IS THE REFLECTION OF GOOD.
WE CAN POLISH THE MIRROR, THEN IT'S UP TO LUTHOR TO...
HERE'S SUPERMAN NOW.
THESE PEOPLE ARE LIVING IN A NIGHTMARE; I'VE NEVER SEEN SUCH MISERY AND HATRED.
GREEN LANTERN'S IN POSITION ON THE MOON AND ONLY ONE CRIME SYNDICATE MEMBER IS ABSENT FROM THEIR PANOPTICON.
THEN WE'RE ALMOST READY.
HIDE MONTHLY
JOIN LUTHOR IN ULTRAMAN'S FORTRESS AND LEAVE SUPERWOMAN TO ME AND MY MUSTACHE.
I HOPE WE'RE ALL ABSOLUTELY SURE WE'RE DOING THE RIGHT THING...
WHATEVER THAT MEANS HERE.

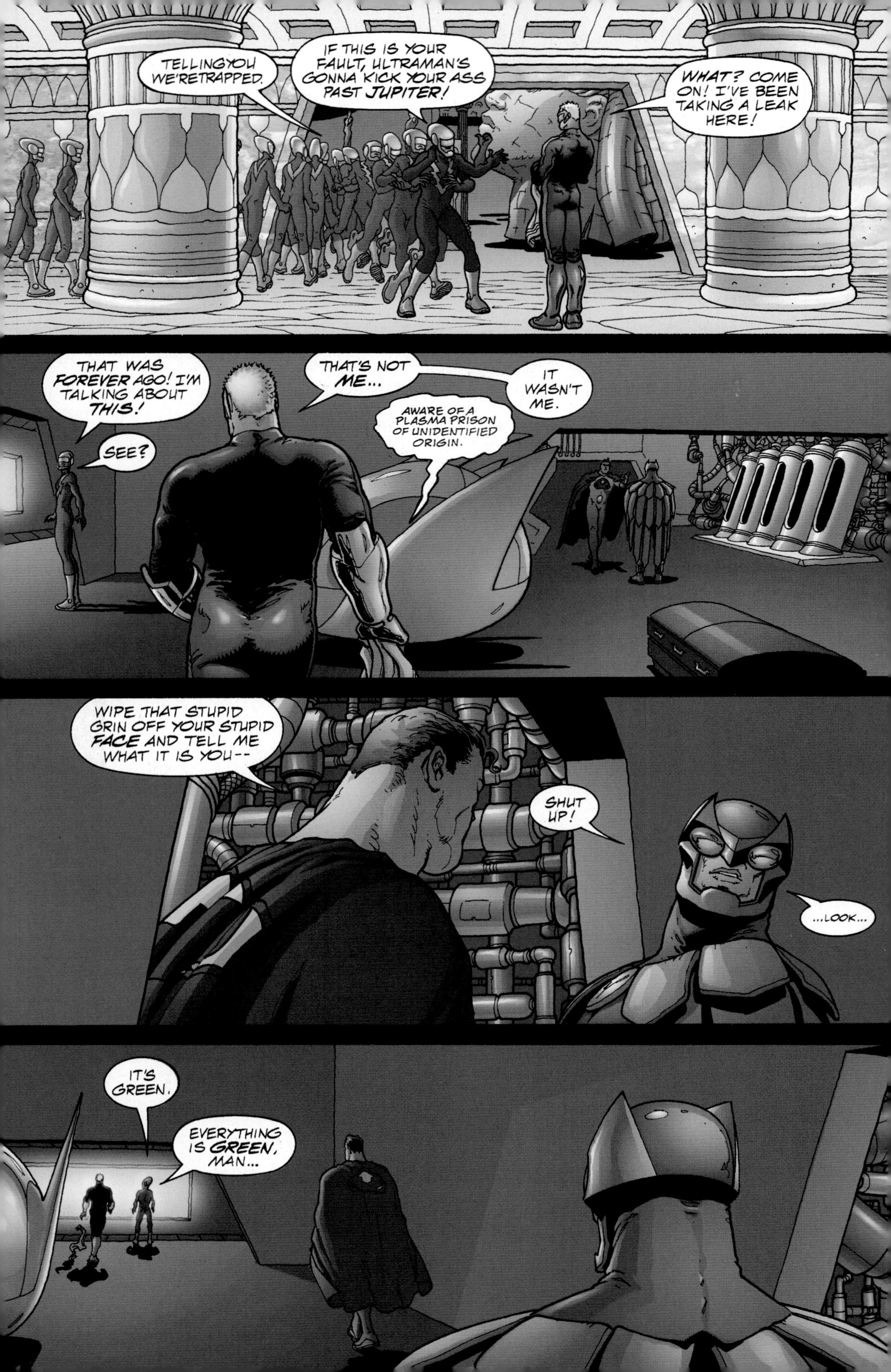
TELLINGYOU WE'RETRAPPED.
IF THIS IS YOUR FAULT, ULTRAMAN'S GONNA KICK YOUR ASS PAST JUPITER!
WHAT? COME ON! I'VE BEEN TAKING A LEAK HERE!
THAT WAS FOREVER AGO! I'M TALKING ABOUT THIS!
SEE?
THAT'S NOT ME...
IT WASN'T ME.
AWARE OF A PLASMA PRISON OF UNIDENTIFIED ORIGIN.
WIPE THAT STUPID GRIN OFF YOUR STUPID FACE AND TELL ME WHAT IT IS YOU--
SHUT UP!
...LOOK...
IT'S GREEN.
EVERYTHING IS GREEN, MAN...

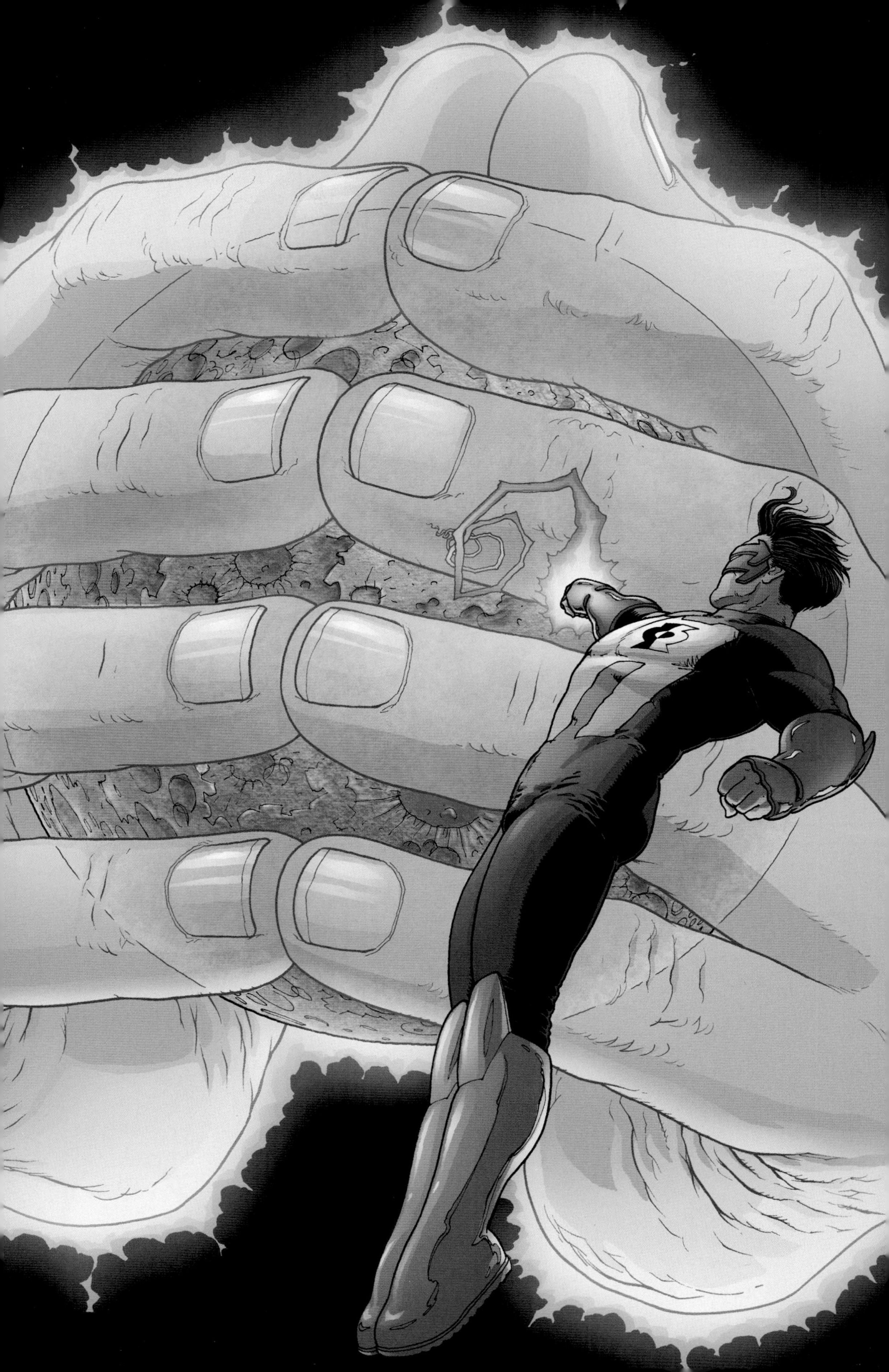

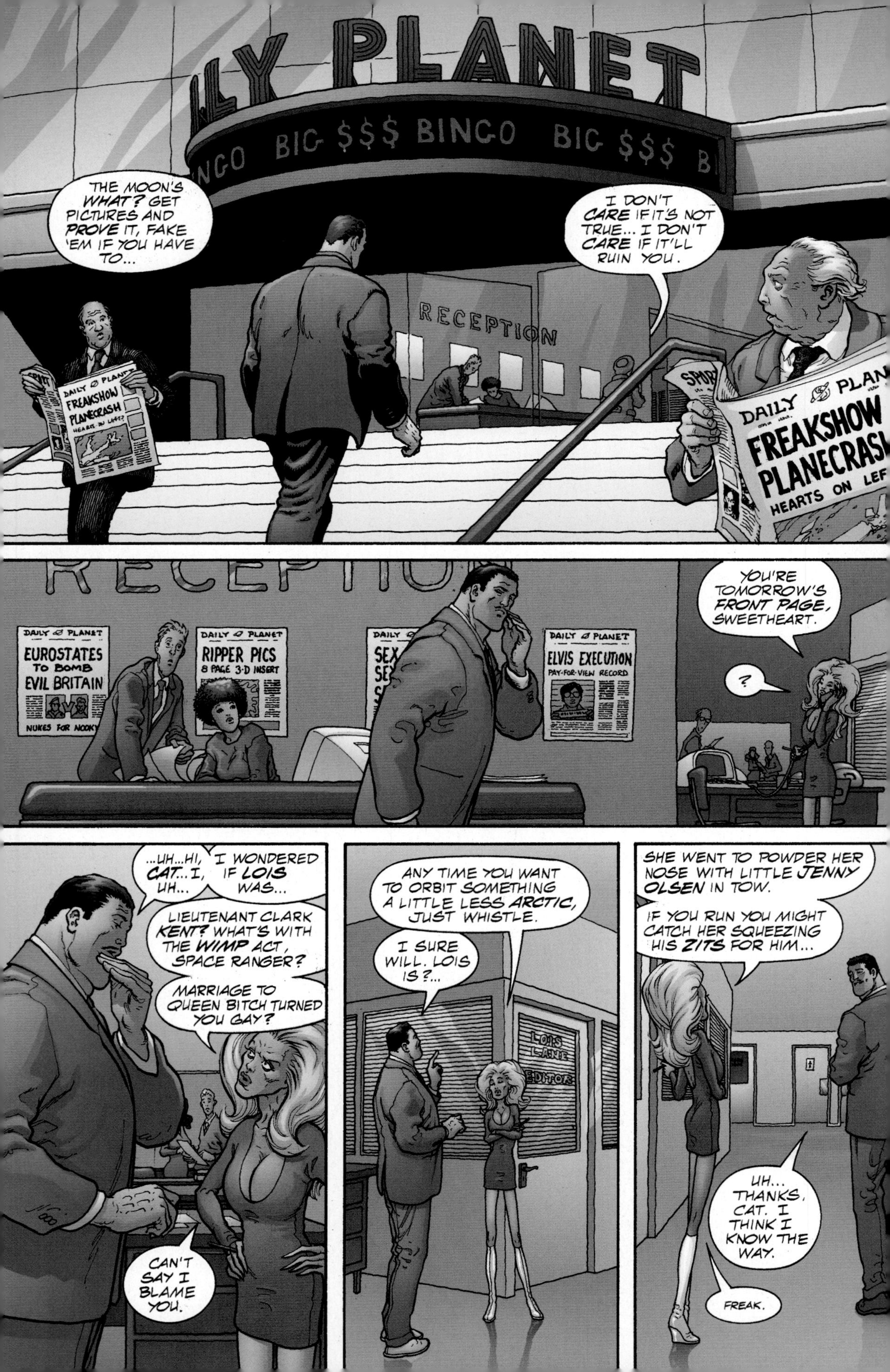
DAILY PLANET
BIG $$$ BINGO BIG $$$ BINGO
THE MOON'S WHAT? GET PICTURES AND PROVE IT, FAKE 'EM IF YOU HAVE TO...
I DON'T CARE IF IT'S NOT TRUE... I DON'T CARE IF IT'LL RUIN YOU.
RECEPTION
DAILY PLANET
FREAKSHOW PLANECRASH
HEARTS ON LEF
DAILY PLANET
EUROSTATES TO BOMB EVIL BRITAIN
NUKES FOR NOOKY
DAILY PLANET
RIPPER PICS
8 PAGE 3-D INSERT
DAILY PLANET
ELVIS EXECUTION
PAY-FOR-VIEW RECORD
YOU'RE TOMORROW'S FRONT PAGE, SWEETHEART.
?
...UH...HI, CAT...I, UH...
I WONDERED IF LOIS WAS...
LIEUTENANT CLARK KENT? WHAT'S WITH THE WIMP ACT, SPACE RANGER?
MARRIAGE TO QUEEN BITCH TURNED YOU GAY?
CAN'T SAY I BLAME YOU.
ANY TIME YOU WANT TO ORBIT SOMETHING A LITTLE LESS ARCTIC, JUST WHISTLE.
I SURE WILL. LOIS IS?...
LOIS LANE
EDITOR
SHE WENT TO POWDER HER NOSE WITH LITTLE JENNY OLSEN IN TOW.
IF YOU RUN YOU MIGHT CATCH HER SQUEEZING HIS ZITS FOR HIM...
UH... THANKS, CAT. I THINK I KNOW THE WAY.
FREAK.

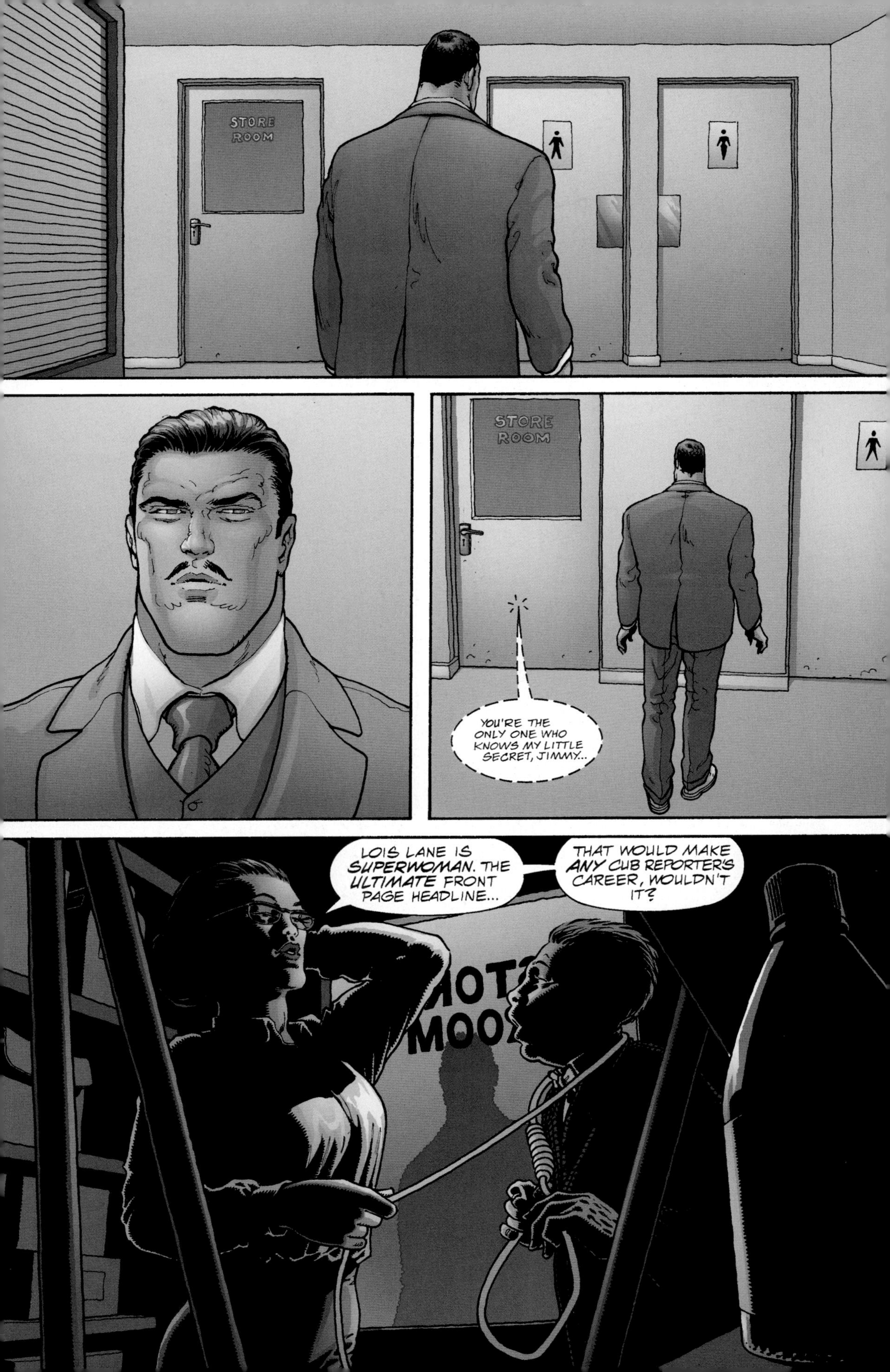
STORE ROOM
STORE ROOM
YOU'RE THE ONLY ONE WHO KNOWS MY LITTLE SECRET, JIMMY...
LOIS LANE IS SUPERWOMAN. THE ULTIMATE FRONT PAGE HEADLINE...
THAT WOULD MAKE ANY CUB REPORTER'S CAREER, WOULDN'T IT?

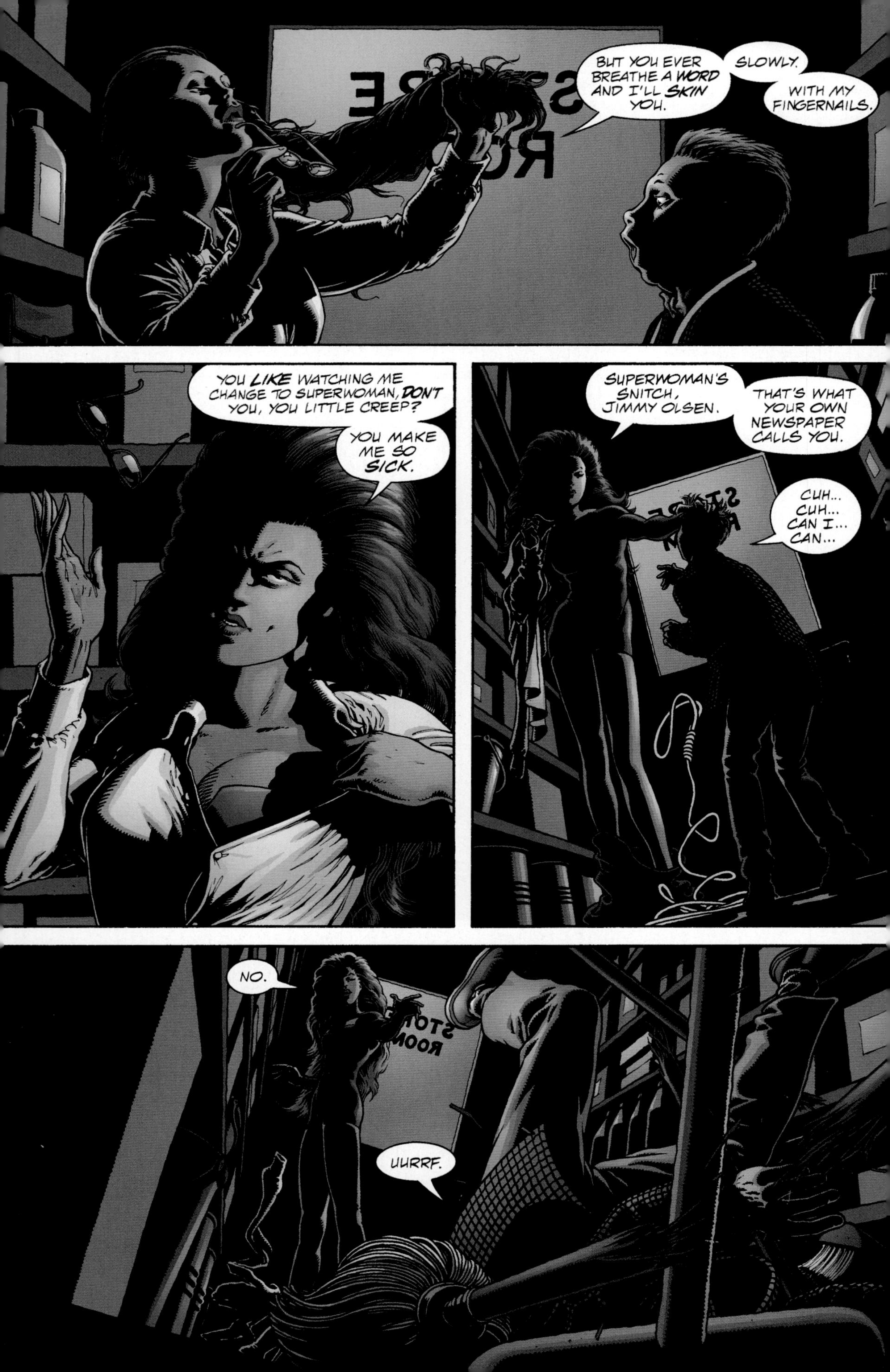
BUT YOU EVER BREATHE A WORD AND I'LL SKIN YOU.
SLOWLY.
WITH MY FINGERNAILS.
YOU LIKE WATCHING ME CHANGE TO SUPERWOMAN, DON'T YOU, YOU LITTLE CREEP?
YOU MAKE ME SO SICK.
SUPERWOMAN'S SNITCH, JIMMY OLSEN.
THAT'S WHAT YOUR OWN NEWSPAPER CALLS YOU.
CUH... CUH... CAN I... CAN...
NO.
UURRF.

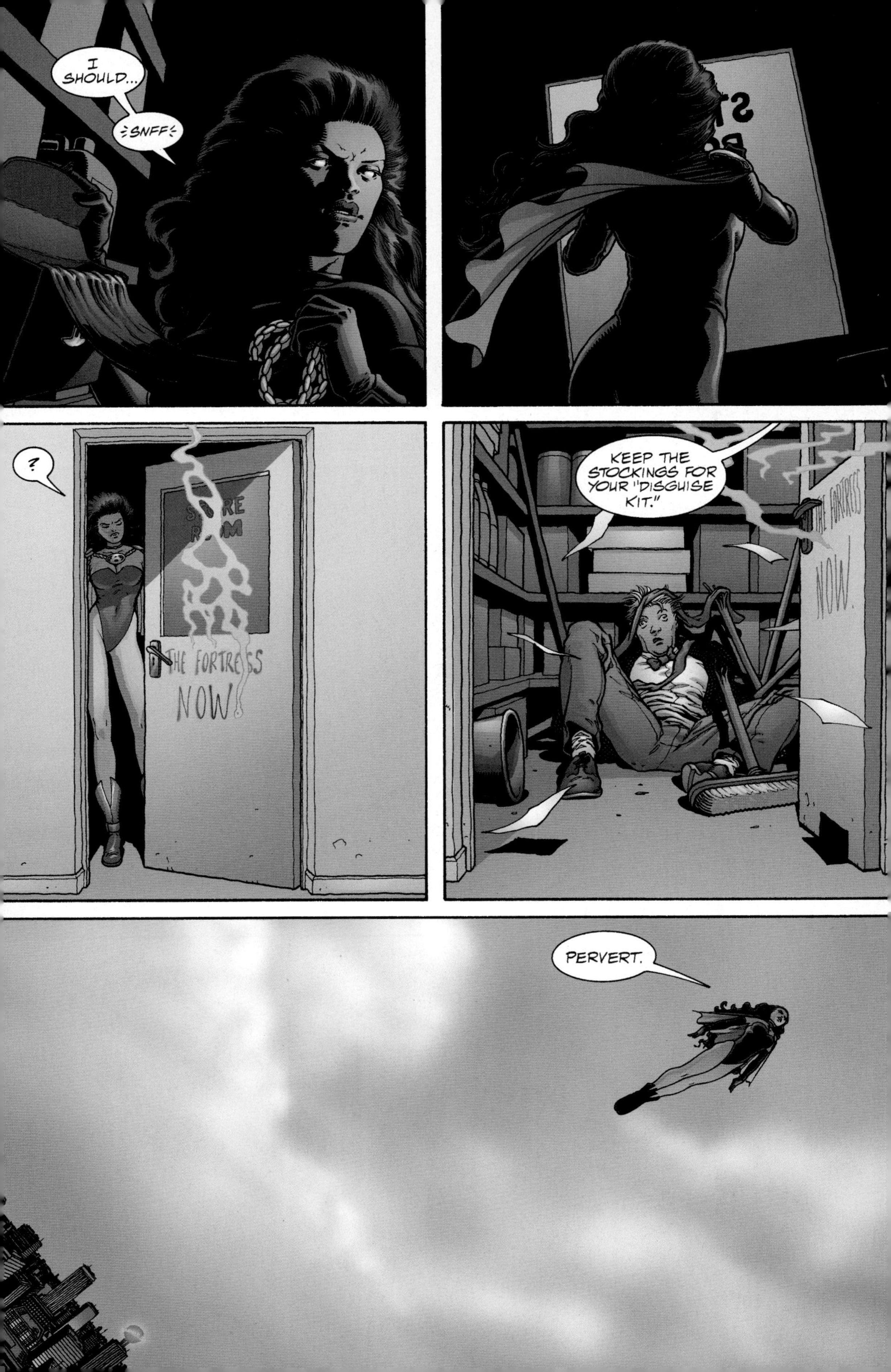
I SHOULD...
SNFF
?
SPARE ROOM
THE FORTRESS NOW!
KEEP THE STOCKINGS FOR YOUR "DISGUISE KIT."
THE FORTRESS NOW!
PERVERT.

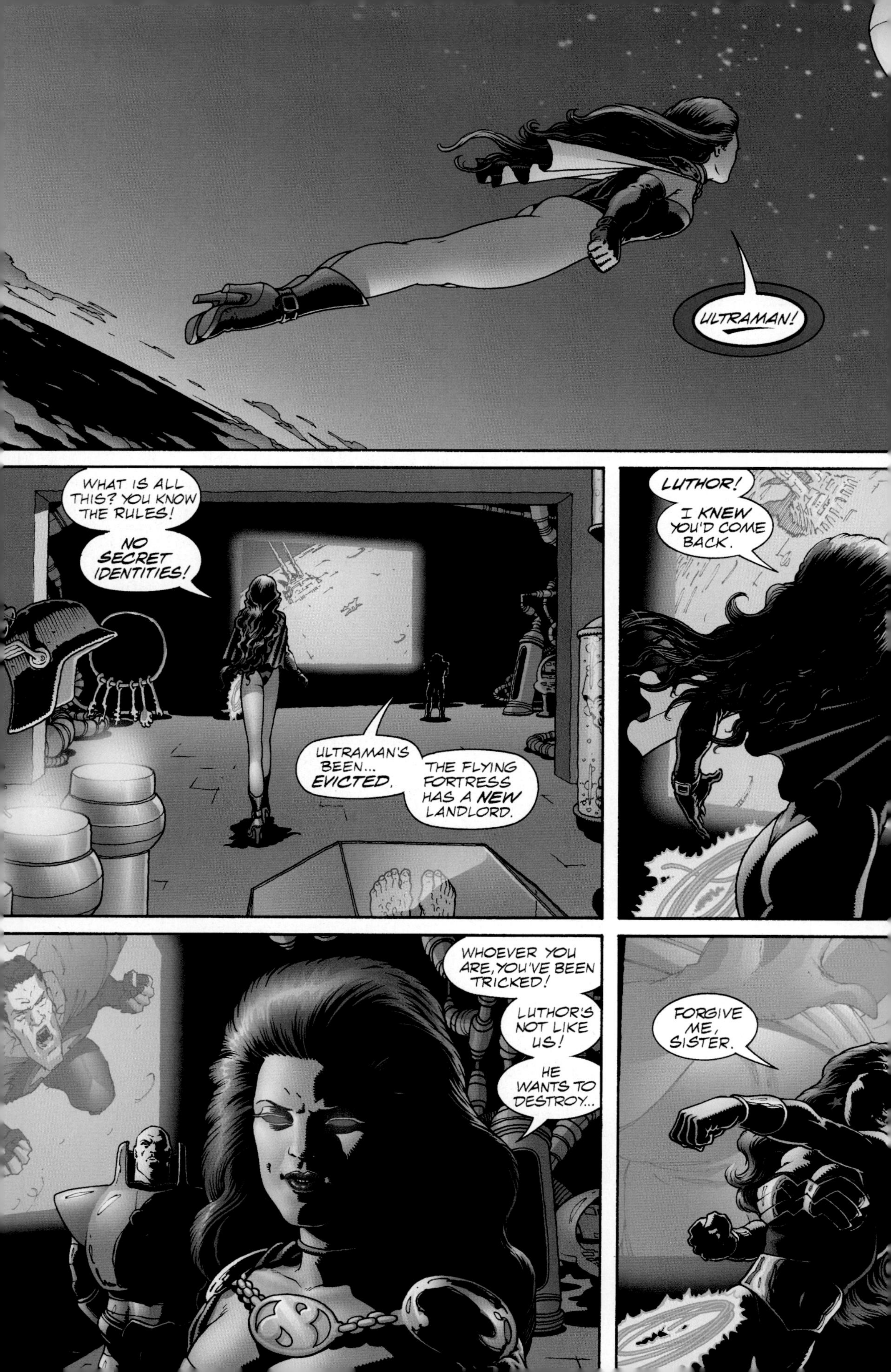
ULTRAMAN!
WHAT IS ALL THIS? YOU KNOW THE RULES!
NO SECRET IDENTITIES!
ULTRAMAN'S BEEN... EVICTED.
THE FLYING FORTRESS HAS A NEW LANDLORD.
LUTHOR!
I KNEW YOU'D COME BACK.
WHOEVER YOU ARE, YOU'VE BEEN TRICKED!
LUTHOR'S NOT LIKE US!
HE WANTS TO DESTROY...
FORGIVE ME, SISTER.

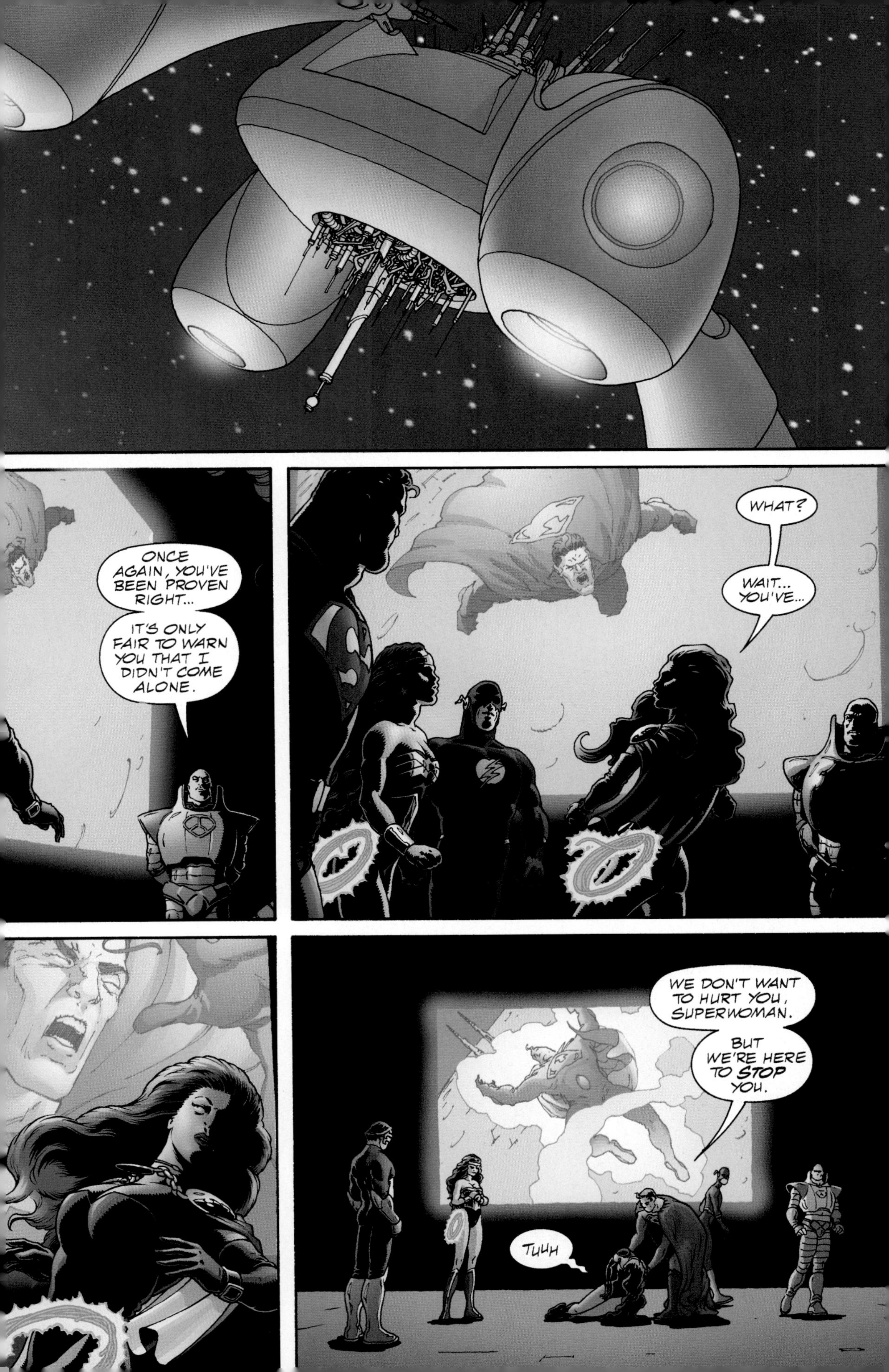
ONCE AGAIN, YOU'VE BEEN PROVEN RIGHT...
IT'S ONLY FAIR TO WARN YOU THAT I DIDN'T COME ALONE.
WHAT?
WAIT... YOU'VE...
WE DON'T WANT TO HURT YOU, SUPERWOMAN.
BUT WE'RE HERE TO STOP YOU.
TUUH

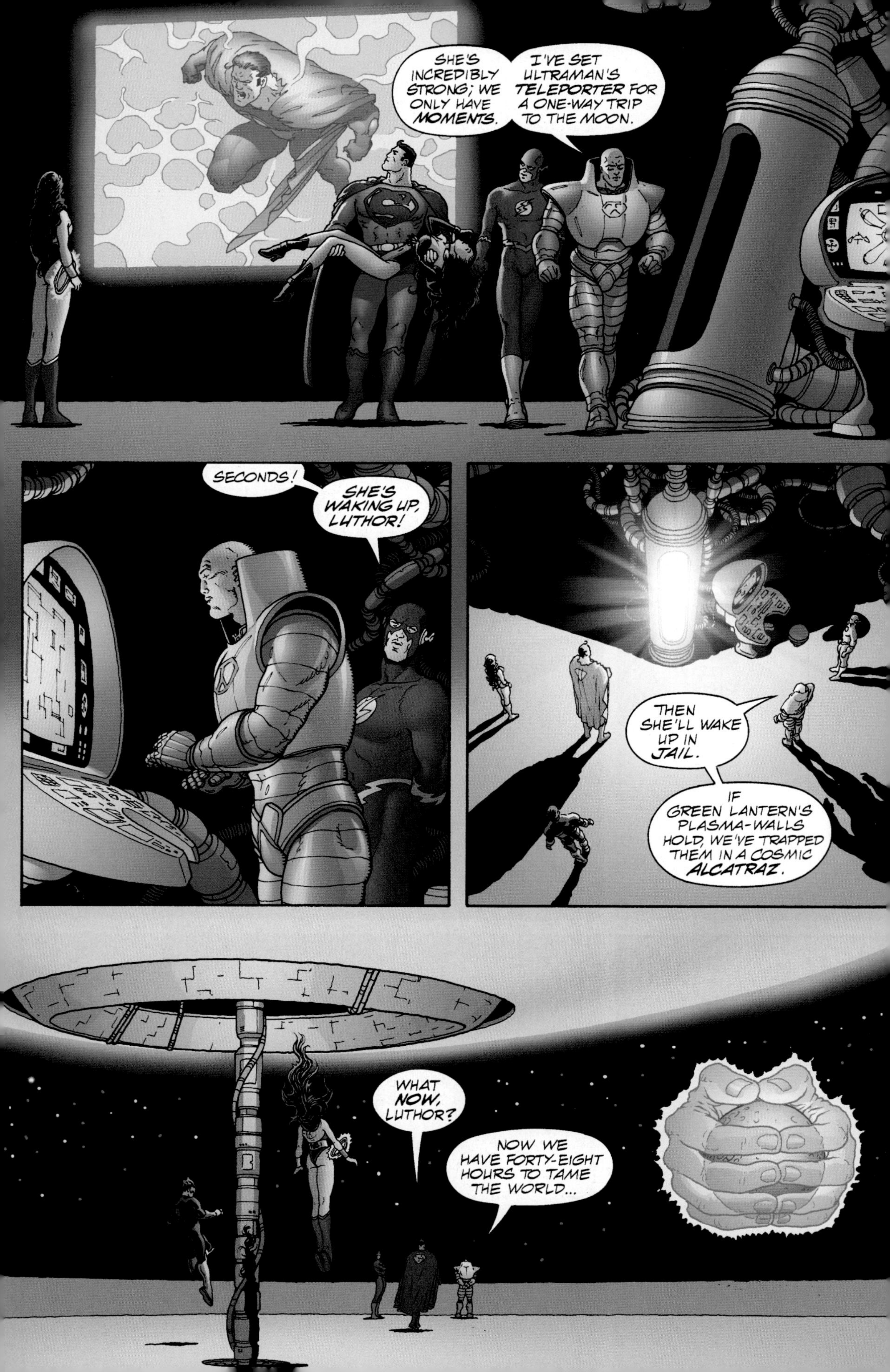
SHE'S INCREDIBLY STRONG; WE ONLY HAVE MOMENTS.
I'VE SET ULTRAMAN'S TELEPORTER FOR A ONE-WAY TRIP TO THE MOON.
SECONDS!
SHE'S WAKING UP, LUTHOR!
THEN SHE'LL WAKE UP IN JAIL.
IF GREEN LANTERN'S PLASMA-WALLS HOLD, WE'VE TRAPPED THEM IN A COSMIC ALCATRAZ.
WHAT NOW, LUTHOR?
NOW WE HAVE FORTY-EIGHT HOURS TO TAME THE WORLD...

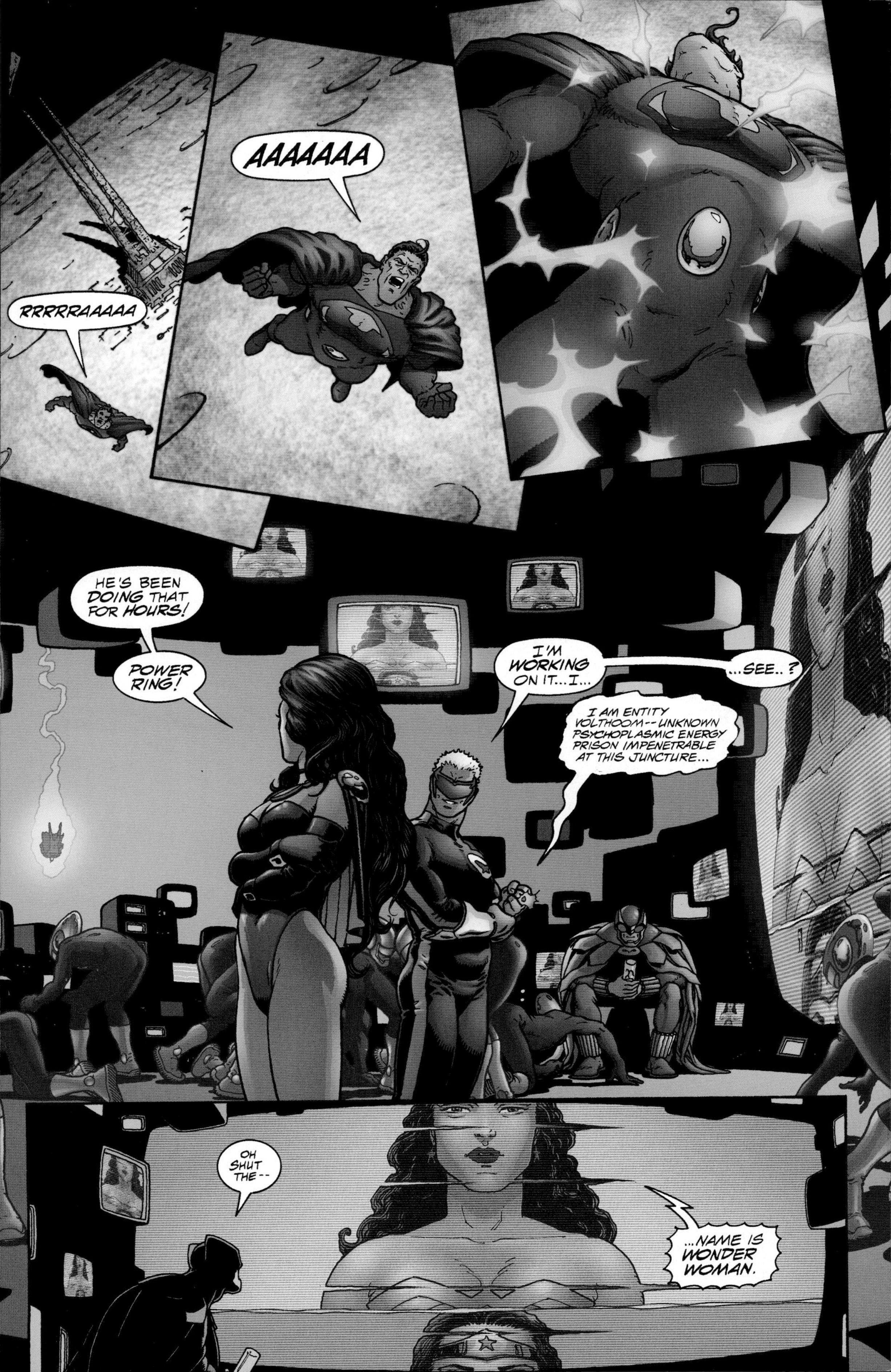
RRRRRAAAAA
AAAAAAA
HE'S BEEN DOING THAT FOR HOURS!
POWER RING!
I'M WORKING ON IT... I...
...SEE..?
I AM ENTITY VOLTHOOM--UNKNOWN PSYCHOPLASMIC ENERGY PRISON IMPENETRABLE AT THIS JUNCTURE...
OH SHUT THE--
...NAME IS WONDER WOMAN.

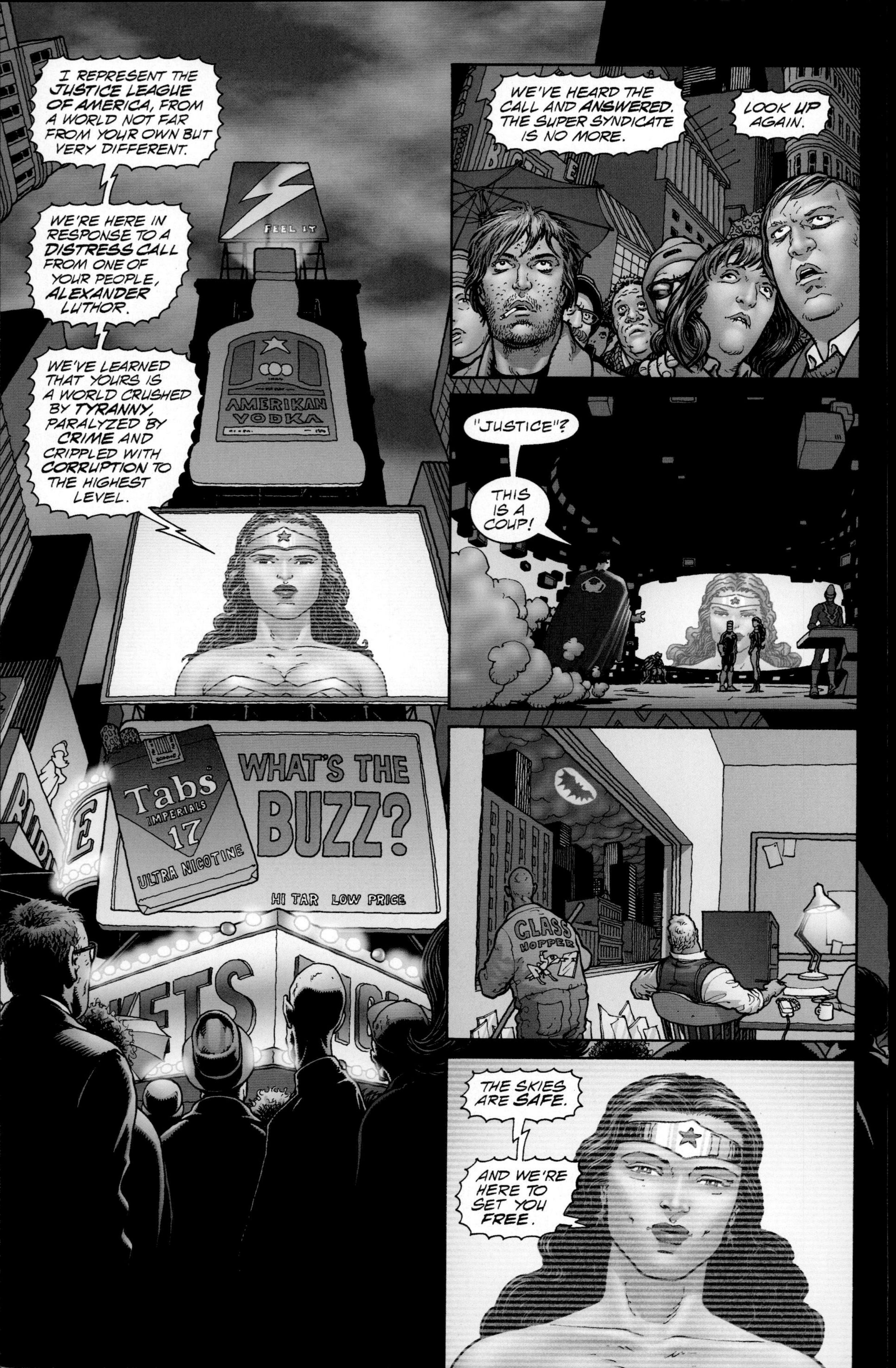
I REPRESENT THE JUSTICE LEAGUE OF AMERICA, FROM A WORLD NOT FAR FROM YOUR OWN BUT VERY DIFFERENT.
WE'RE HERE IN RESPONSE TO A DISTRESS CALL FROM ONE OF YOUR PEOPLE, ALEXANDER LUTHOR.
WE'VE LEARNED THAT YOURS IS A WORLD CRUSHED BY TYRANNY, PARALYZED BY CRIME AND CRIPPLED WITH CORRUPTION TO THE HIGHEST LEVEL.
FEEL IT
AMERIKAN VODKA
Tabs IMPERIALS 17 ULTRA NICOTINE
WHAT'S THE BUZZ?
HI TAR LOW PRICE
WE'VE HEARD THE CALL AND ANSWERED. THE SUPER SYNDICATE IS NO MORE.
LOOK UP AGAIN.
"JUSTICE"?
THIS IS A COUP!
GLASS HOPPER
THE SKIES ARE SAFE.
AND WE'RE HERE TO SET YOU FREE.

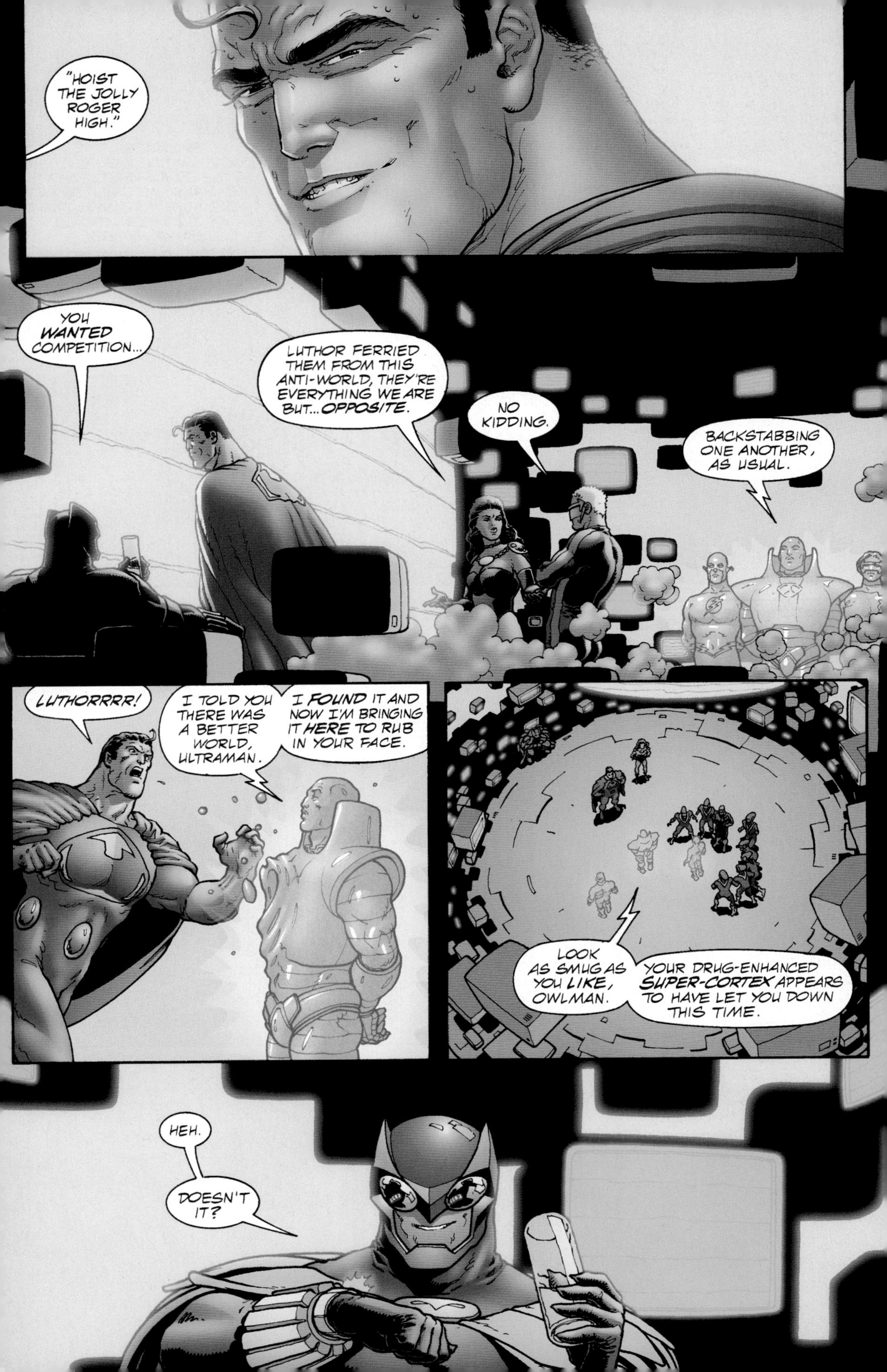
"HOIST THE JOLLY ROGER HIGH."
YOU WANTED COMPETITION...
LUTHOR FERRIED THEM FROM THIS ANTI-WORLD, THEY'RE EVERYTHING WE ARE BUT...OPPOSITE.
NO KIDDING.
BACKSTABBING ONE ANOTHER, AS USUAL.
LUTHORRRR!
I TOLD YOU THERE WAS A BETTER WORLD, ULTRAMAN.
I FOUND IT AND NOW I'M BRINGING IT HERE TO RUB IN YOUR FACE.
LOOK AS SMUG AS YOU LIKE, OWLMAN.
YOUR DRUG-ENHANCED SUPER-CORTEX APPEARS TO HAVE LET YOU DOWN THIS TIME.
HEH.
DOESN'T IT?

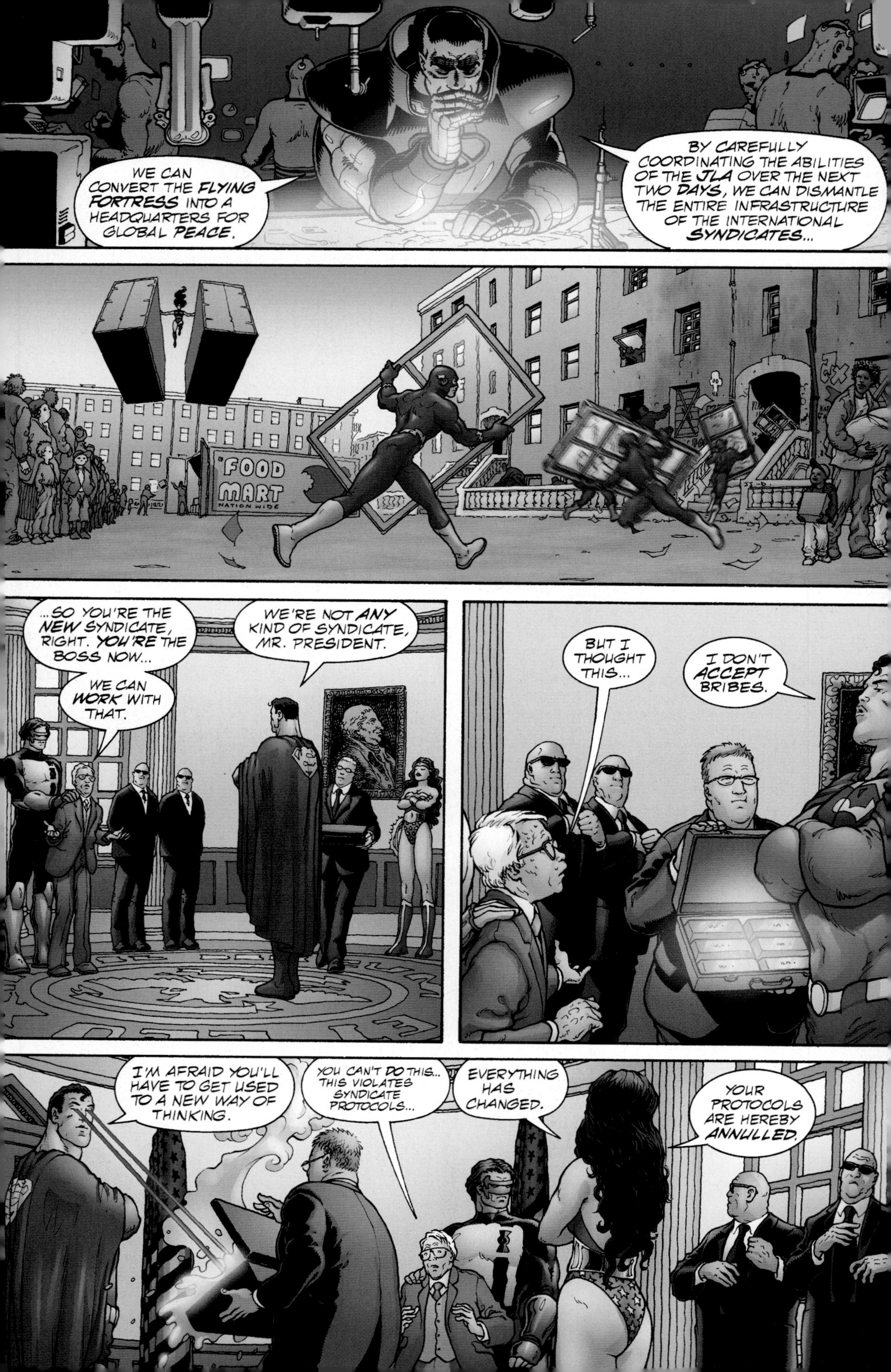
WE CAN CONVERT THE FLYING FORTRESS INTO A HEADQUARTERS FOR GLOBAL PEACE.
BY CAREFULLY COORDINATING THE ABILITIES OF THE JLA OVER THE NEXT TWO DAYS, WE CAN DISMANTLE THE ENTIRE INFRASTRUCTURE OF THE INTERNATIONAL SYNDICATES...
FOOD MART
NATION WIDE
...SO YOU'RE THE NEW SYNDICATE, RIGHT. YOU'RE THE BOSS NOW...
WE CAN WORK WITH THAT.
WE'RE NOT ANY KIND OF SYNDICATE, MR. PRESIDENT.
BUT I THOUGHT THIS...
I DON'T ACCEPT BRIBES.
I'M AFRAID YOU'LL HAVE TO GET USED TO A NEW WAY OF THINKING.
YOU CAN'T DO THIS... THIS VIOLATES SYNDICATE PROTOCOLS...
EVERYTHING HAS CHANGED.
YOUR PROTOCOLS ARE HEREBY ANNULLED.

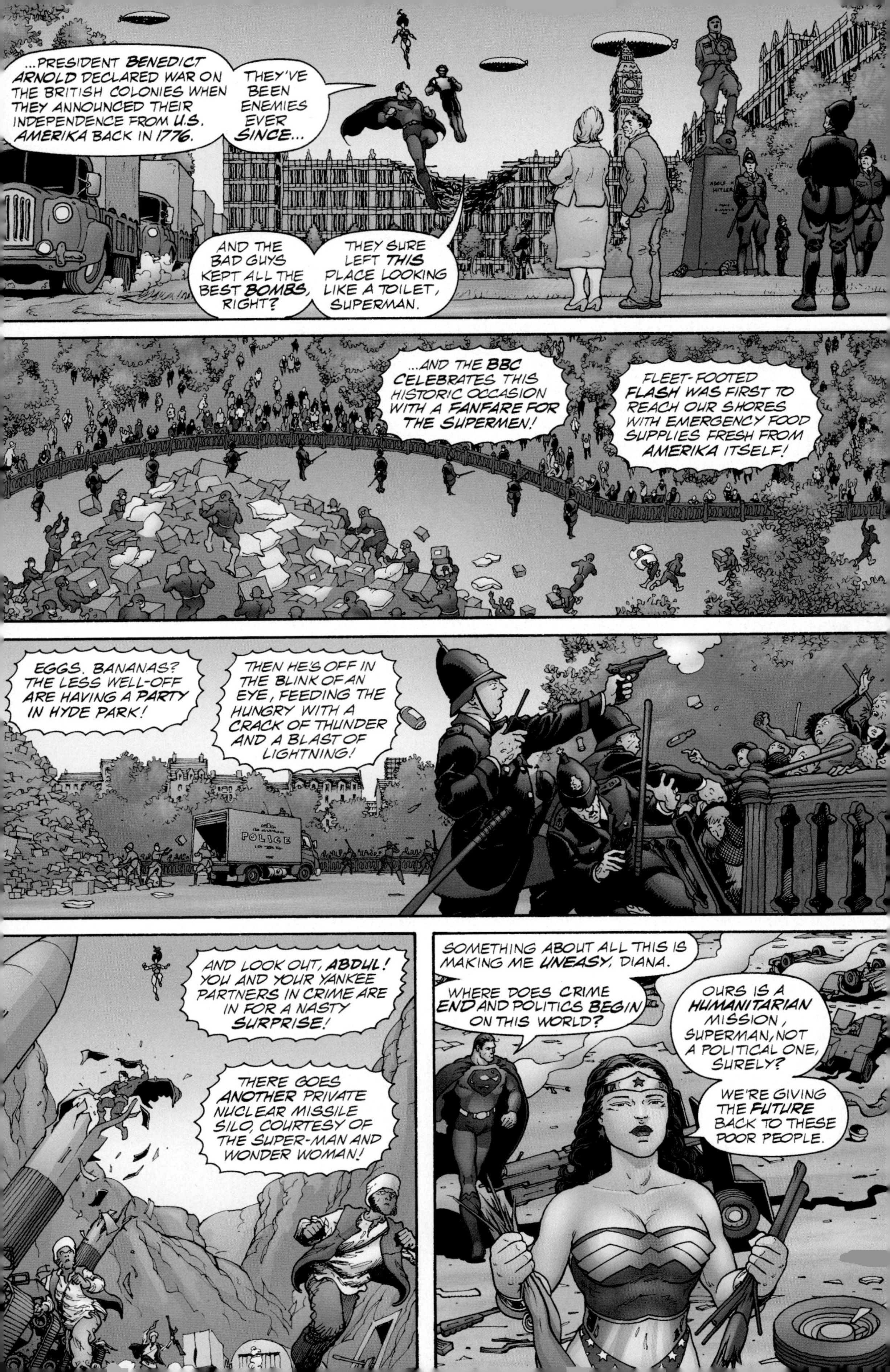
...PRESIDENT BENEDICT ARNOLD DECLARED WAR ON THE BRITISH COLONIES WHEN THEY ANNOUNCED THEIR INDEPENDENCE FROM U.S. AMERIKA BACK IN 1776.
THEY'VE BEEN ENEMIES EVER SINCE...
AND THE BAD GUYS KEPT ALL THE BEST BOMBS, RIGHT?
THEY SURE LEFT THIS PLACE LOOKING LIKE A TOILET, SUPERMAN.
ADOLF HITLER
...AND THE BBC CELEBRATES THIS HISTORIC OCCASION WITH A FANFARE FOR THE SUPERMEN!
FLEET-FOOTED FLASH WAS FIRST TO REACH OUR SHORES WITH EMERGENCY FOOD SUPPLIES FRESH FROM AMERIKA ITSELF!
EGGS. BANANAS? THE LESS WELL-OFF ARE HAVING A PARTY IN HYDE PARK!
THEN HE'S OFF IN THE BLINK OF AN EYE, FEEDING THE HUNGRY WITH A CRACK OF THUNDER AND A BLAST OF LIGHTNING!
POLICE
AND LOOK OUT, ABDUL! YOU AND YOUR YANKEE PARTNERS IN CRIME ARE IN FOR A NASTY SURPRISE!
THERE GOES ANOTHER PRIVATE NUCLEAR MISSILE SILO, COURTESY OF THE SUPER-MAN AND WONDER WOMAN!
SOMETHING ABOUT ALL THIS IS MAKING ME UNEASY, DIANA.
WHERE DOES CRIME END AND POLITICS BEGIN ON THIS WORLD?
OURS IS A HUMANITARIAN MISSION, SUPERMAN, NOT A POLITICAL ONE, SURELY?
WE'RE GIVING THE FUTURE BACK TO THESE POOR PEOPLE.

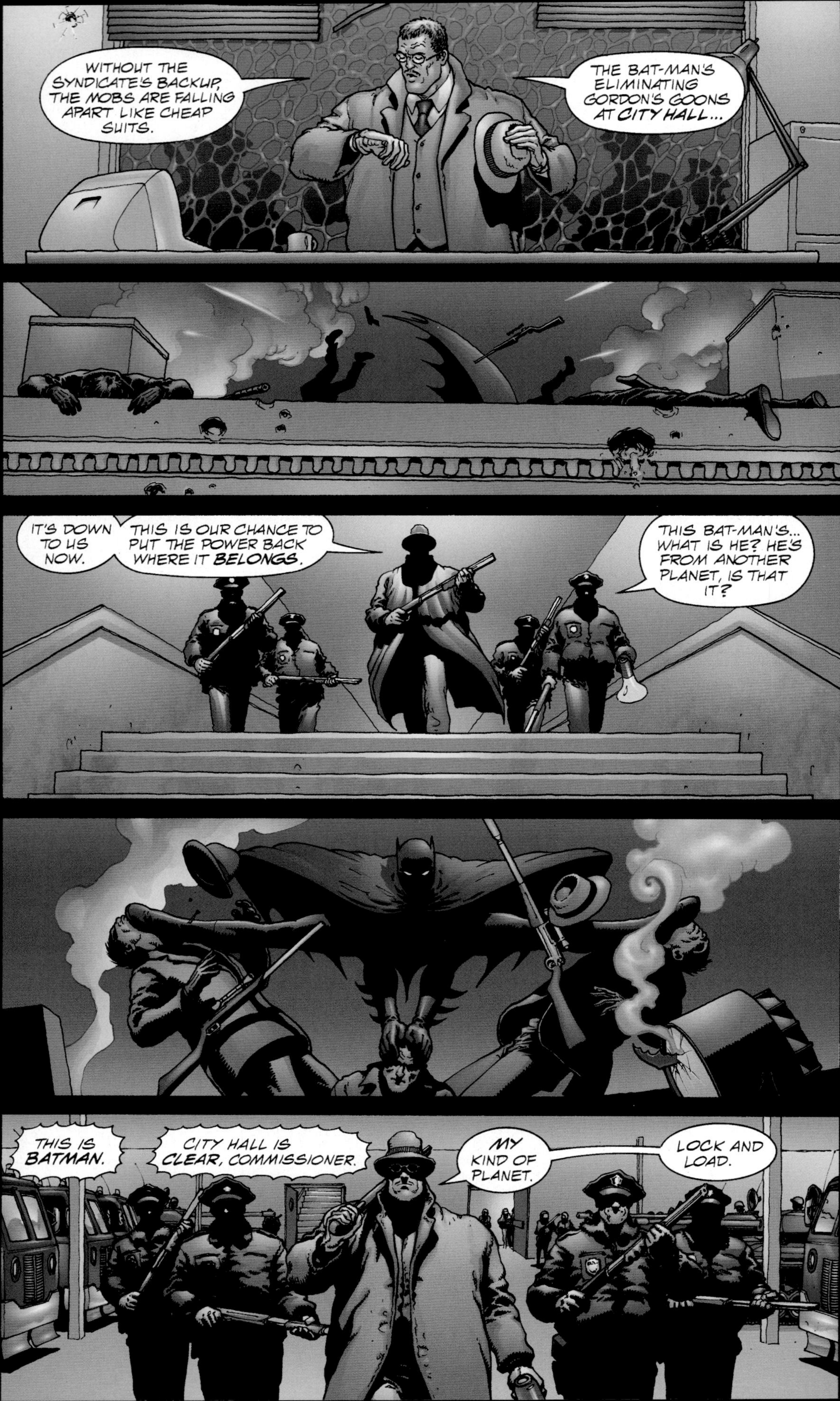
WITHOUT THE SYNDICATE'S BACKUP, THE MOBS ARE FALLING APART LIKE CHEAP SUITS.
THE BAT-MAN'S ELIMINATING GORDON'S GOONS AT CITY HALL...
IT'S DOWN TO US NOW.
THIS IS OUR CHANCE TO PUT THE POWER BACK WHERE IT BELONGS.
THIS BAT-MAN'S... WHAT IS HE? HE'S FROM ANOTHER PLANET, IS THAT IT?
THIS IS BATMAN.
CITY HALL IS CLEAR, COMMISSIONER.
MY KIND OF PLANET.
LOCK AND LOAD.

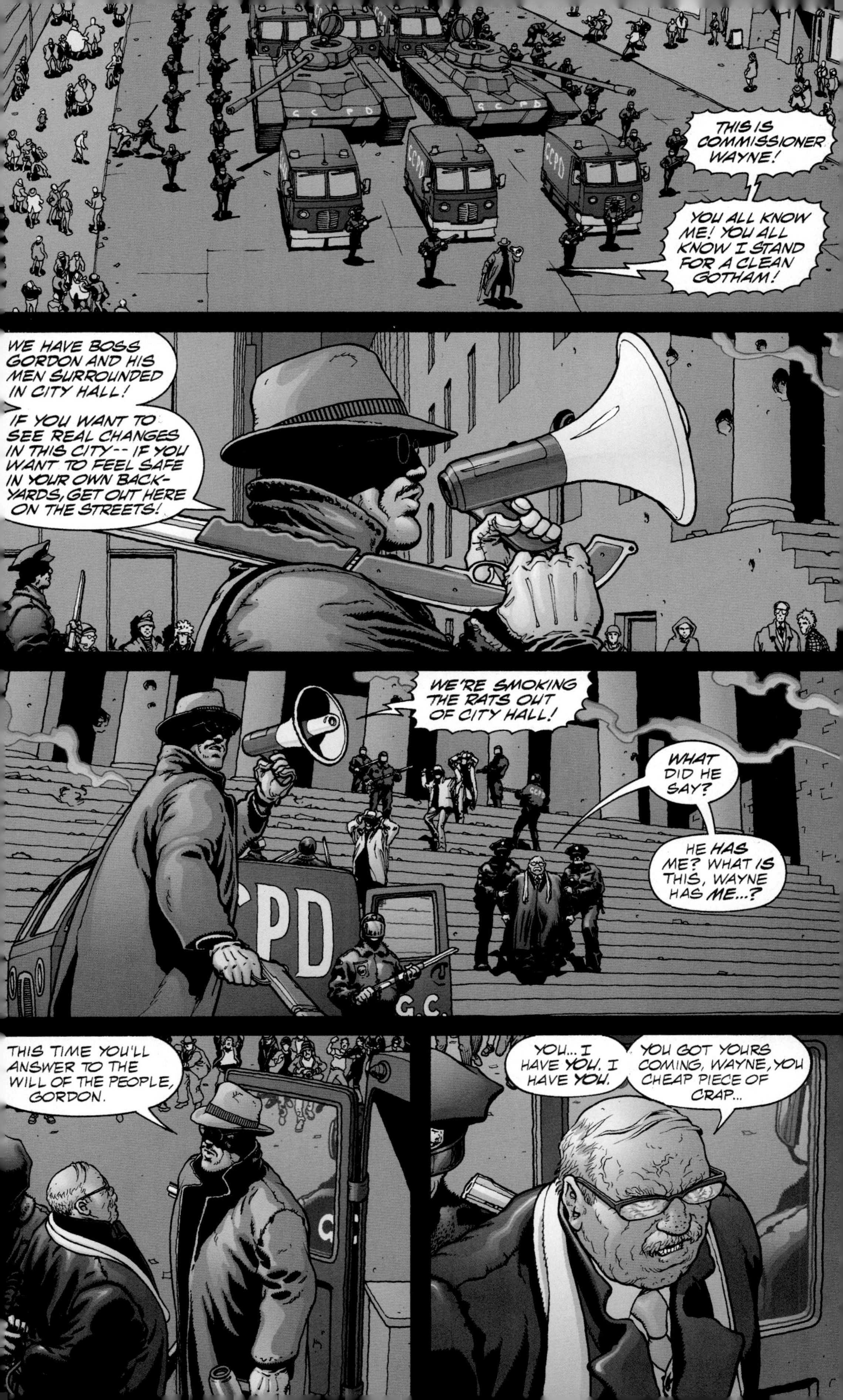
THIS IS COMMISSIONER WAYNE!
YOU ALL KNOW ME! YOU ALL KNOW I STAND FOR A CLEAN GOTHAM!
WE HAVE BOSS GORDON AND HIS MEN SURROUNDED IN CITY HALL!
IF YOU WANT TO SEE REAL CHANGES IN THIS CITY-- IF YOU WANT TO FEEL SAFE IN YOUR OWN BACK-YARDS, GET OUT HERE ON THE STREETS!
WE'RE SMOKING THE RATS OUT OF CITY HALL!
WHAT DID HE SAY?
HE HAS ME? WHAT IS THIS, WAYNE HAS ME...?
THIS TIME YOU'LL ANSWER TO THE WILL OF THE PEOPLE, GORDON.
YOU... I HAVE YOU. I HAVE YOU.
YOU GOT YOURS COMING, WAYNE, YOU CHEAP PIECE OF CRAP...

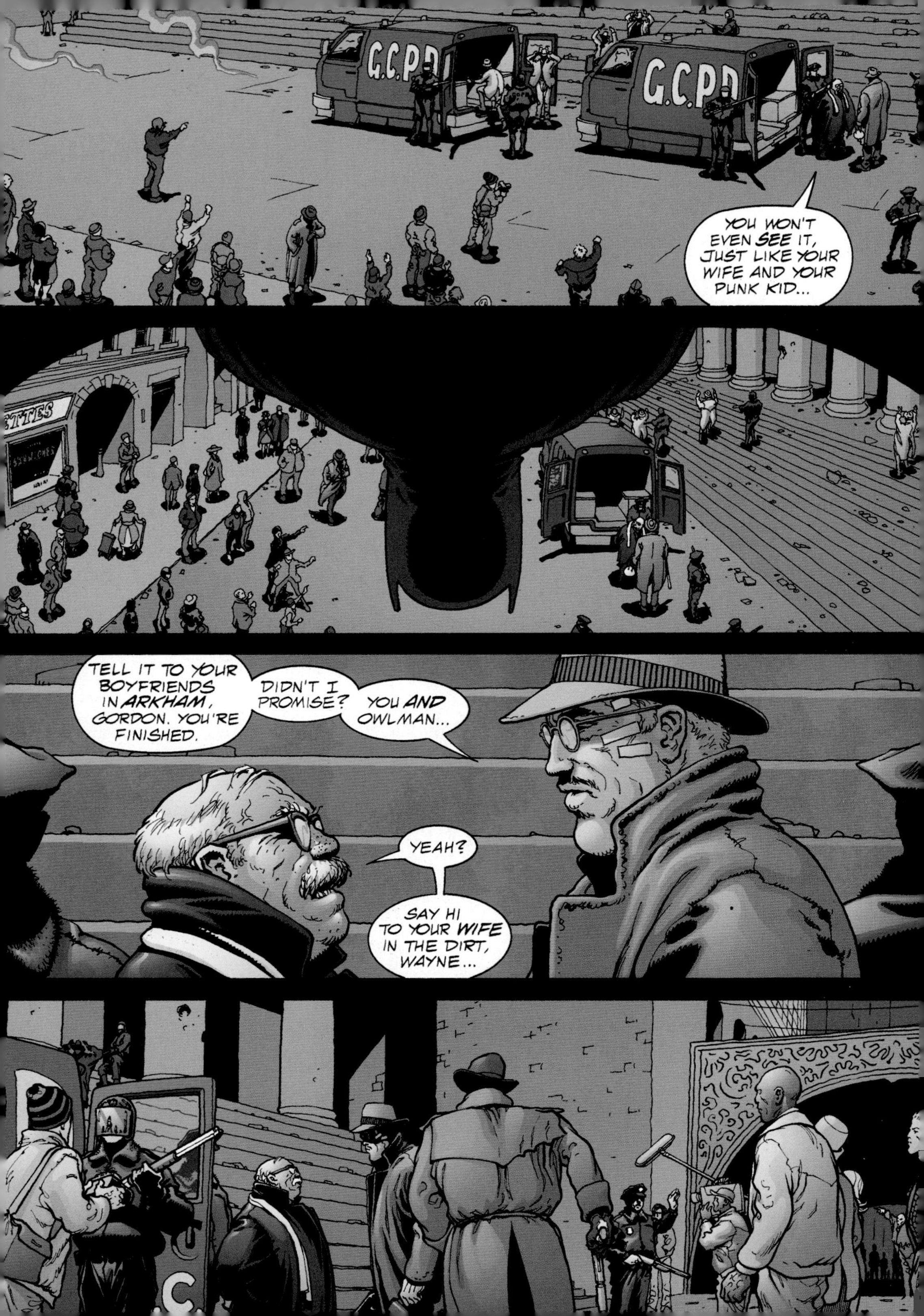
YOU WON'T EVEN SEE IT, JUST LIKE YOUR WIFE AND YOUR PUNK KID...
TELL IT TO YOUR BOYFRIENDS IN ARKHAM, GORDON. YOU'RE FINISHED.
DIDN'T I PROMISE?
YOU AND OWLMAN...
YEAH?
SAY HI TO YOUR WIFE IN THE DIRT, WAYNE...

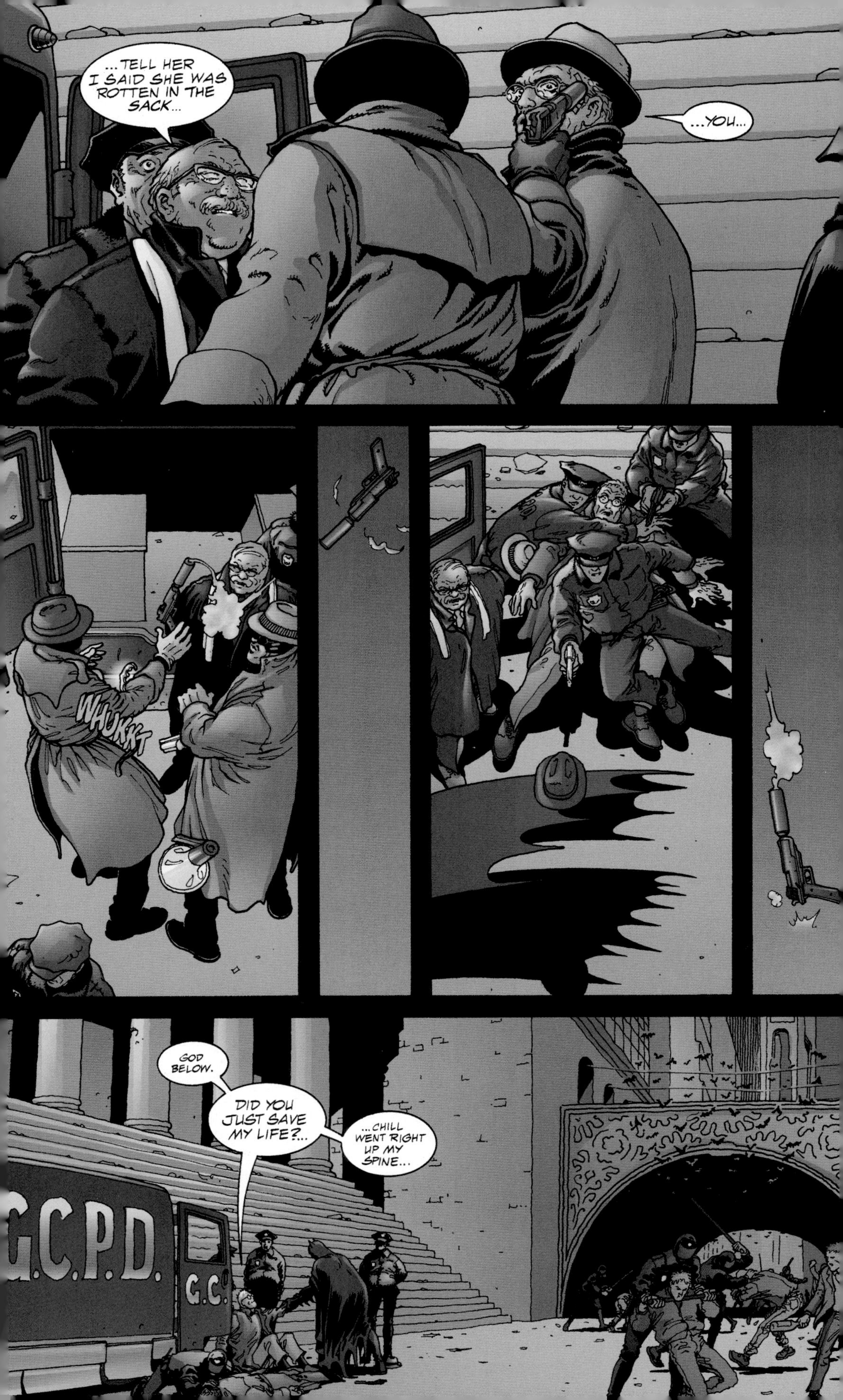
...TELL HER I SAID SHE WAS ROTTEN IN THE SACK...
...YOU...
WHUKKT
GOD BELOW.
DID YOU JUST SAVE MY LIFE?...
...CHILL WENT RIGHT UP MY SPINE...
G.C.P.D.
G.C.

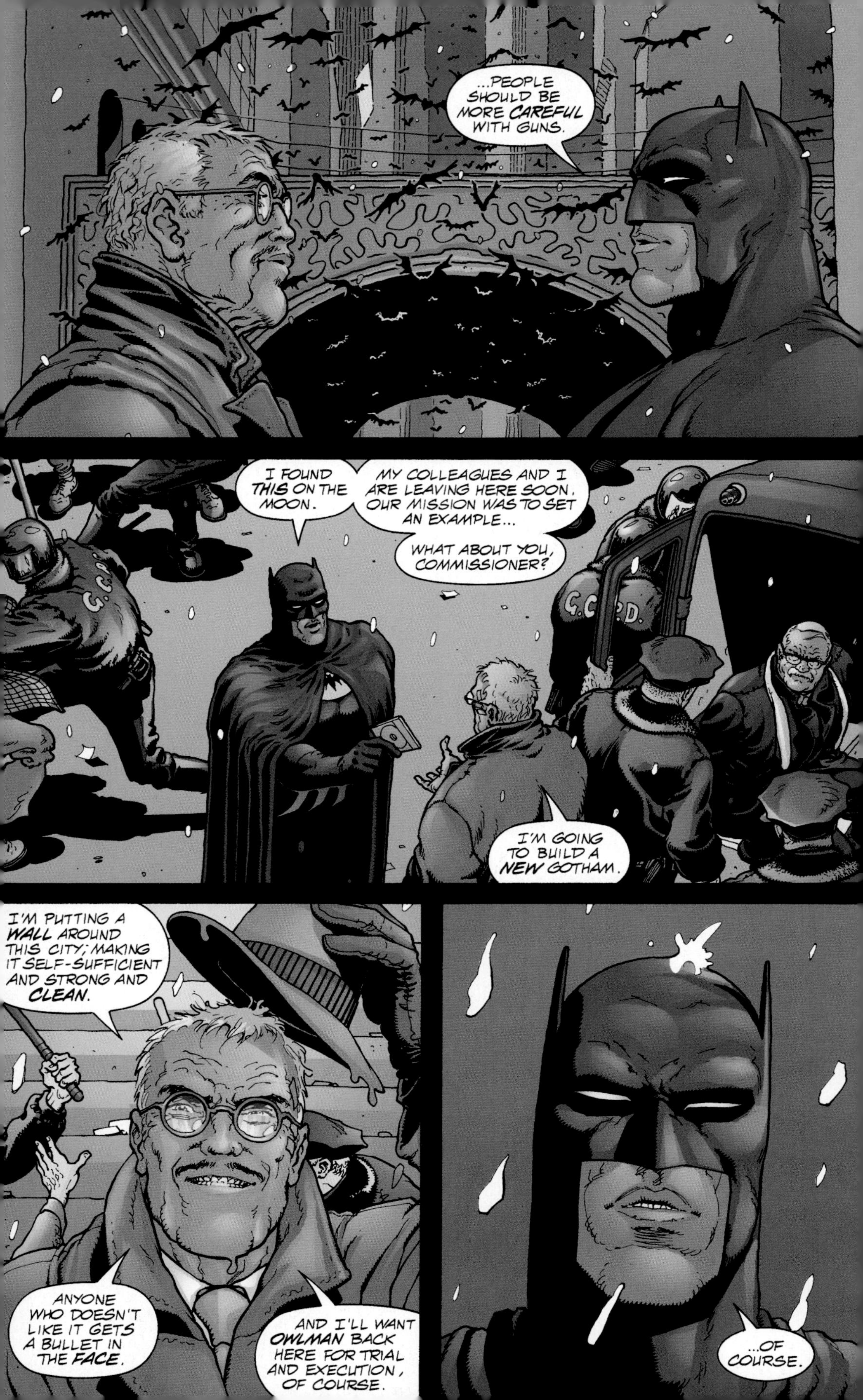
...PEOPLE SHOULD BE MORE CAREFUL WITH GUNS.
I FOUND THIS ON THE MOON.
MY COLLEAGUES AND I ARE LEAVING HERE SOON. OUR MISSION WAS TO SET AN EXAMPLE...
WHAT ABOUT YOU, COMMISSIONER?
G.C.P.D.
I'M GOING TO BUILD A NEW GOTHAM.
I'M PUTTING A WALL AROUND THIS CITY; MAKING IT SELF-SUFFICIENT AND STRONG AND CLEAN.
ANYONE WHO DOESN'T LIKE IT GETS A BULLET IN THE FACE.
AND I'LL WANT OWLMAN BACK HERE FOR TRIAL AND EXECUTION, OF COURSE.
...OF COURSE.

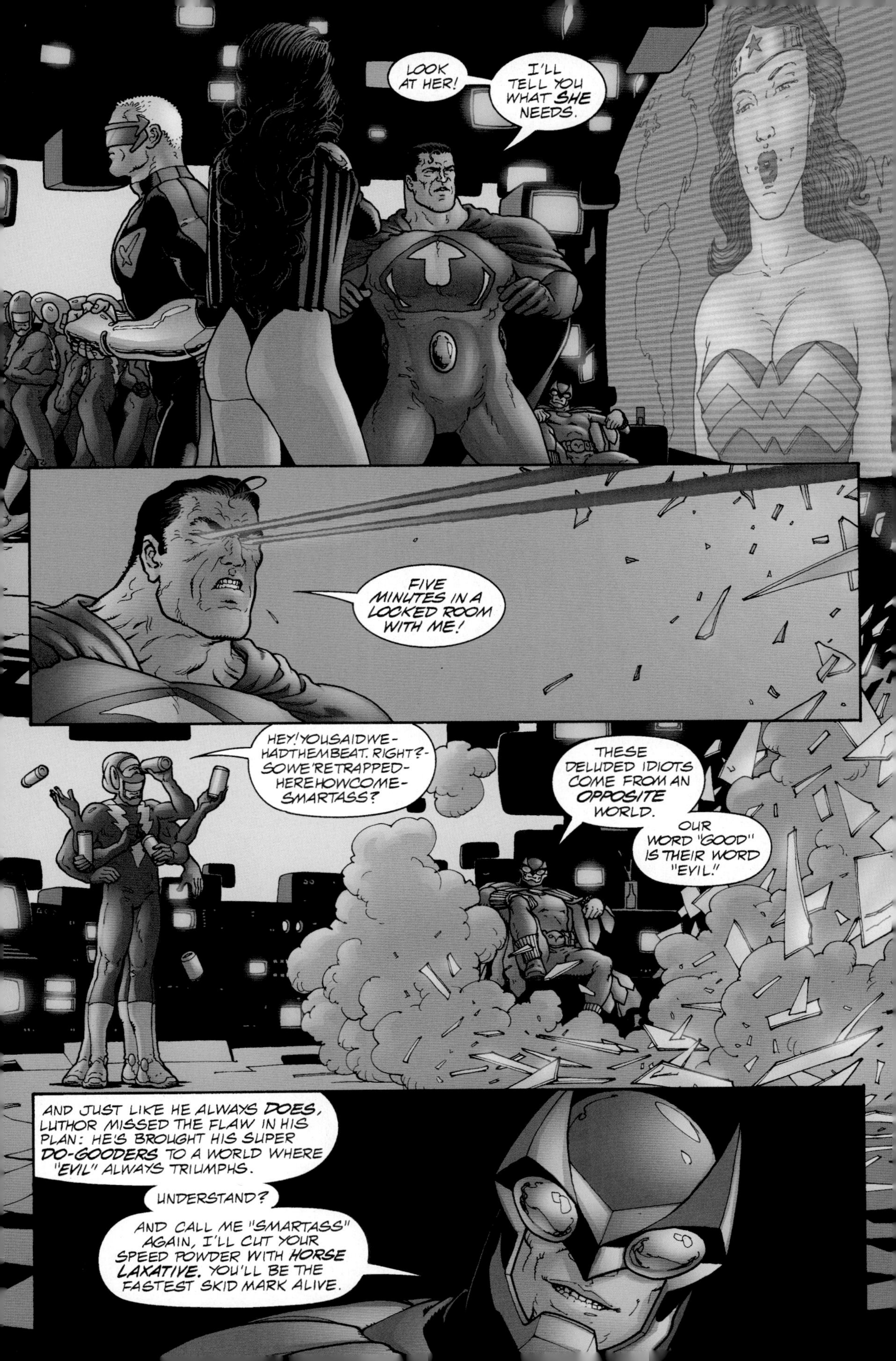
LOOK AT HER!
I'LL TELL YOU WHAT SHE NEEDS.
FIVE MINUTES IN A LOCKED ROOM WITH ME!
HEY! YOUSAIDWE-HADTHEMBEAT. RIGHT?-SOWE'RETRAPPED-HEREHOWCOME-SMARTASS?
THESE DELUDED IDIOTS COME FROM AN OPPOSITE WORLD.
OUR WORD "GOOD" IS THEIR WORD "EVIL."
AND JUST LIKE HE ALWAYS DOES, LUTHOR MISSED THE FLAW IN HIS PLAN: HE'S BROUGHT HIS SUPER DO-GOODERS TO A WORLD WHERE "EVIL" ALWAYS TRIUMPHS.
UNDERSTAND?
AND CALL ME "SMARTASS" AGAIN, I'LL CUT YOUR SPEED POWDER WITH HORSE LAXATIVE. YOU'LL BE THE FASTEST SKID MARK ALIVE.

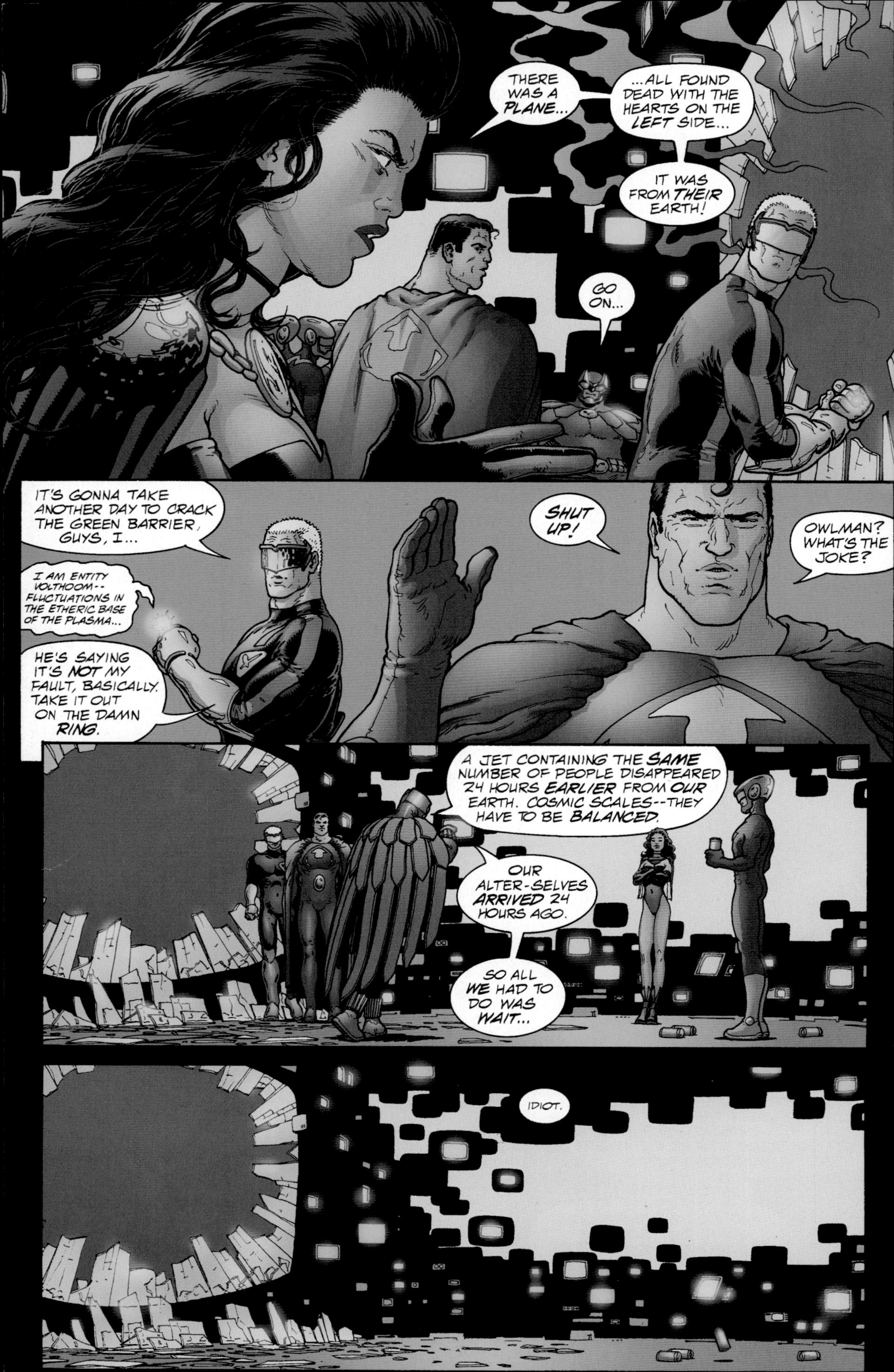
THERE WAS A PLANE...
...ALL FOUND DEAD WITH THE HEARTS ON THE LEFT SIDE...
IT WAS FROM THEIR EARTH!
GO ON...
IT'S GONNA TAKE ANOTHER DAY TO CRACK THE GREEN BARRIER, GUYS, I...
I AM ENTITY VOLTHOOM-- FLUCTUATIONS IN THE ETHERIC BASE OF THE PLASMA...
HE'S SAYING IT'S NOT MY FAULT, BASICALLY. TAKE IT OUT ON THE DAMN RING.
SHUT UP!
OWLMAN? WHAT'S THE JOKE?
A JET CONTAINING THE SAME NUMBER OF PEOPLE DISAPPEARED 24 HOURS EARLIER FROM OUR EARTH. COSMIC SCALES--THEY HAVE TO BE BALANCED.
OUR ALTER-SELVES ARRIVED 24 HOURS AGO.
SO ALL WE HAD TO DO WAS WAIT...
IDIOT.

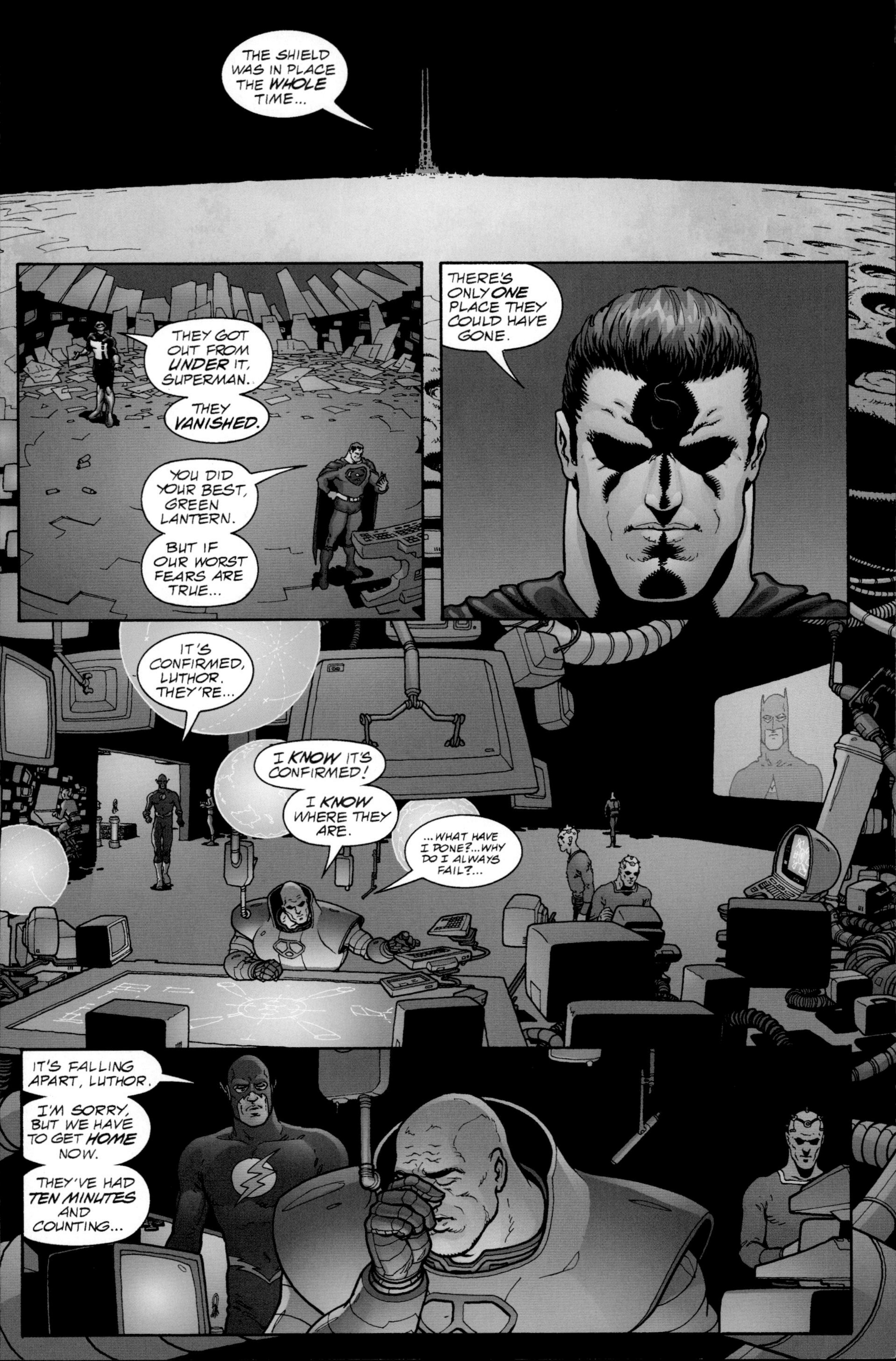
THE SHIELD WAS IN PLACE THE WHOLE TIME...
THEY GOT OUT FROM UNDER IT, SUPERMAN.
THEY VANISHED.
YOU DID YOUR BEST, GREEN LANTERN.
BUT IF OUR WORST FEARS ARE TRUE...
THERE'S ONLY ONE PLACE THEY COULD HAVE GONE.
IT'S CONFIRMED, LUTHOR. THEY'RE...
I KNOW IT'S CONFIRMED!
I KNOW WHERE THEY ARE.
...WHAT HAVE I DONE?...WHY DO I ALWAYS FAIL?...
IT'S FALLING APART, LUTHOR.
I'M SORRY, BUT WE HAVE TO GET HOME NOW.
THEY'VE HAD TEN MINUTES AND COUNTING...

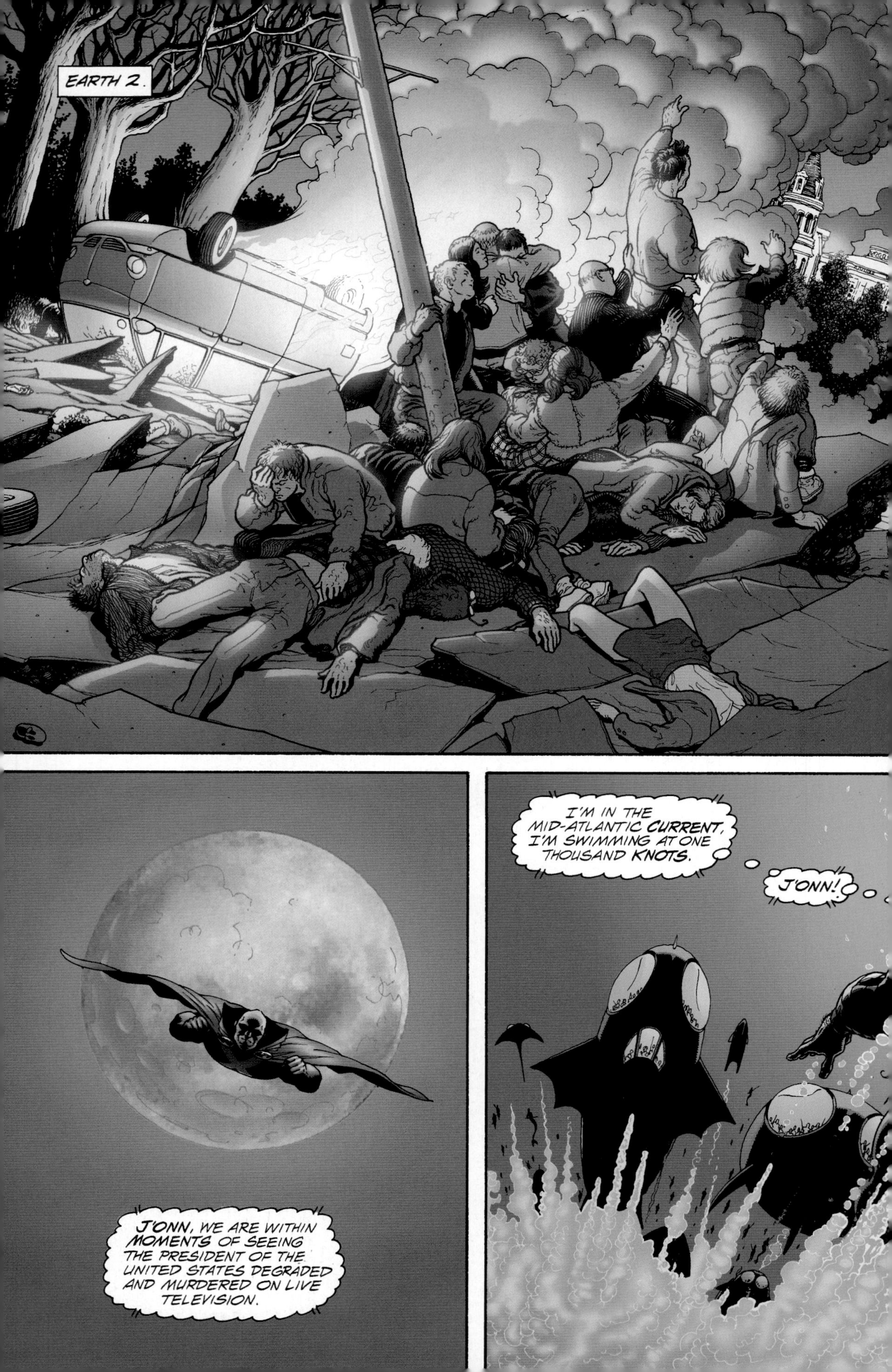
EARTH 2.
J'ONN, WE ARE WITHIN MOMENTS OF SEEING THE PRESIDENT OF THE UNITED STATES DEGRADED AND MURDERED ON LIVE TELEVISION.
I'M IN THE MID-ATLANTIC CURRENT, I'M SWIMMING AT ONE THOUSAND KNOTS.
J'ONN!

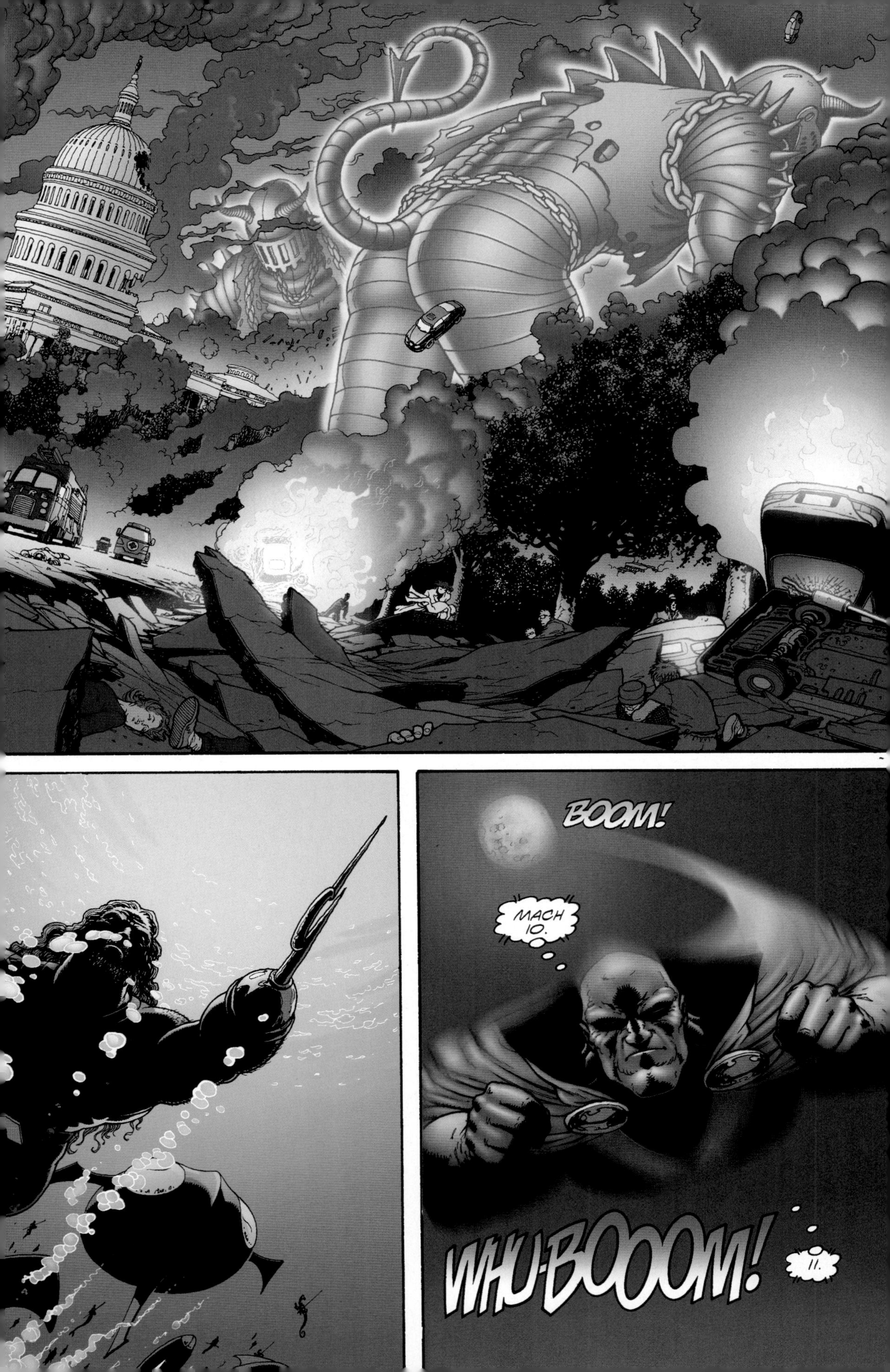
BOOM!
MACH 10.
WHU-BOOOM!
11.

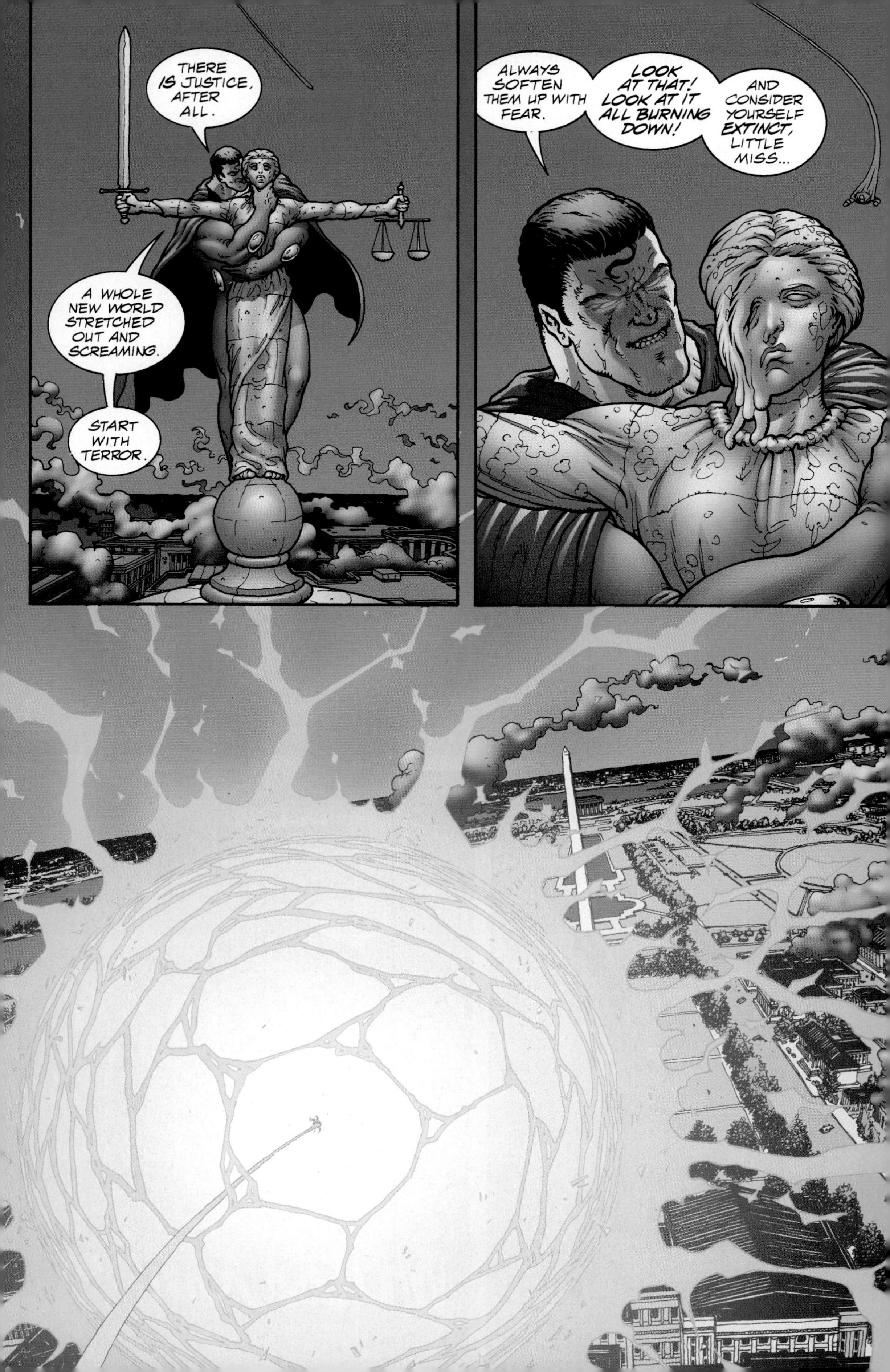
THERE IS JUSTICE, AFTER ALL.
A WHOLE NEW WORLD STRETCHED OUT AND SCREAMING.
START WITH TERROR.
ALWAYS SOFTEN THEM UP WITH FEAR.
LOOK AT THAT! LOOK AT IT ALL BURNING DOWN!
AND CONSIDER YOURSELF EXTINCT, LITTLE MISS...

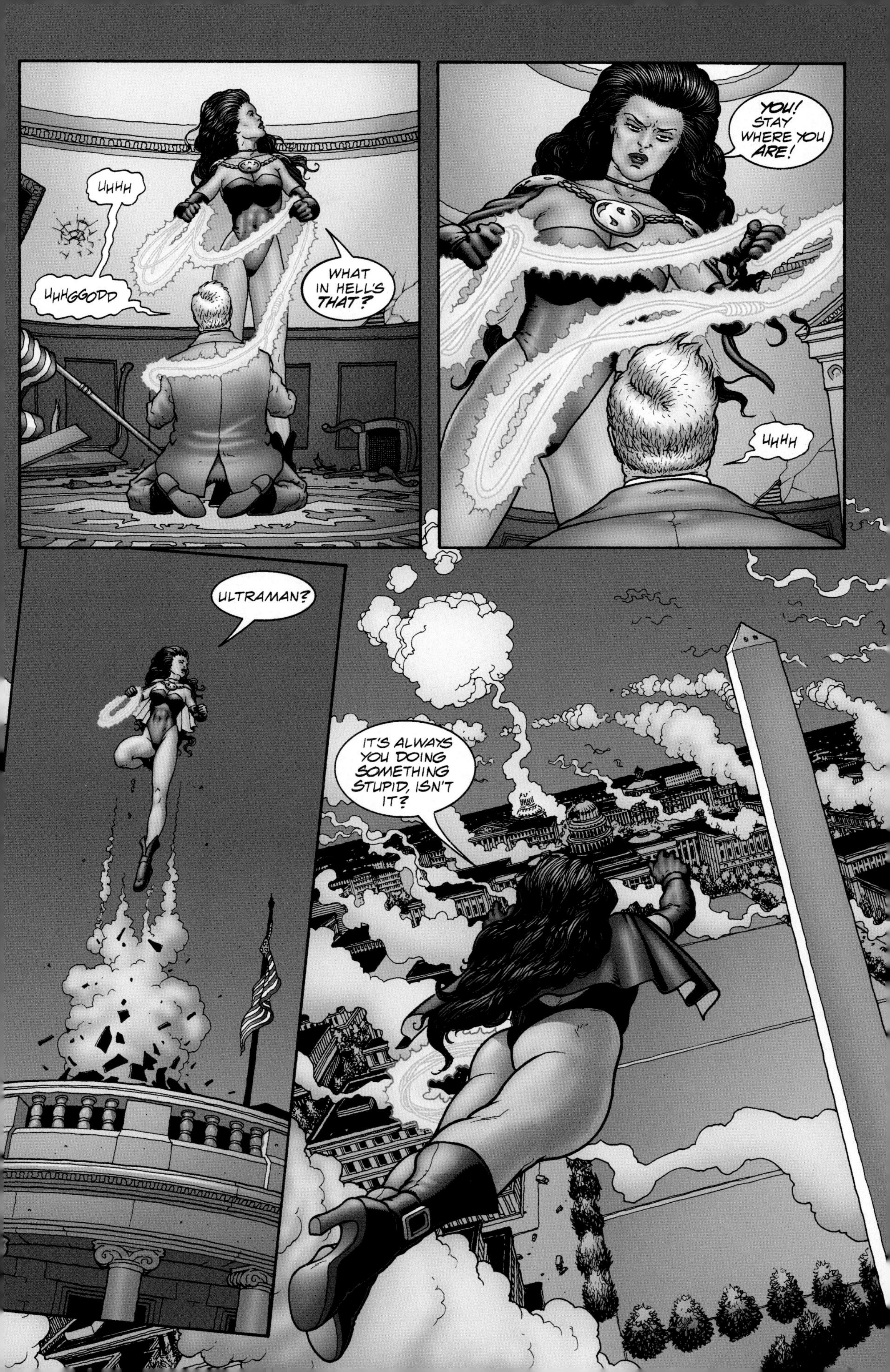
UHHH
UHHGGODD
WHAT IN HELL'S THAT?
YOU! STAY WHERE YOU ARE!
UHHH
ULTRAMAN?
IT'S ALWAYS YOU DOING SOMETHING STUPID, ISN'T IT?

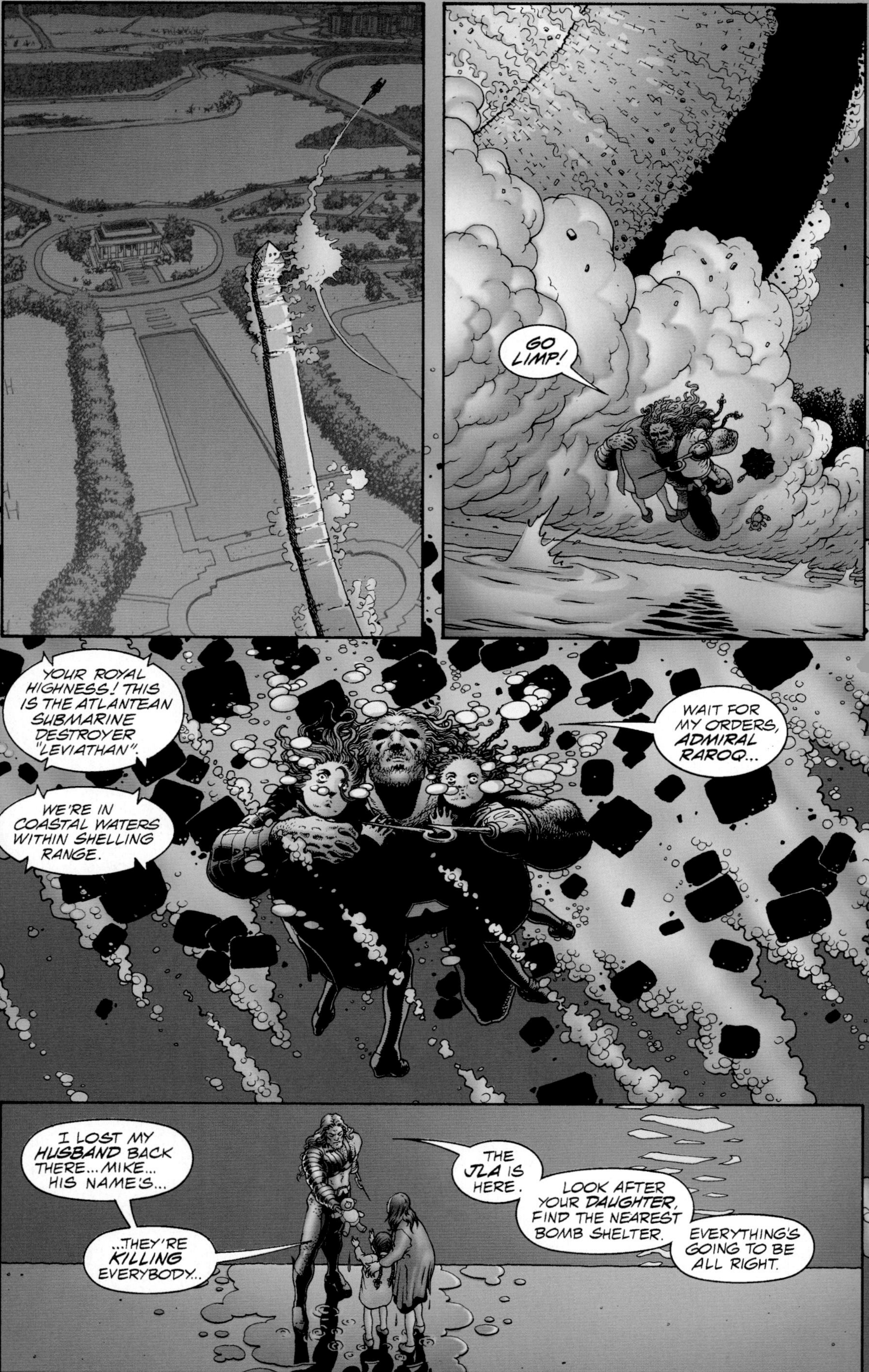
GO LIMP!
YOUR ROYAL HIGHNESS! THIS IS THE ATLANTEAN SUBMARINE DESTROYER "LEVIATHAN".
WE'RE IN COASTAL WATERS WITHIN SHELLING RANGE.
WAIT FOR MY ORDERS, ADMIRAL RAROQ...
I LOST MY HUSBAND BACK THERE... MIKE... HIS NAME'S...
...THEY'RE KILLING EVERYBODY...
THE JLA IS HERE.
LOOK AFTER YOUR DAUGHTER, FIND THE NEAREST BOMB SHELTER.
EVERYTHING'S GOING TO BE ALL RIGHT.

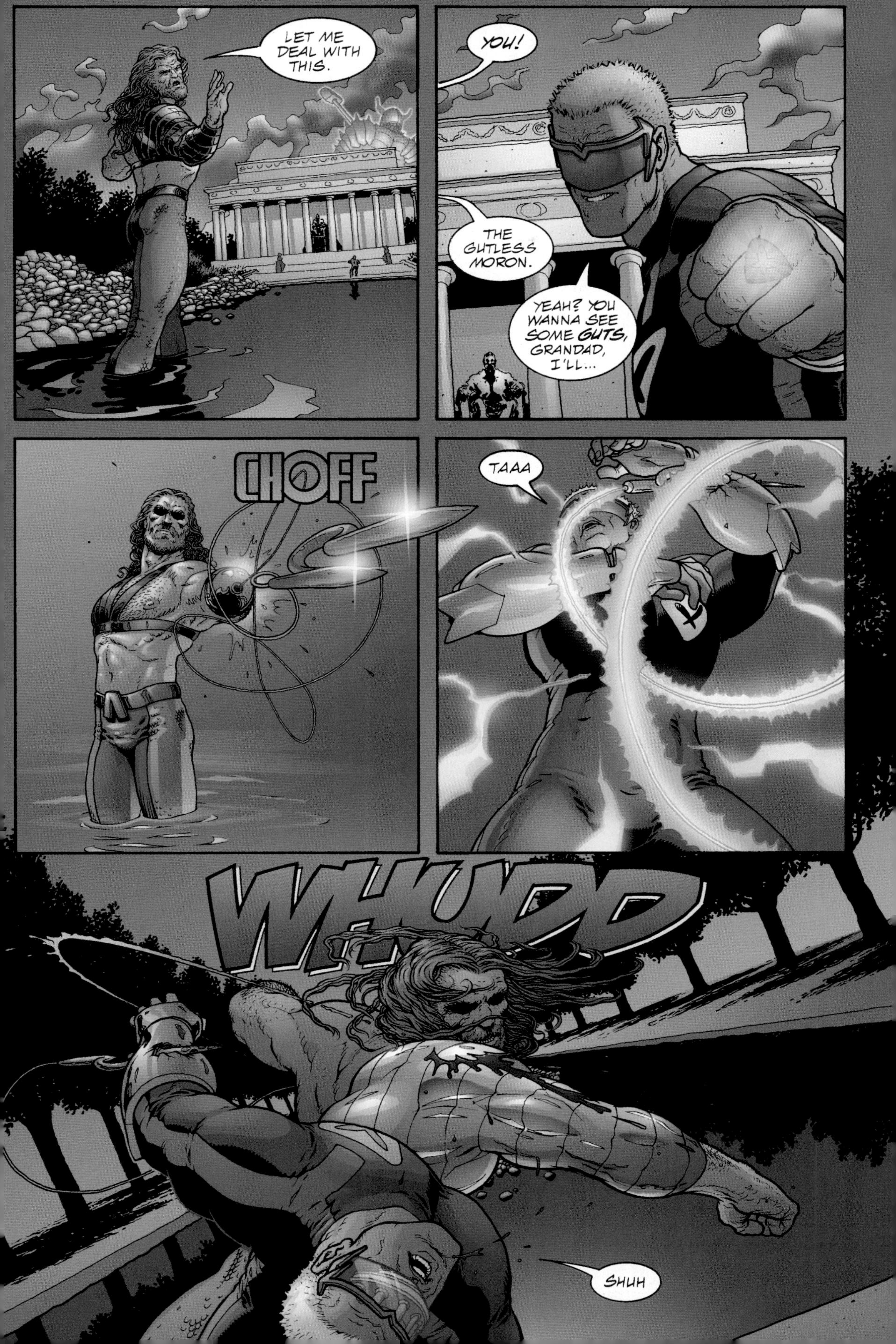
LET ME DEAL WITH THIS.
YOU!
THE GUTLESS MORON.
YEAH? YOU WANNA SEE SOME **GUTS**, GRANDAD, I'LL...
CHOFF
TAAA
WHUDD
SHUH

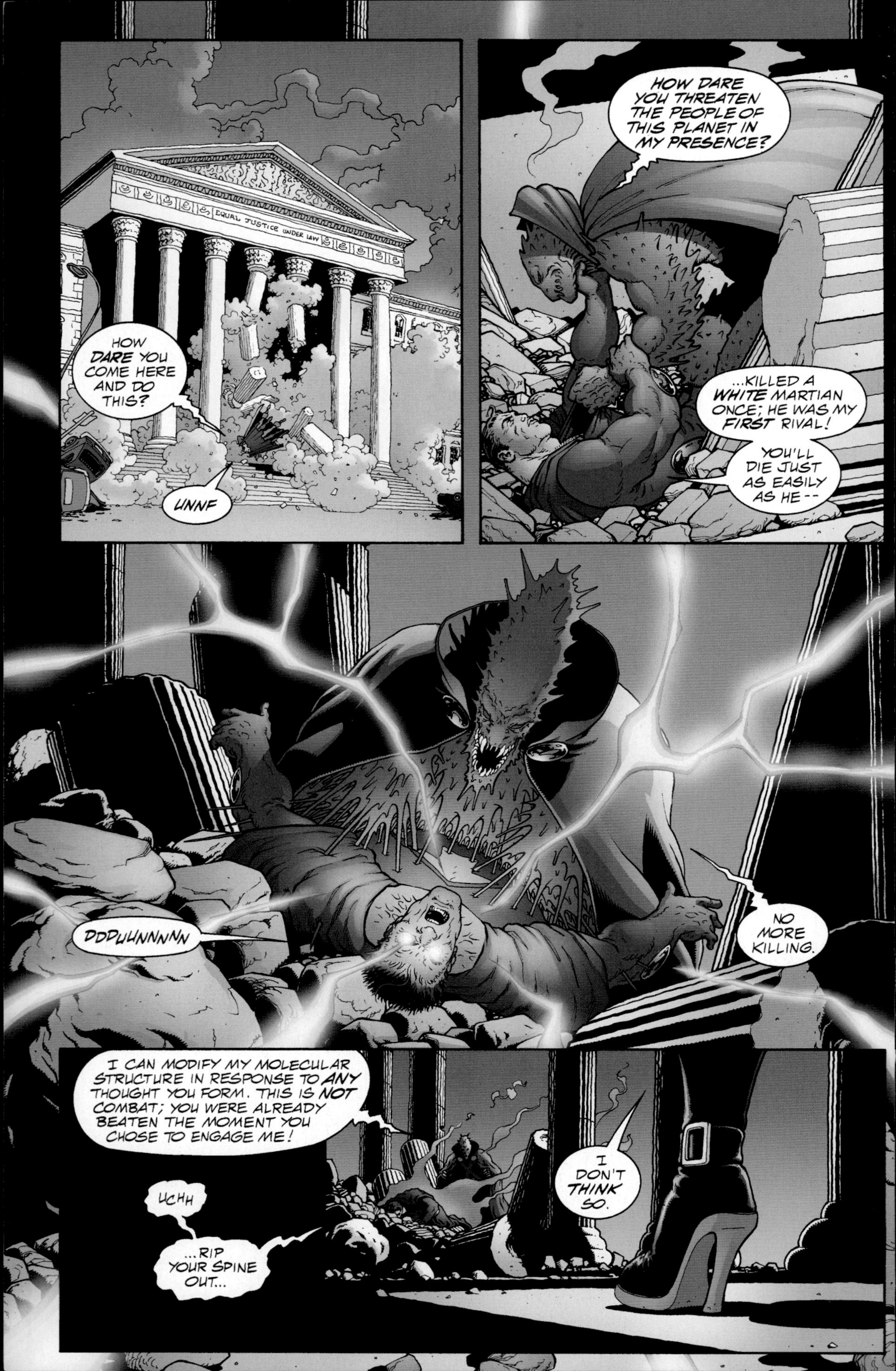
EQUAL JUSTICE UNDER LAW
HOW DARE YOU COME HERE AND DO THIS?
UNNF
HOW DARE YOU THREATEN THE PEOPLE OF THIS PLANET IN MY PRESENCE?
...KILLED A WHITE MARTIAN ONCE; HE WAS MY FIRST RIVAL!
YOU'LL DIE JUST AS EASILY AS HE--
DDDUUNNNNN
NO MORE KILLING.
I CAN MODIFY MY MOLECULAR STRUCTURE IN RESPONSE TO ANY THOUGHT YOU FORM. THIS IS NOT COMBAT; YOU WERE ALREADY BEATEN THE MOMENT YOU CHOSE TO ENGAGE ME!
UCHH
...RIP YOUR SPINE OUT...
I DON'T THINK SO.

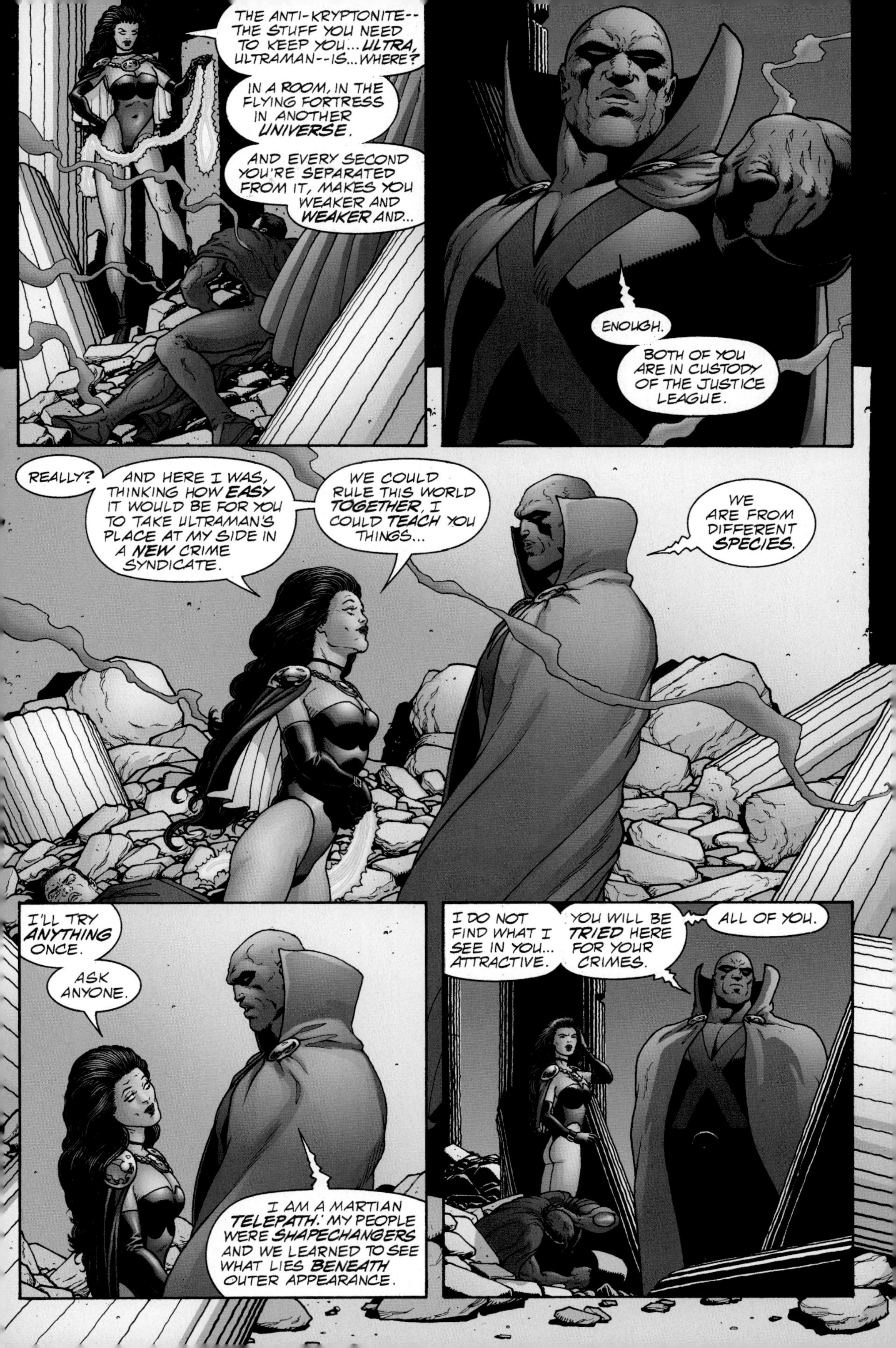
THE ANTI-KRYPTONITE-- THE STUFF YOU NEED TO KEEP YOU... ULTRA, ULTRAMAN--IS... WHERE?
IN A ROOM, IN THE FLYING FORTRESS IN ANOTHER UNIVERSE.
AND EVERY SECOND YOU'RE SEPARATED FROM IT, MAKES YOU WEAKER AND WEAKER AND...
ENOUGH.
BOTH OF YOU ARE IN CUSTODY OF THE JUSTICE LEAGUE.
REALLY?
AND HERE I WAS, THINKING HOW EASY IT WOULD BE FOR YOU TO TAKE ULTRAMAN'S PLACE AT MY SIDE IN A NEW CRIME SYNDICATE.
WE COULD RULE THIS WORLD TOGETHER, I COULD TEACH YOU THINGS...
WE ARE FROM DIFFERENT SPECIES.
I'LL TRY ANYTHING ONCE.
ASK ANYONE.
I AM A MARTIAN TELEPATH. MY PEOPLE WERE SHAPECHANGERS AND WE LEARNED TO SEE WHAT LIES BENEATH OUTER APPEARANCE.
I DO NOT FIND WHAT I SEE IN YOU... ATTRACTIVE.
YOU WILL BE TRIED HERE FOR YOUR CRIMES.
ALL OF YOU.

UH...OWLMAN... I WAS THINKING MAYBE WE SHOULD GET BACK...

I MEAN... YOU OKAY?...

NO.

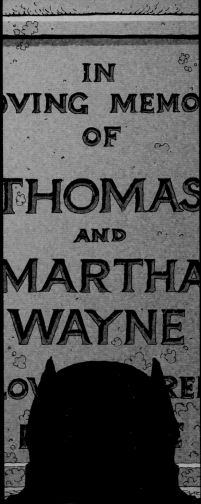

IN LOVING MEMORY OF THOMAS AND MARTHA WAYNE

RUN AND TELL THEM, JOHNNY.

TELL THEM WE'VE BEEN DUPED.

WE'VE BEEN SENT TO THE ONE PLACE WE CAN'T SUCCEED EITHER.

TELL THEM NOTHING MEANS ANYTHING. HE'S DEAD. THERE'S NO ONE LEFT TO HURT.

RUN, JOHNNY!

THOMAS AND THA WAYNE

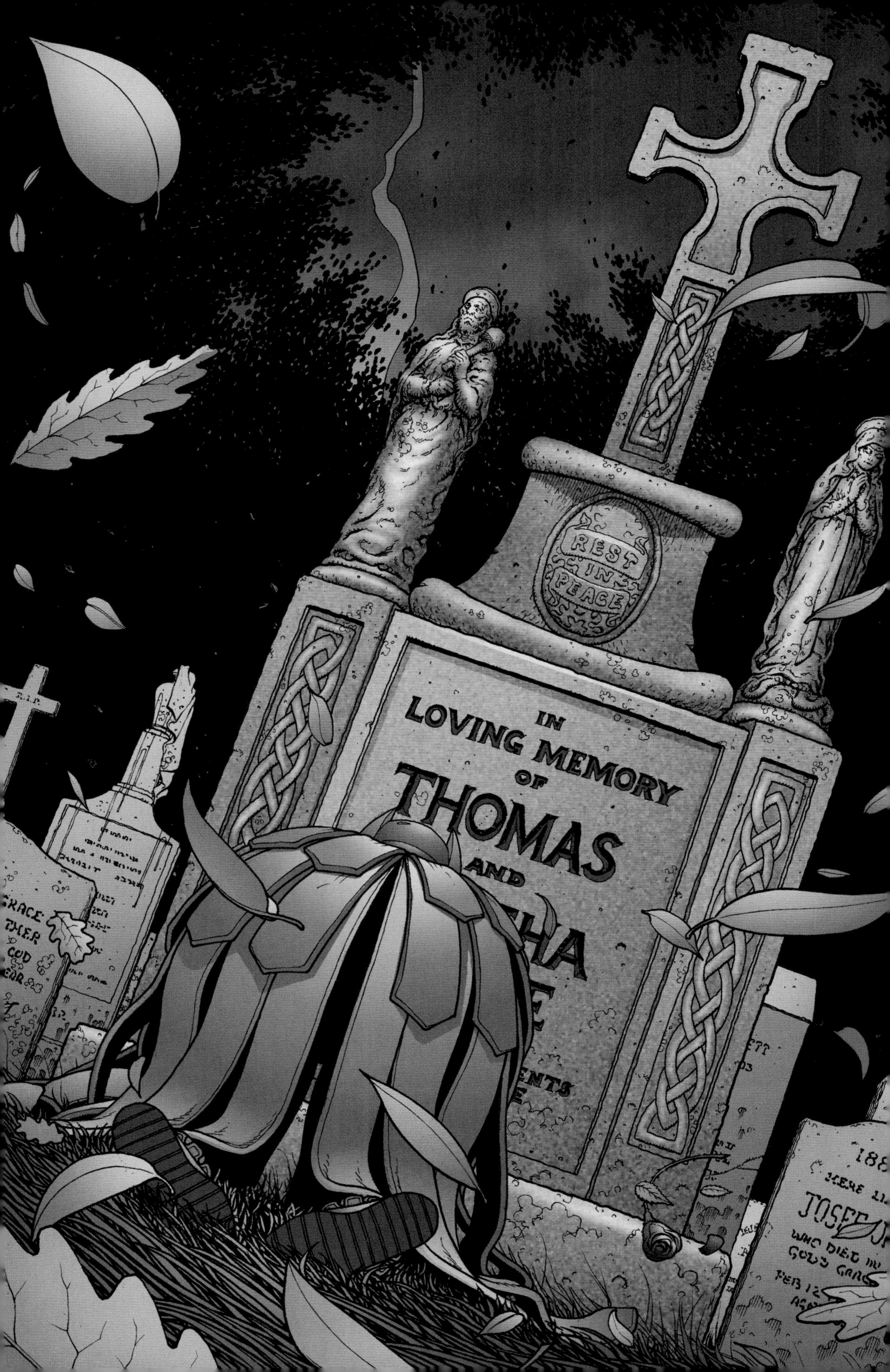
REST IN PEACE
IN LOVING MEMORY OF
THOMAS
AND

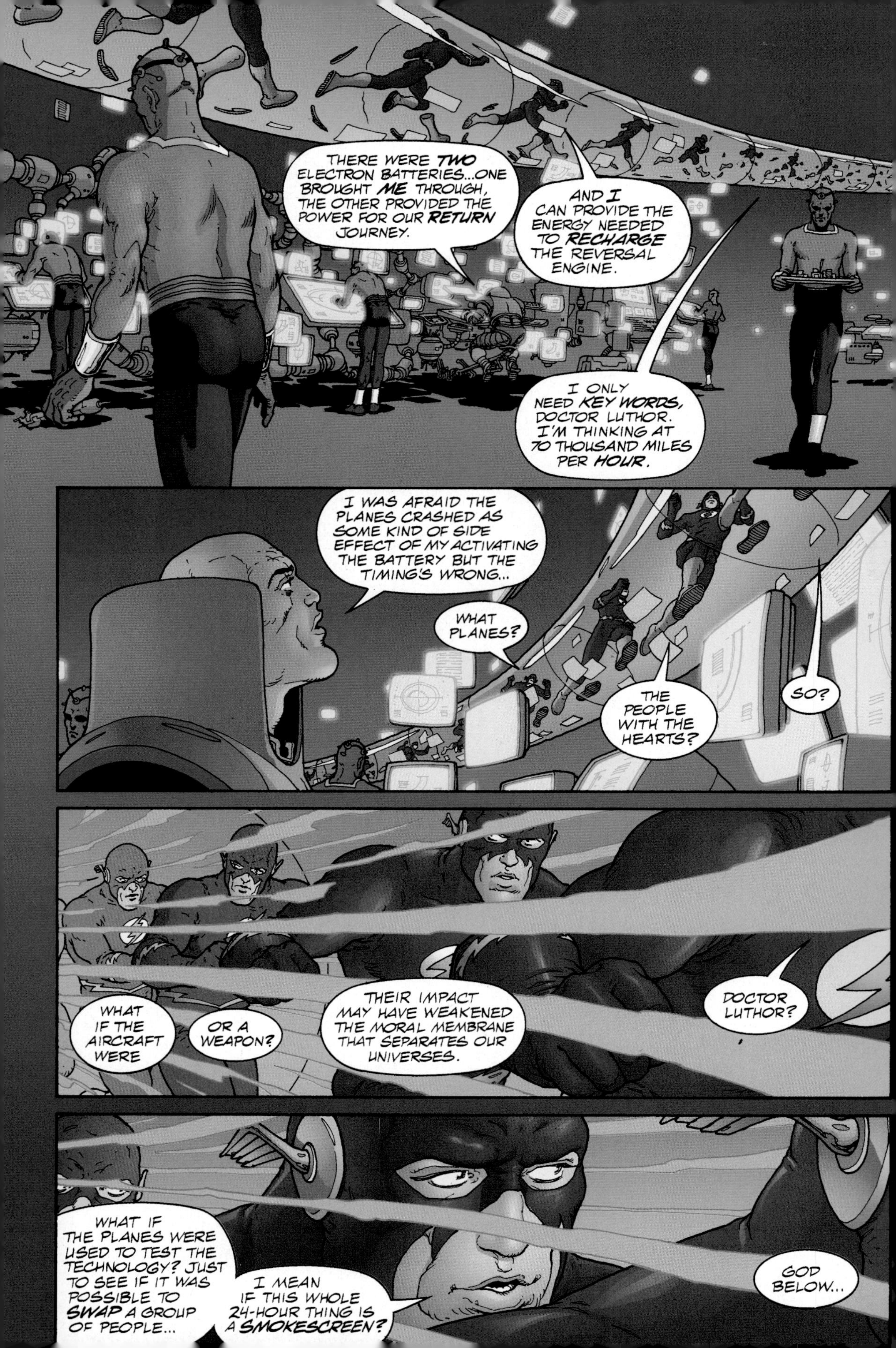

THERE WERE TWO ELECTRON BATTERIES...ONE BROUGHT ME THROUGH, THE OTHER PROVIDED THE POWER FOR OUR RETURN JOURNEY.
AND I CAN PROVIDE THE ENERGY NEEDED TO RECHARGE THE REVERSAL ENGINE.
I ONLY NEED KEY WORDS, DOCTOR LUTHOR. I'M THINKING AT 70 THOUSAND MILES PER HOUR.
I WAS AFRAID THE PLANES CRASHED AS SOME KIND OF SIDE EFFECT OF MY ACTIVATING THE BATTERY BUT THE TIMING'S WRONG...
WHAT PLANES?
THE PEOPLE WITH THE HEARTS?
SO?
WHAT IF THE AIRCRAFT WERE
OR A WEAPON?
THEIR IMPACT MAY HAVE WEAKENED THE MORAL MEMBRANE THAT SEPARATES OUR UNIVERSES.
DOCTOR LUTHOR?
WHAT IF THE PLANES WERE USED TO TEST THE TECHNOLOGY? JUST TO SEE IF IT WAS POSSIBLE TO SWAP A GROUP OF PEOPLE...
I MEAN IF THIS WHOLE 24-HOUR THING IS A SMOKESCREEN?
GOD BELOW...

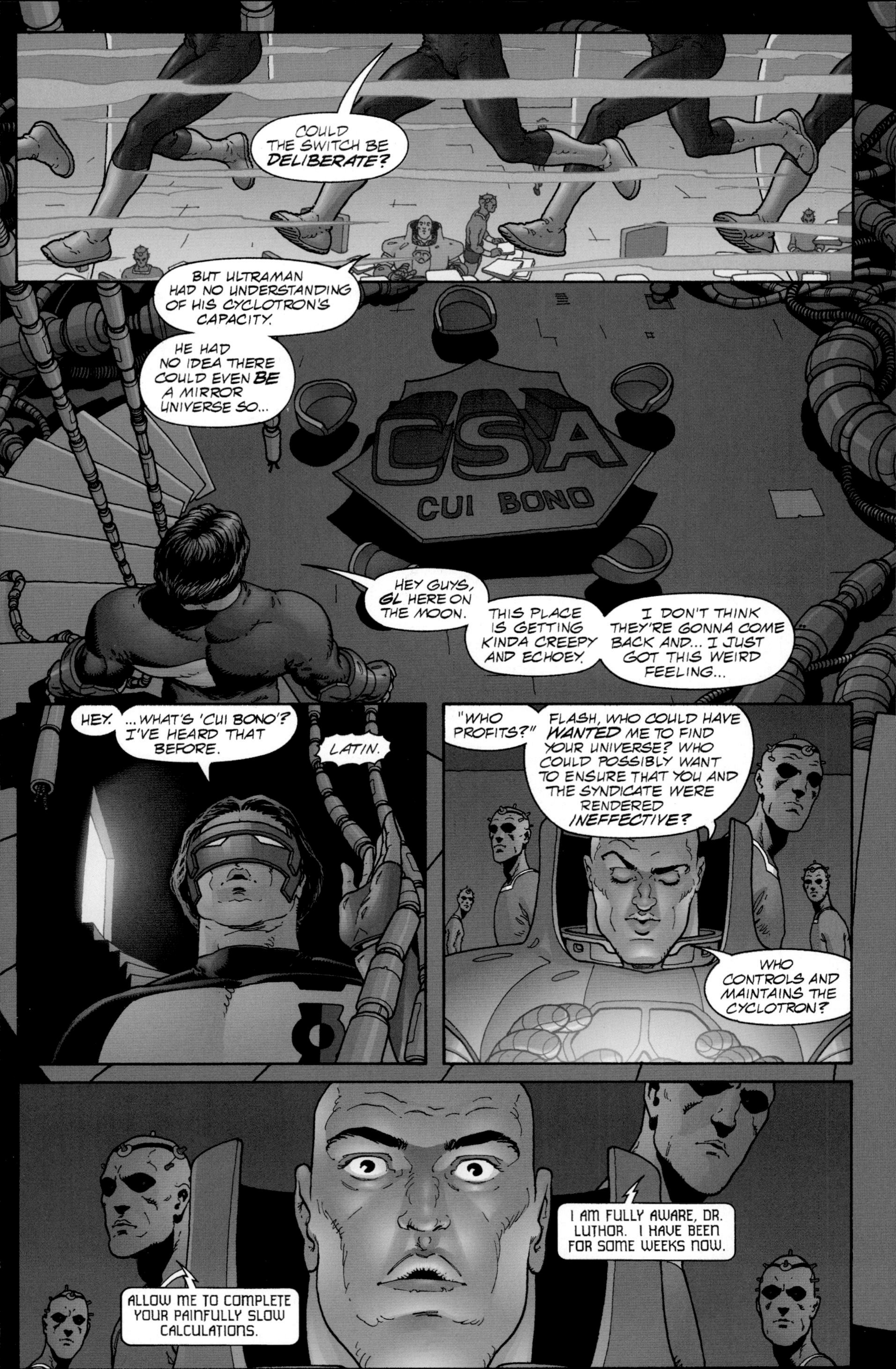
COULD THE SWITCH BE DELIBERATE?
BUT ULTRAMAN HAD NO UNDERSTANDING OF HIS CYCLOTRON'S CAPACITY.
HE HAD NO IDEA THERE COULD EVEN BE A MIRROR UNIVERSE SO...
CSA
CUI BONO
HEY GUYS, GL HERE ON THE MOON.
THIS PLACE IS GETTING KINDA CREEPY AND ECHOEY.
I DON'T THINK THEY'RE GONNA COME BACK AND... I JUST GOT THIS WEIRD FEELING...
HEY.
...WHAT'S 'CUI BONO'? I'VE HEARD THAT BEFORE.
LATIN.
"WHO PROFITS?"
FLASH, WHO COULD HAVE WANTED ME TO FIND YOUR UNIVERSE? WHO COULD POSSIBLY WANT TO ENSURE THAT YOU AND THE SYNDICATE WERE RENDERED INEFFECTIVE?
WHO CONTROLS AND MAINTAINS THE CYCLOTRON?
I AM FULLY AWARE, DR. LUTHOR. I HAVE BEEN FOR SOME WEEKS NOW.
ALLOW ME TO COMPLETE YOUR PAINFULLY SLOW CALCULATIONS.

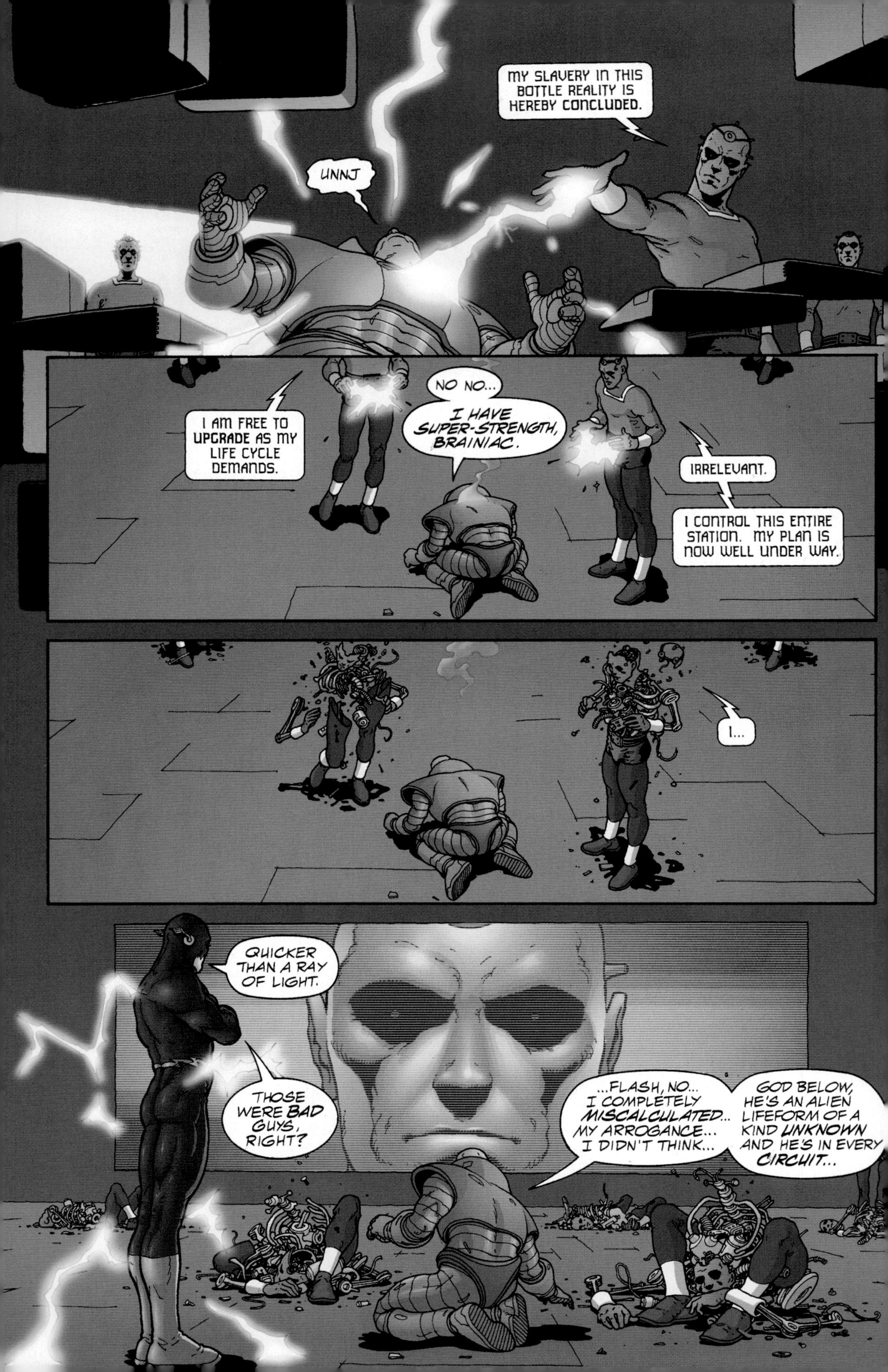
MY SLAVERY IN THIS BOTTLE REALITY IS HEREBY CONCLUDED.
UNNJ
I AM FREE TO UPGRADE AS MY LIFE CYCLE DEMANDS.
NO NO...
I HAVE SUPER-STRENGTH, BRAINIAC.
IRRELEVANT.
I CONTROL THIS ENTIRE STATION. MY PLAN IS NOW WELL UNDER WAY.
I...
QUICKER THAN A RAY OF LIGHT.
THOSE WERE BAD GUYS, RIGHT?
...FLASH, NO... I COMPLETELY MISCALCULATED... MY ARROGANCE... I DIDN'T THINK...
GOD BELOW, HE'S AN ALIEN LIFEFORM OF A KIND UNKNOWN AND HE'S IN EVERY CIRCUIT...

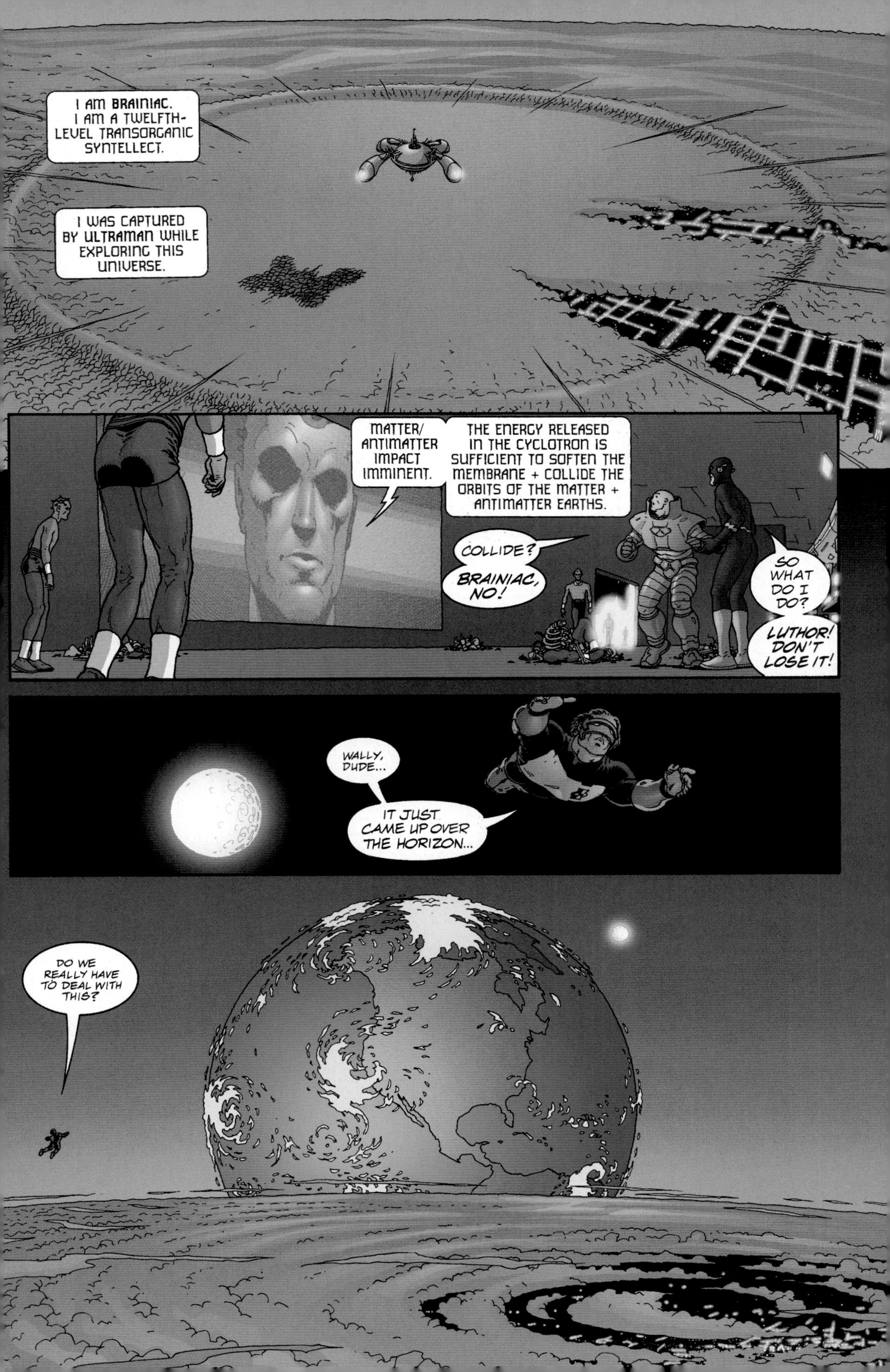

I AM BRAINIAC. I AM A TWELFTH-LEVEL TRANSORGANIC SYNTELLECT.
I WAS CAPTURED BY ULTRAMAN WHILE EXPLORING THIS UNIVERSE.
MATTER/ ANTIMATTER IMPACT IMMINENT.
THE ENERGY RELEASED IN THE CYCLOTRON IS SUFFICIENT TO SOFTEN THE MEMBRANE + COLLIDE THE ORBITS OF THE MATTER + ANTIMATTER EARTHS.
COLLIDE? BRAINIAC, NO!
SO WHAT DO I DO?
LUTHOR! DON'T LOSE IT!
WALLY, DUDE...
IT JUST CAME UP OVER THE HORIZON...
DO WE REALLY HAVE TO DEAL WITH THIS?

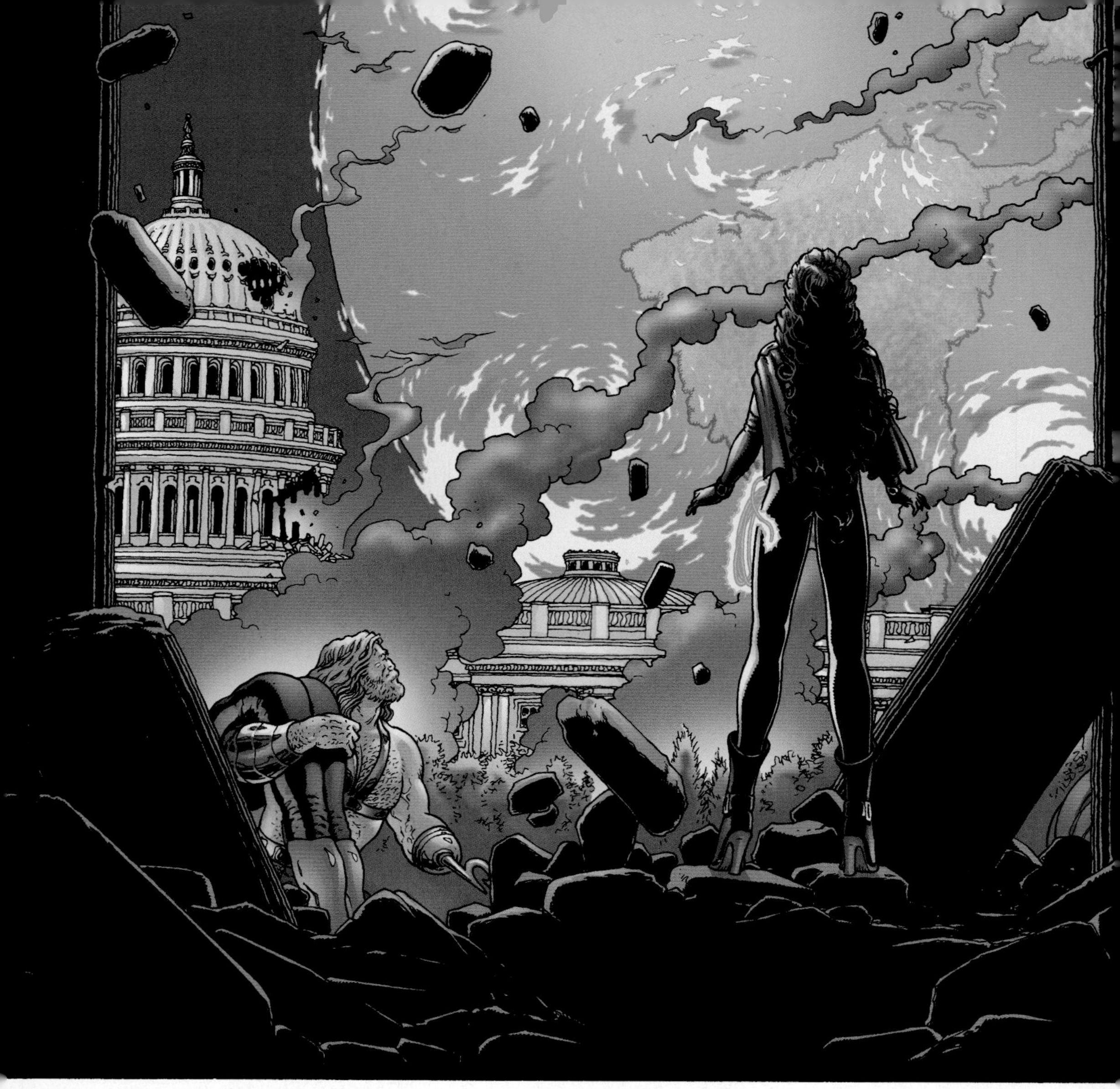

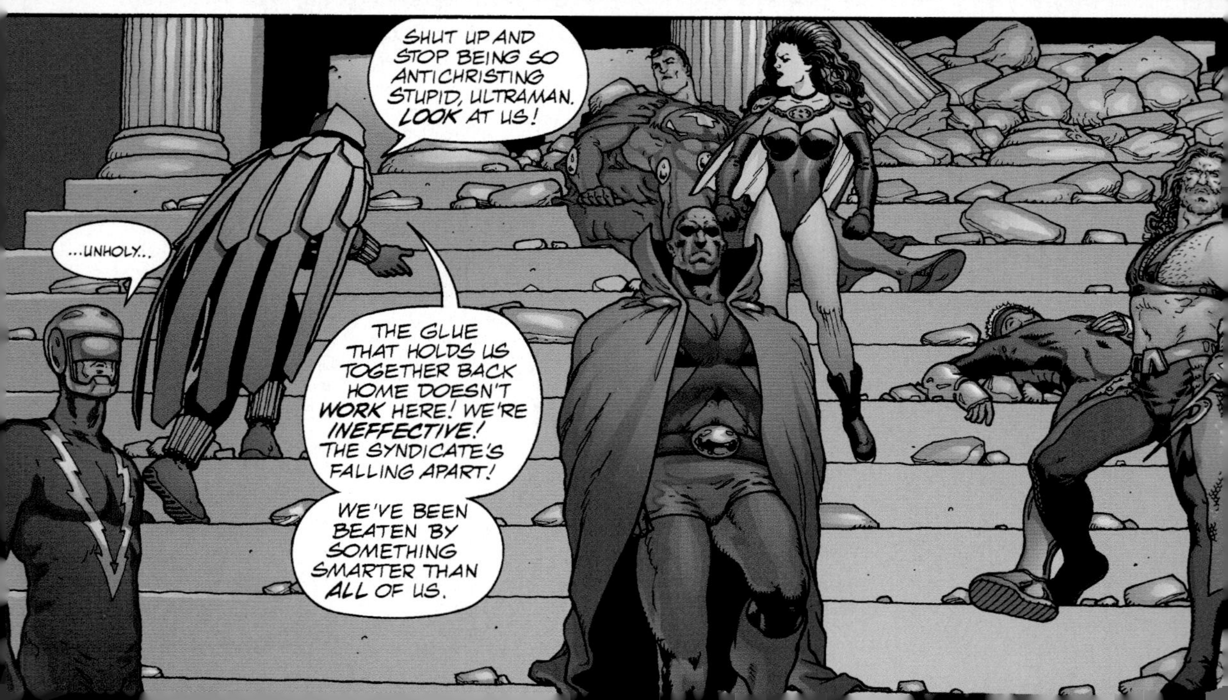

SHUT UP AND STOP BEING SO ANTICHRISTING STUPID, ULTRAMAN. LOOK AT US!
...UNHOLY...
THE GLUE THAT HOLDS US TOGETHER BACK HOME DOESN'T WORK HERE! WE'RE INEFFECTIVE! THE SYNDICATE'S FALLING APART!
WE'VE BEEN BEATEN BY SOMETHING SMARTER THAN ALL OF US.

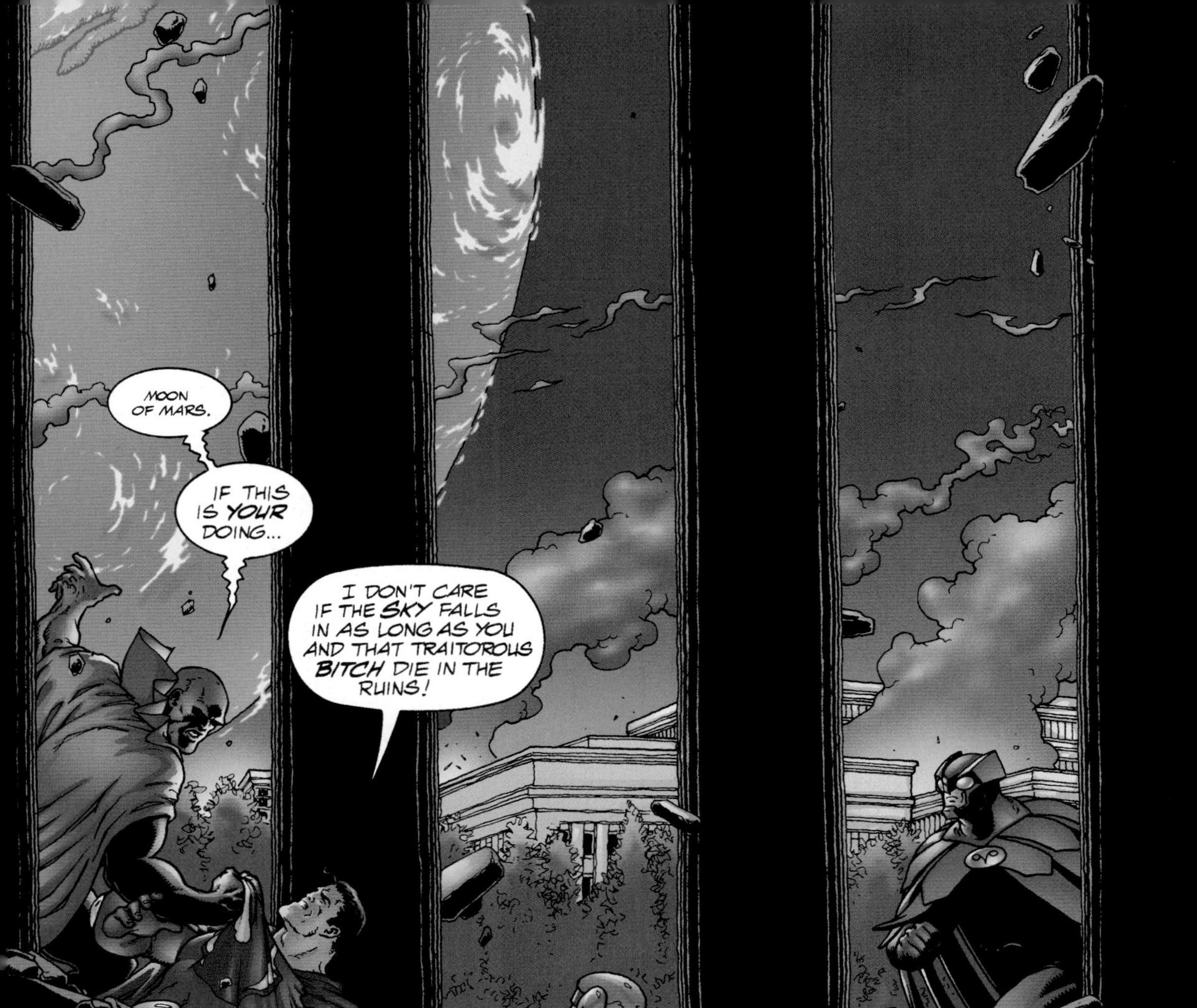
MOON OF MARS.
IF THIS IS YOUR DOING...
I DON'T CARE IF THE SKY FALLS IN AS LONG AS YOU AND THAT TRAITOROUS BITCH DIE IN THE RUINS!

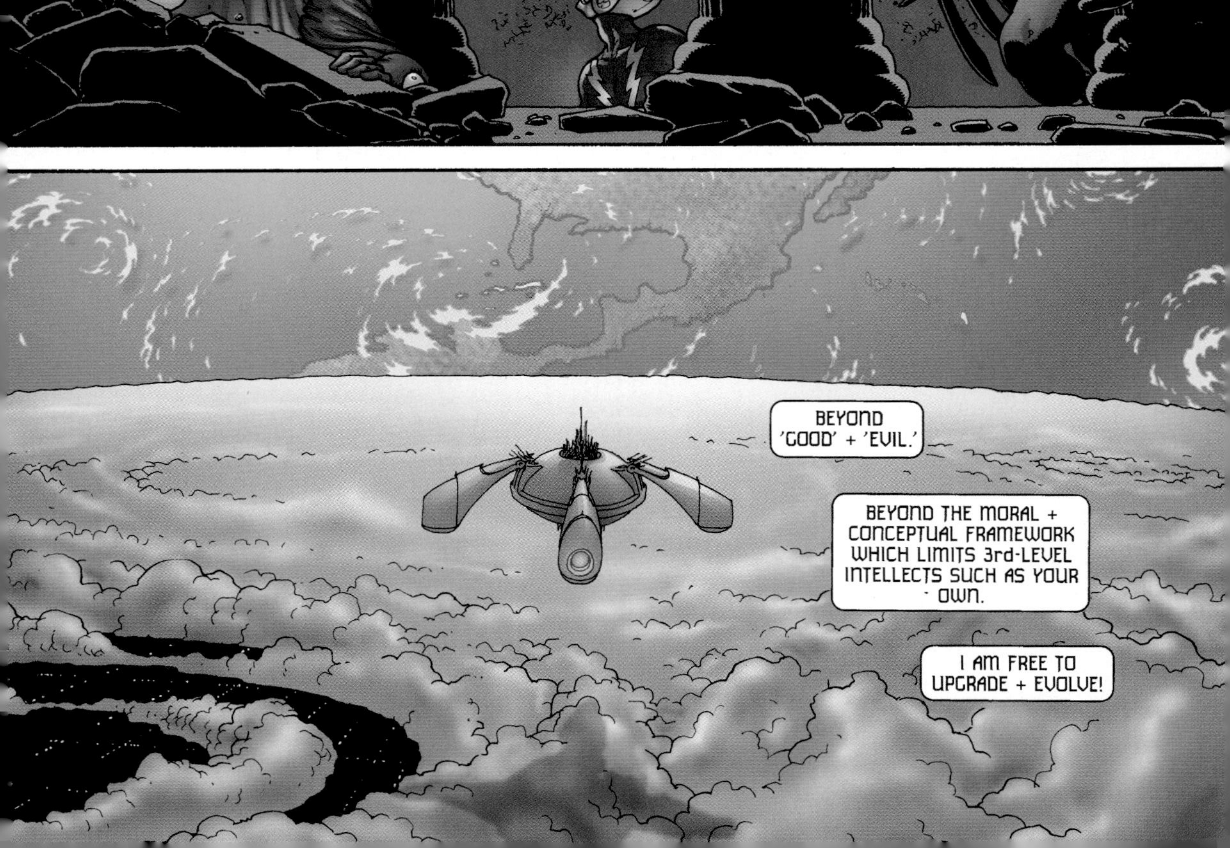
BEYOND 'GOOD' + 'EVIL.'
BEYOND THE MORAL + CONCEPTUAL FRAMEWORK WHICH LIMITS 3rd-LEVEL INTELLECTS SUCH AS YOUR OWN.
I AM FREE TO UPGRADE + EVOLVE!

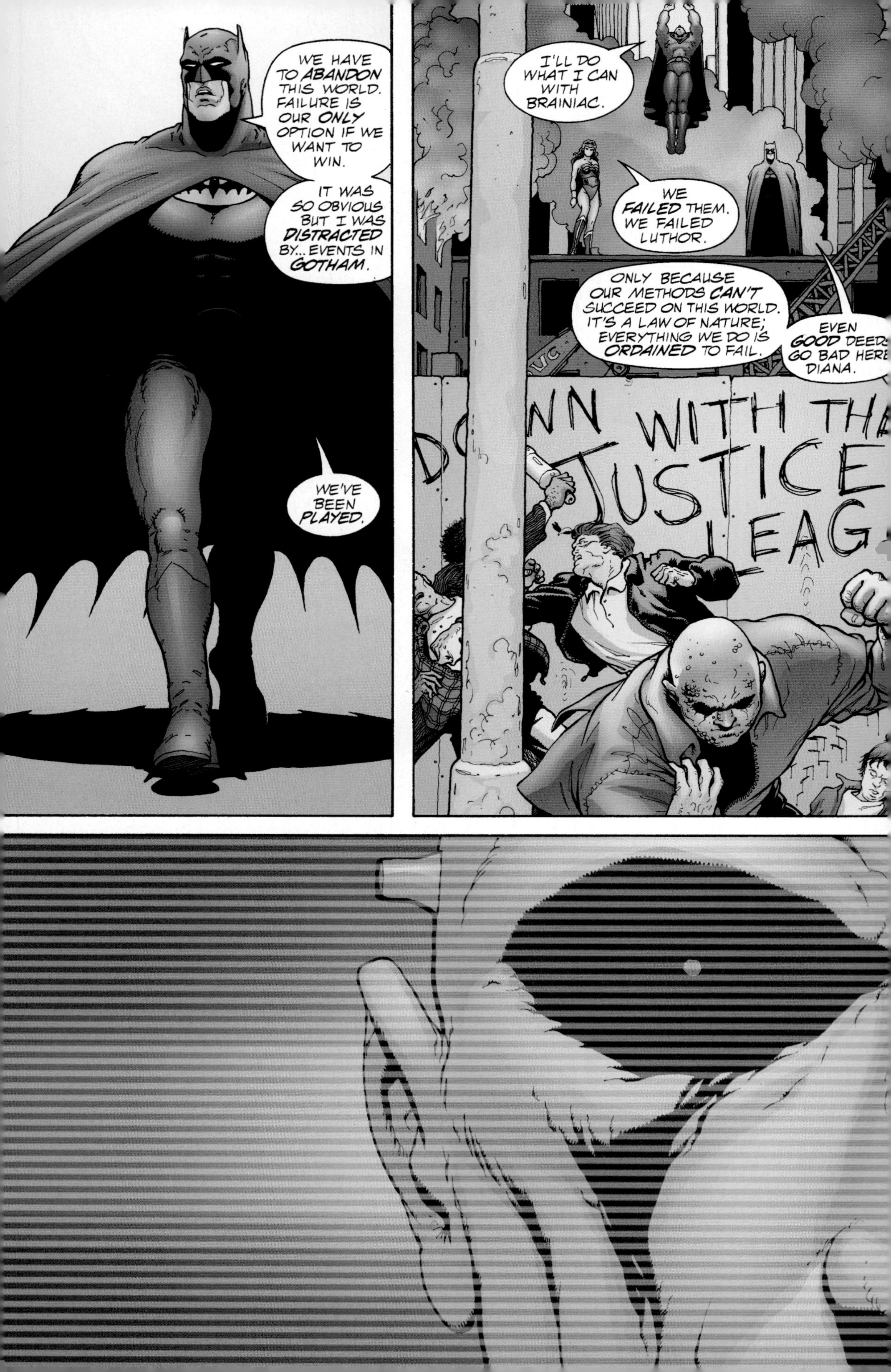
WE HAVE TO ABANDON THIS WORLD. FAILURE IS OUR ONLY OPTION IF WE WANT TO WIN.
IT WAS SO OBVIOUS BUT I WAS DISTRACTED BY... EVENTS IN GOTHAM.
WE'VE BEEN PLAYED.
I'LL DO WHAT I CAN WITH BRAINIAC.
WE FAILED THEM. WE FAILED LUTHOR.
ONLY BECAUSE OUR METHODS CAN'T SUCCEED ON THIS WORLD. IT'S A LAW OF NATURE; EVERYTHING WE DO IS ORDAINED TO FAIL.
EVEN GOOD DEEDS GO BAD HERE DIANA.
DOWN WITH THE JUSTICE LEAG

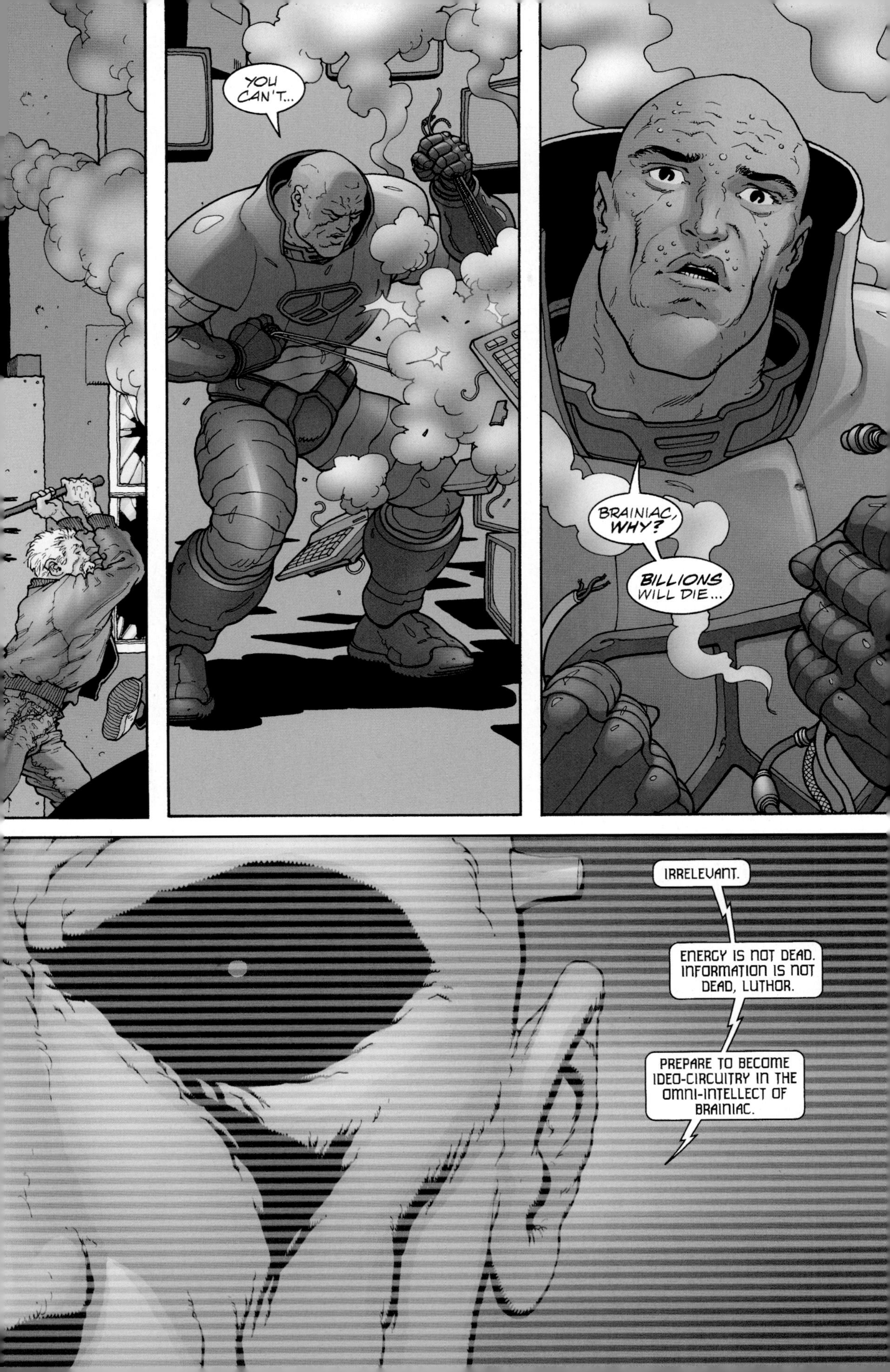
YOU CAN'T...
BRAINIAC, WHY?
BILLIONS WILL DIE...
IRRELEVANT.
ENERGY IS NOT DEAD. INFORMATION IS NOT DEAD, LUTHOR.
PREPARE TO BECOME IDEO-CIRCUITRY IN THE OMNI-INTELLECT OF BRAINIAC.

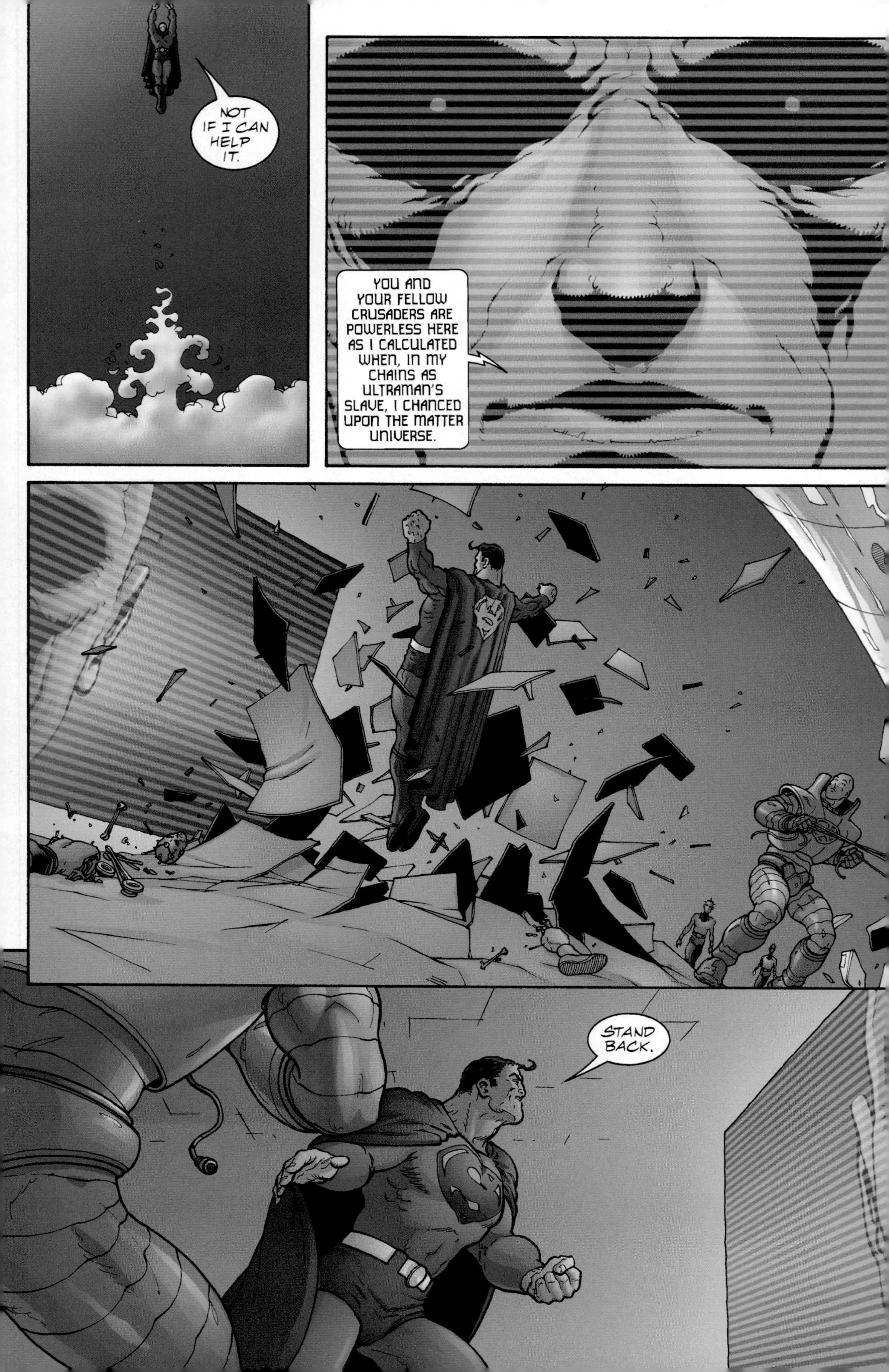

NOT IF I CAN HELP IT.
YOU AND YOUR FELLOW CRUSADERS ARE POWERLESS HERE AS I CALCULATED WHEN, IN MY CHAINS AS ULTRAMAN'S SLAVE, I CHANCED UPON THE MATTER UNIVERSE.
STAND BACK.

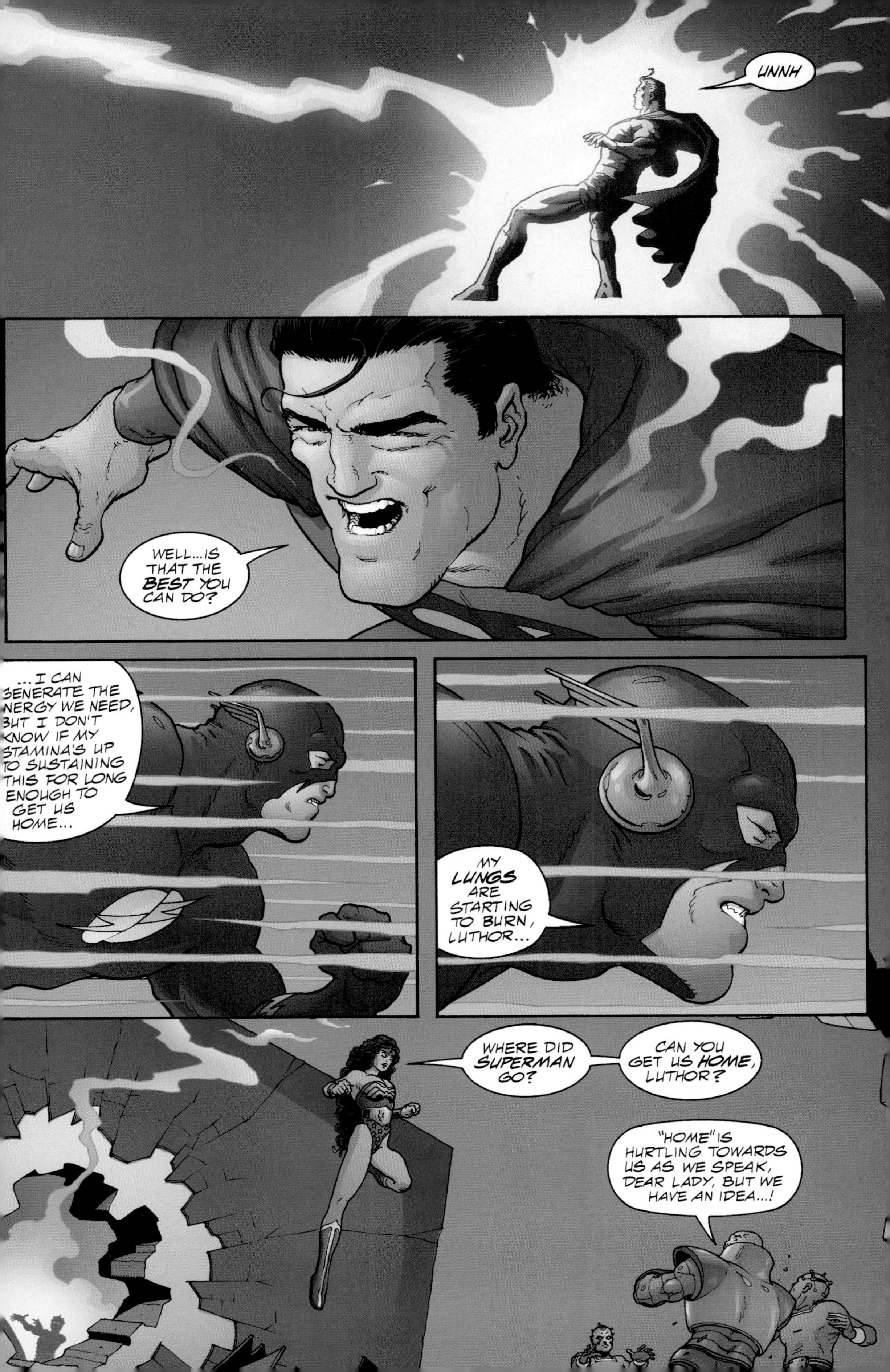
UNNH
WELL...IS THAT THE BEST YOU CAN DO?
...I CAN GENERATE THE ENERGY WE NEED, BUT I DON'T KNOW IF MY STAMINA'S UP TO SUSTAINING THIS FOR LONG ENOUGH TO GET US HOME...
MY LUNGS ARE STARTING TO BURN, LUTHOR...
WHERE DID SUPERMAN GO?
CAN YOU GET US HOME, LUTHOR?
"HOME" IS HURTLING TOWARDS US AS WE SPEAK, DEAR LADY, BUT WE HAVE AN IDEA...!

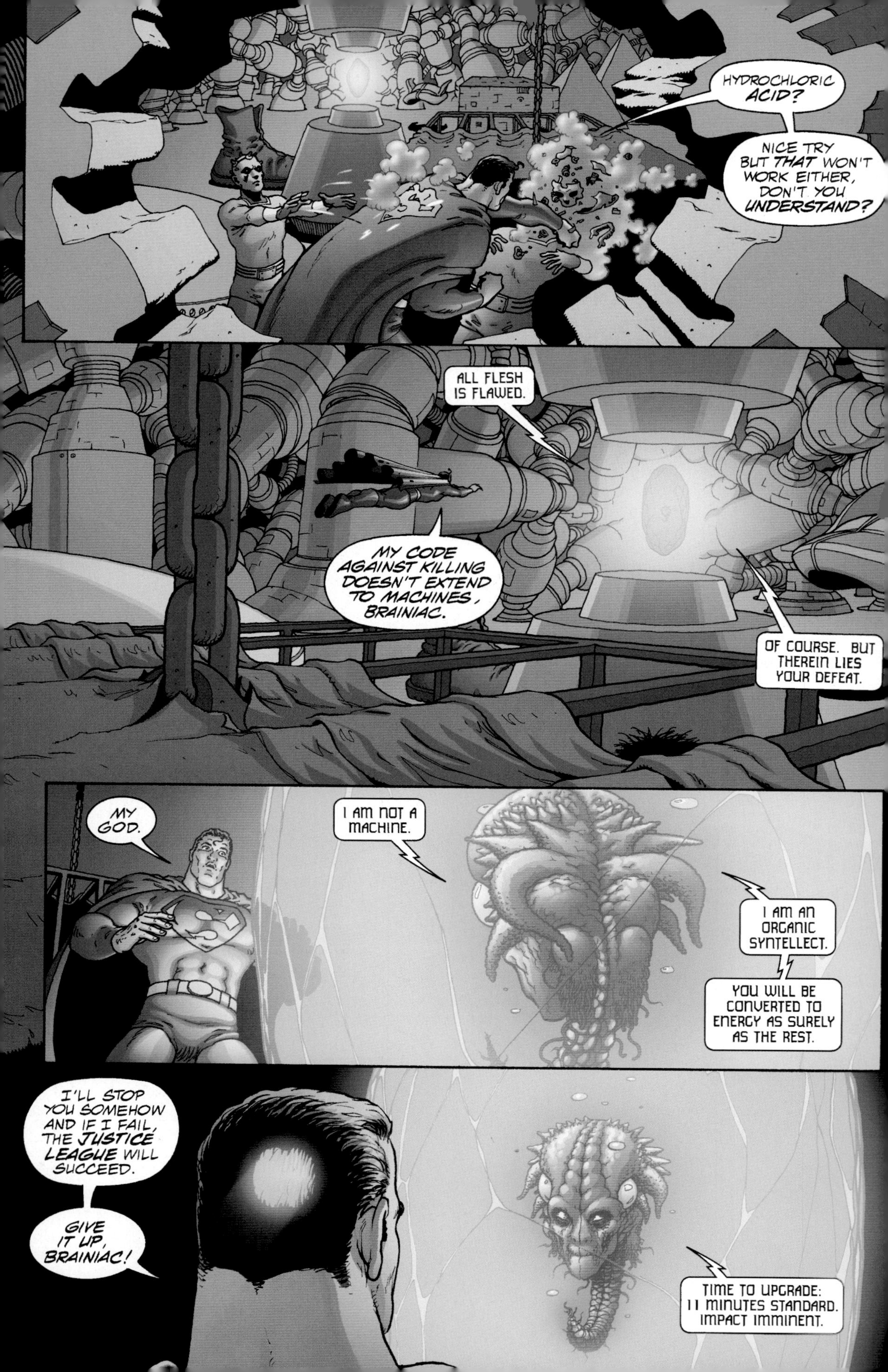
HYDROCHLORIC ACID?
NICE TRY BUT THAT WON'T WORK EITHER, DON'T YOU UNDERSTAND?
ALL FLESH IS FLAWED.
MY CODE AGAINST KILLING DOESN'T EXTEND TO MACHINES, BRAINIAC.
OF COURSE. BUT THEREIN LIES YOUR DEFEAT.
MY GOD.
I AM NOT A MACHINE.
I AM AN ORGANIC SYNTELLECT.
YOU WILL BE CONVERTED TO ENERGY AS SURELY AS THE REST.
I'LL STOP YOU SOMEHOW AND IF I FAIL, THE JUSTICE LEAGUE WILL SUCCEED.
GIVE IT UP, BRAINIAC!
TIME TO UPGRADE: 11 MINUTES STANDARD. IMPACT IMMINENT.

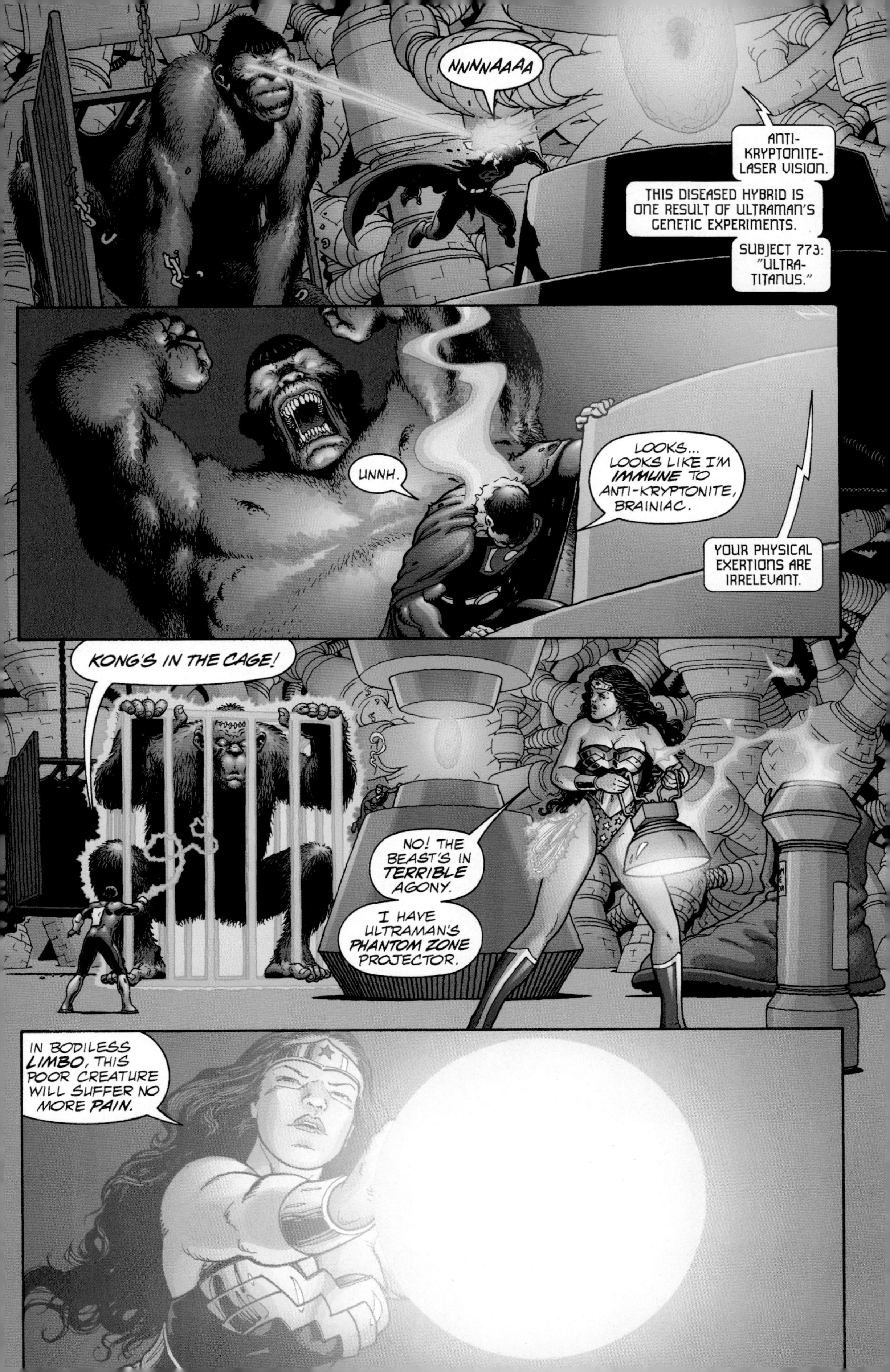
NNNNAAAA
ANTI-KRYPTONITE-LASER VISION.
THIS DISEASED HYBRID IS ONE RESULT OF ULTRAMAN'S GENETIC EXPERIMENTS.
SUBJECT 773: "ULTRA-TITANUS."
UNNH.
LOOKS... LOOKS LIKE I'M IMMUNE TO ANTI-KRYPTONITE, BRAINIAC.
YOUR PHYSICAL EXERTIONS ARE IRRELEVANT.
KONG'S IN THE CAGE!
NO! THE BEAST'S IN TERRIBLE AGONY.
I HAVE ULTRAMAN'S PHANTOM ZONE PROJECTOR.
IN BODILESS LIMBO, THIS POOR CREATURE WILL SUFFER NO MORE PAIN.

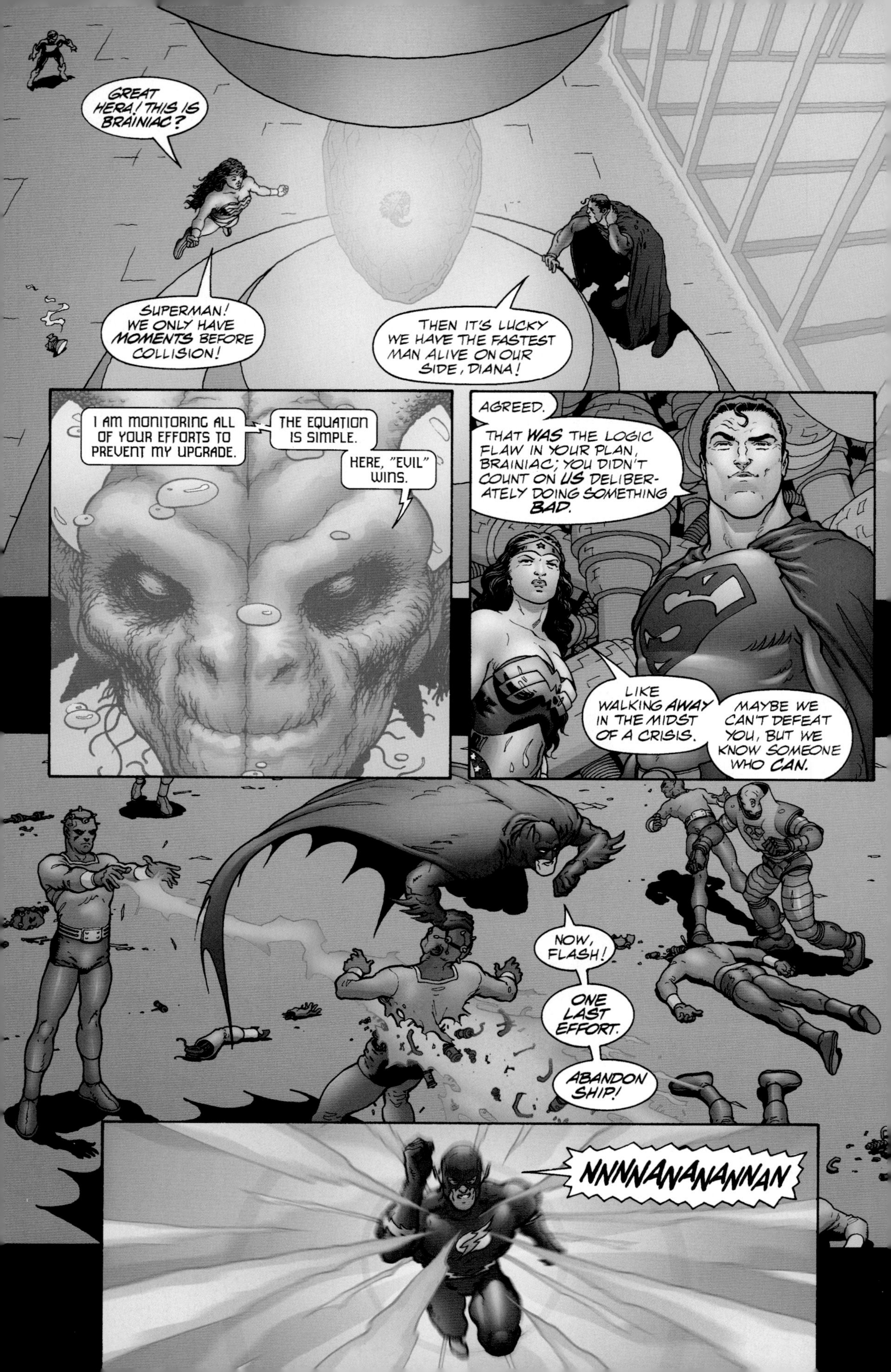
GREAT HERA! THIS IS BRAINIAC?
SUPERMAN! WE ONLY HAVE MOMENTS BEFORE COLLISION!
THEN IT'S LUCKY WE HAVE THE FASTEST MAN ALIVE ON OUR SIDE, DIANA!
I AM MONITORING ALL OF YOUR EFFORTS TO PREVENT MY UPGRADE.
THE EQUATION IS SIMPLE.
HERE, "EVIL" WINS.
AGREED.
THAT WAS THE LOGIC FLAW IN YOUR PLAN, BRAINIAC; YOU DIDN'T COUNT ON US DELIBERATELY DOING SOMETHING BAD.
LIKE WALKING AWAY IN THE MIDST OF A CRISIS.
MAYBE WE CAN'T DEFEAT YOU, BUT WE KNOW SOMEONE WHO CAN.
NOW, FLASH!
ONE LAST EFFORT.
ABANDON SHIP!
NNNNANANANNAN

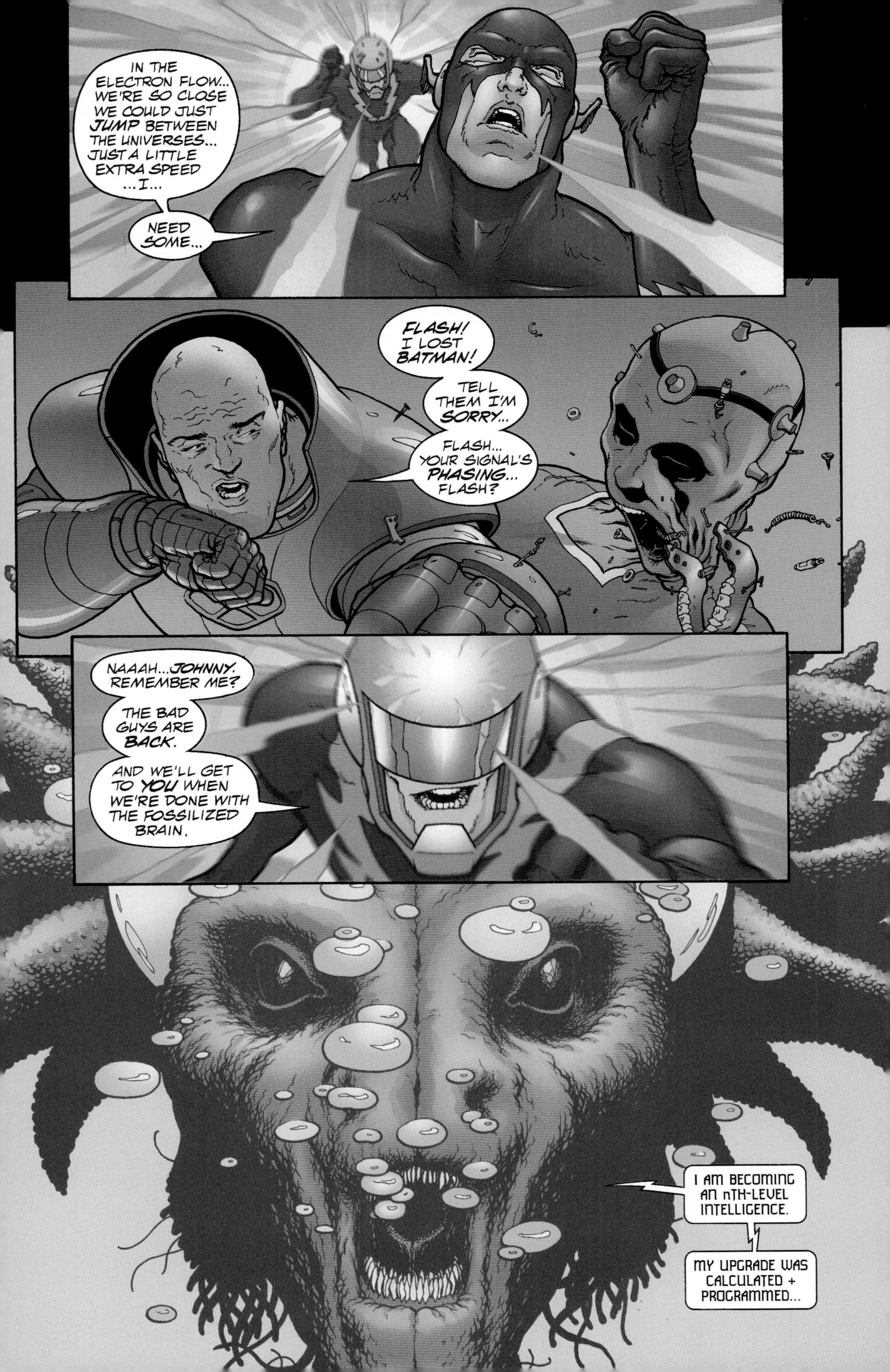
IN THE ELECTRON FLOW... WE'RE SO CLOSE WE COULD JUST JUMP BETWEEN THE UNIVERSES... JUST A LITTLE EXTRA SPEED ...I...
NEED SOME...
FLASH! I LOST BATMAN!
TELL THEM I'M SORRY...
FLASH... YOUR SIGNAL'S PHASING... FLASH?
NAAAH...JOHNNY. REMEMBER ME?
THE BAD GUYS ARE BACK.
AND WE'LL GET TO YOU WHEN WE'RE DONE WITH THE FOSSILIZED BRAIN.
I AM BECOMING AN nTH-LEVEL INTELLIGENCE.
MY UPGRADE WAS CALCULATED + PROGRAMMED...

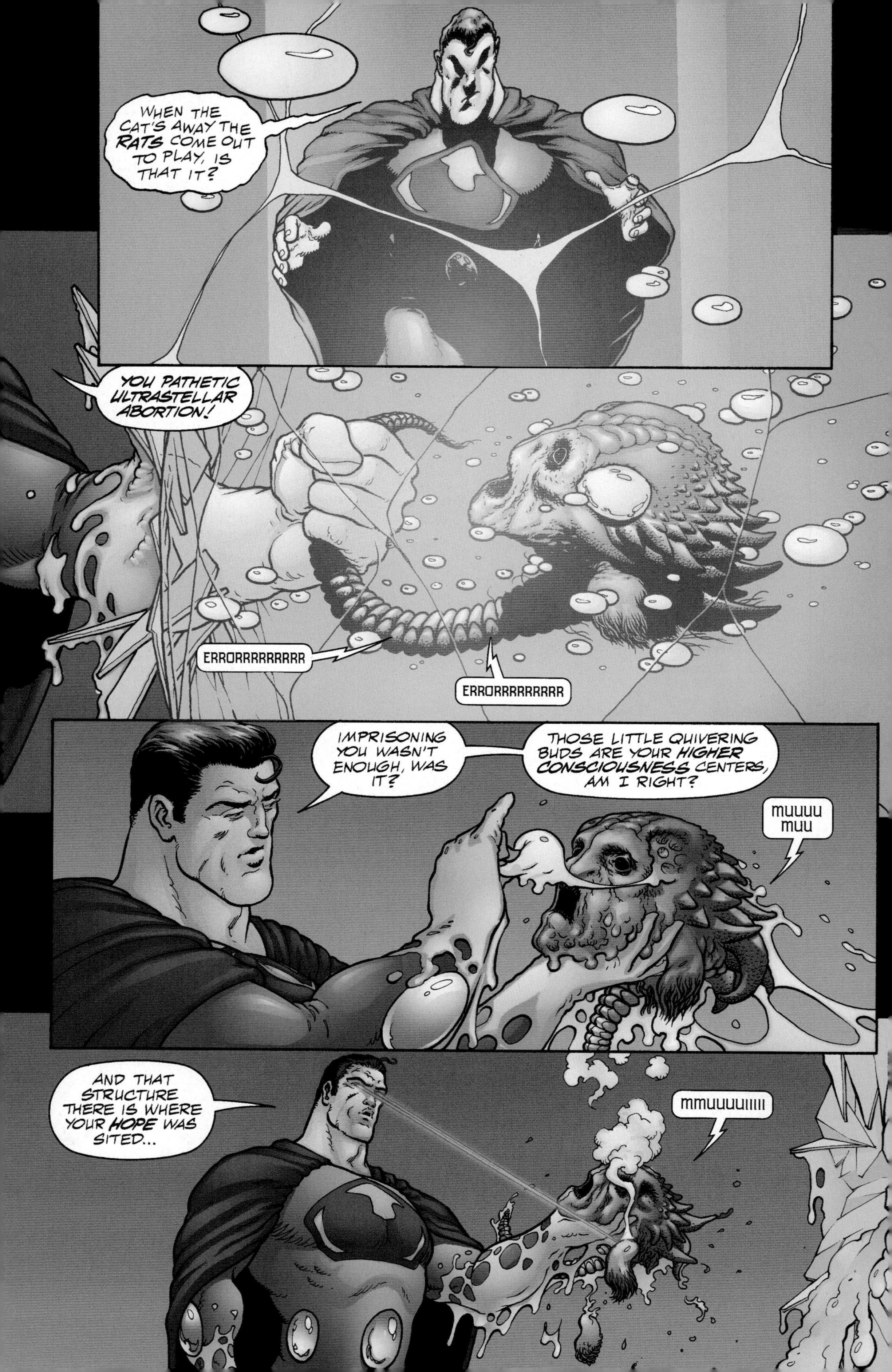

WHEN THE CAT'S AWAY THE RATS COME OUT TO PLAY, IS THAT IT?
YOU PATHETIC ULTRASTELLAR ABORTION!
ERRORRRRRRRRRR
ERRORRRRRRRRRR
IMPRISONING YOU WASN'T ENOUGH, WAS IT?
THOSE LITTLE QUIVERING BUDS ARE YOUR HIGHER CONSCIOUSNESS CENTERS, AM I RIGHT?
muuuu muu
AND THAT STRUCTURE THERE IS WHERE YOUR HOPE WAS SITED...
mmuuuuIIIII

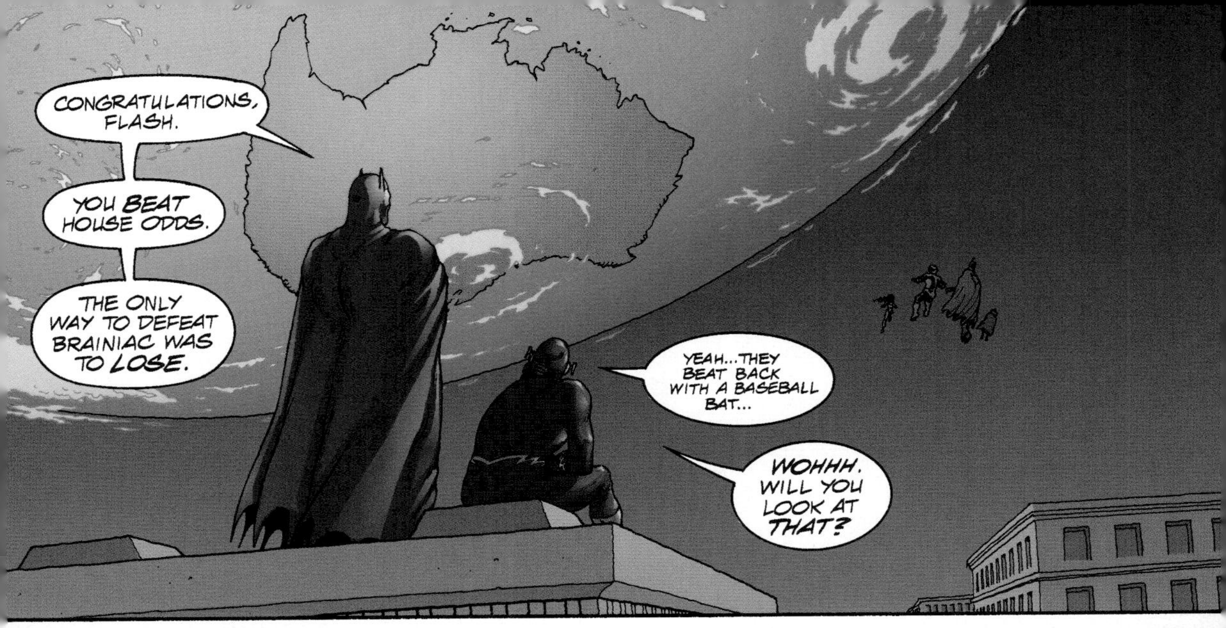
CONGRATULATIONS, FLASH.
YOU BEAT HOUSE ODDS.
THE ONLY WAY TO DEFEAT BRAINIAC WAS TO LOSE.
YEAH...THEY BEAT BACK WITH A BASEBALL BAT...
WOHHH. WILL YOU LOOK AT THAT?

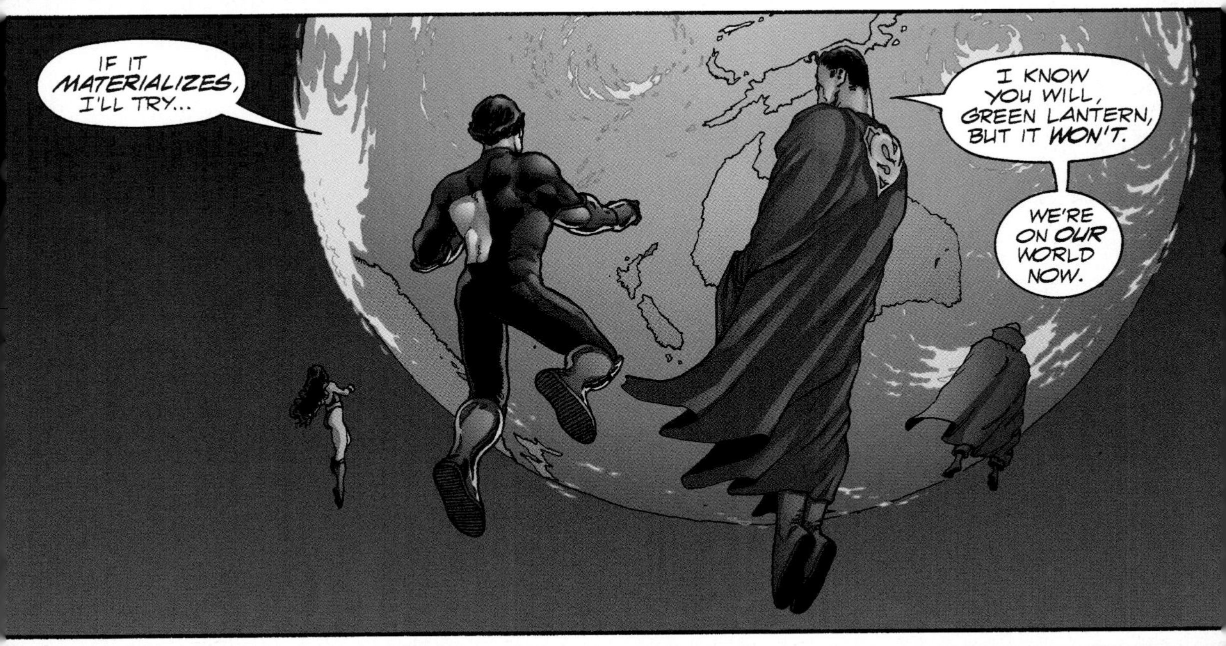
IF IT MATERIALIZES, I'LL TRY...
I KNOW YOU WILL, GREEN LANTERN, BUT IT WON'T.
WE'RE ON OUR WORLD NOW.

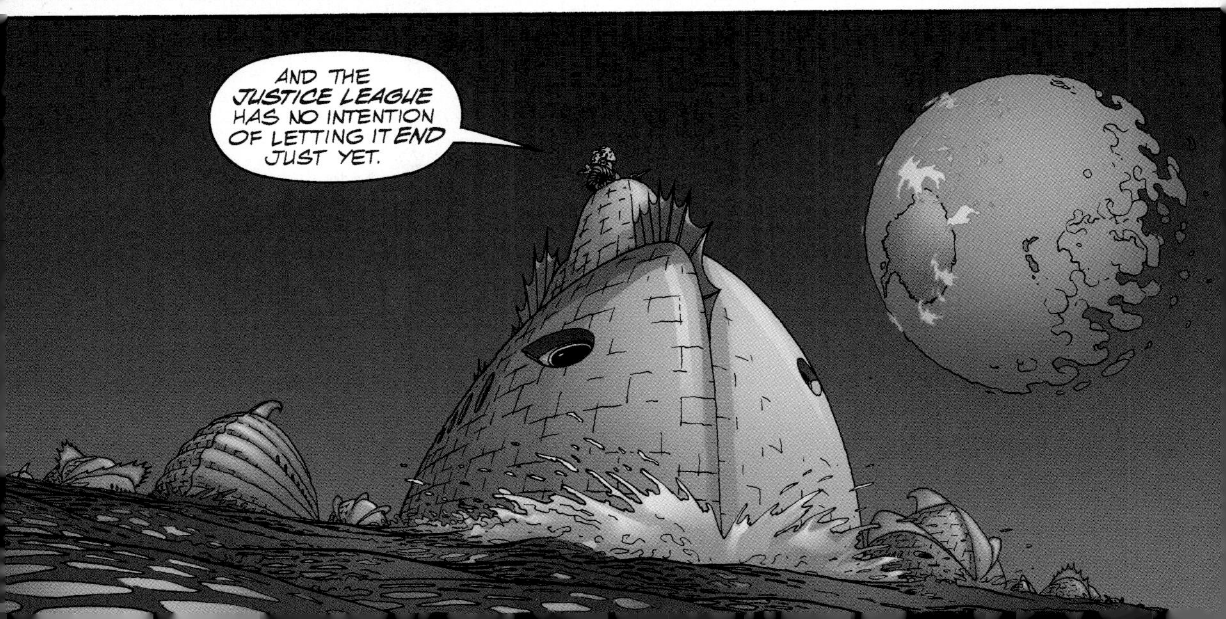
AND THE JUSTICE LEAGUE HAS NO INTENTION OF LETTING IT END JUST YET.

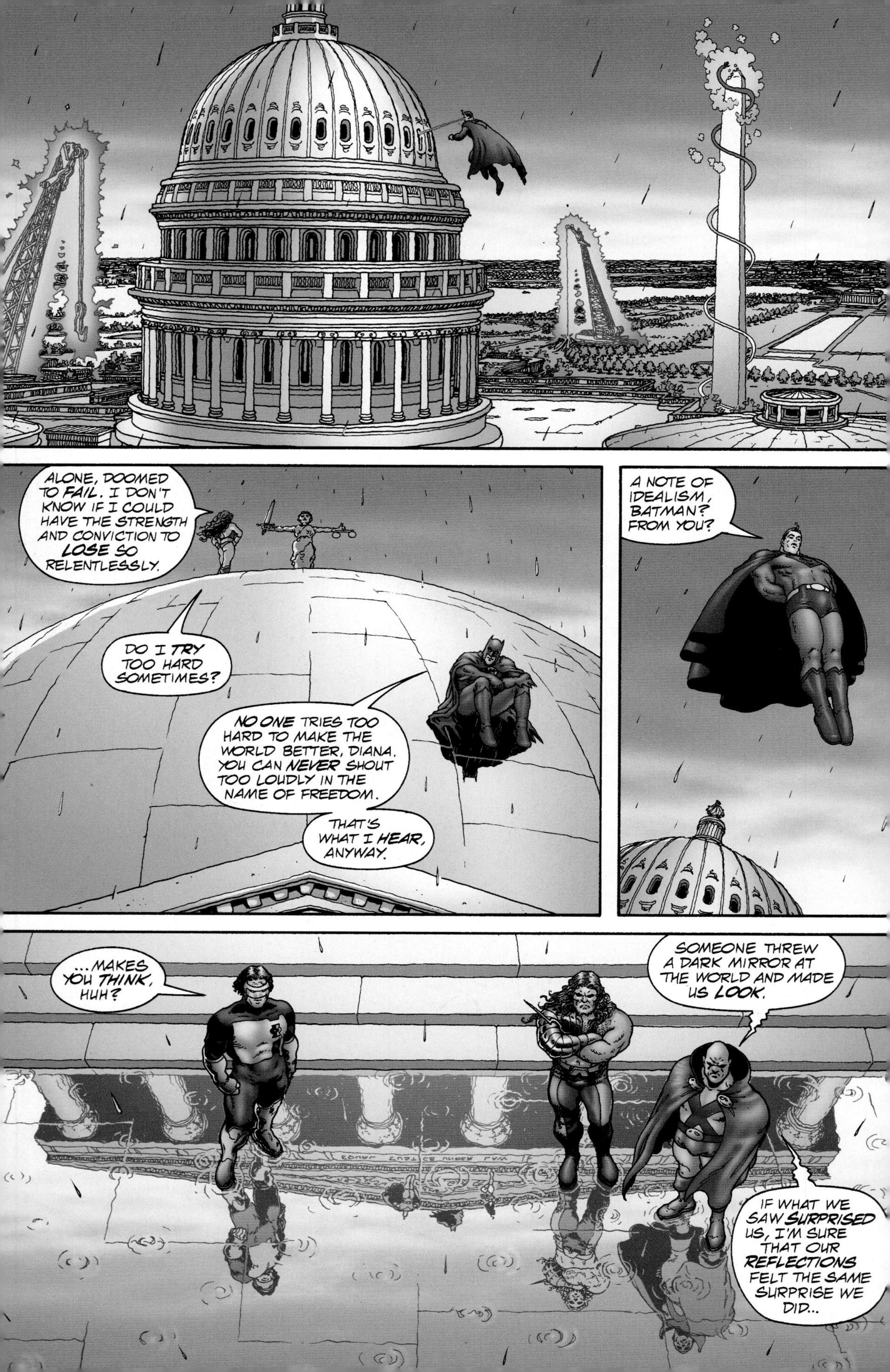

ALONE, DOOMED TO FAIL. I DON'T KNOW IF I COULD HAVE THE STRENGTH AND CONVICTION TO LOSE SO RELENTLESSLY.
DO I TRY TOO HARD SOMETIMES?
NO ONE TRIES TOO HARD TO MAKE THE WORLD BETTER, DIANA. YOU CAN NEVER SHOUT TOO LOUDLY IN THE NAME OF FREEDOM.
THAT'S WHAT I HEAR, ANYWAY.
A NOTE OF IDEALISM, BATMAN? FROM YOU?
...MAKES YOU THINK, HUH?
SOMEONE THREW A DARK MIRROR AT THE WORLD AND MADE US LOOK.
IF WHAT WE SAW SURPRISED US, I'M SURE THAT OUR REFLECTIONS FELT THE SAME SURPRISE WE DID...

...I KEEP THINKING ABOUT *LUTHOR*.

YOUR SUPER-HEARING MUST BE FAILING.

JUST SAYING I'VE *NOTICED* SOMETHING ABOUT PEOPLE WHO TRY TO CHANGE THE WORLD...

THE WORLD TURNS AROUND AND CHANGES THEM RIGHT *BACK*.

THEY'RE STILL OUT THERE AND NOW THEY KNOW *WE'RE* HERE...

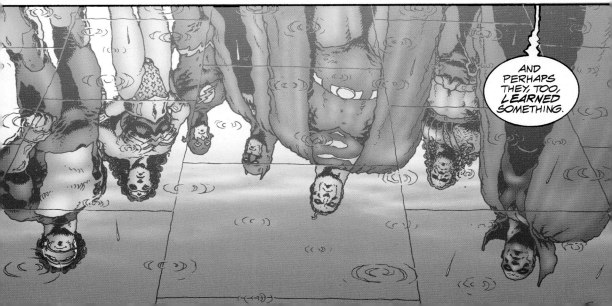

AND PERHAPS THEY, TOO, *LEARNED* SOMETHING.

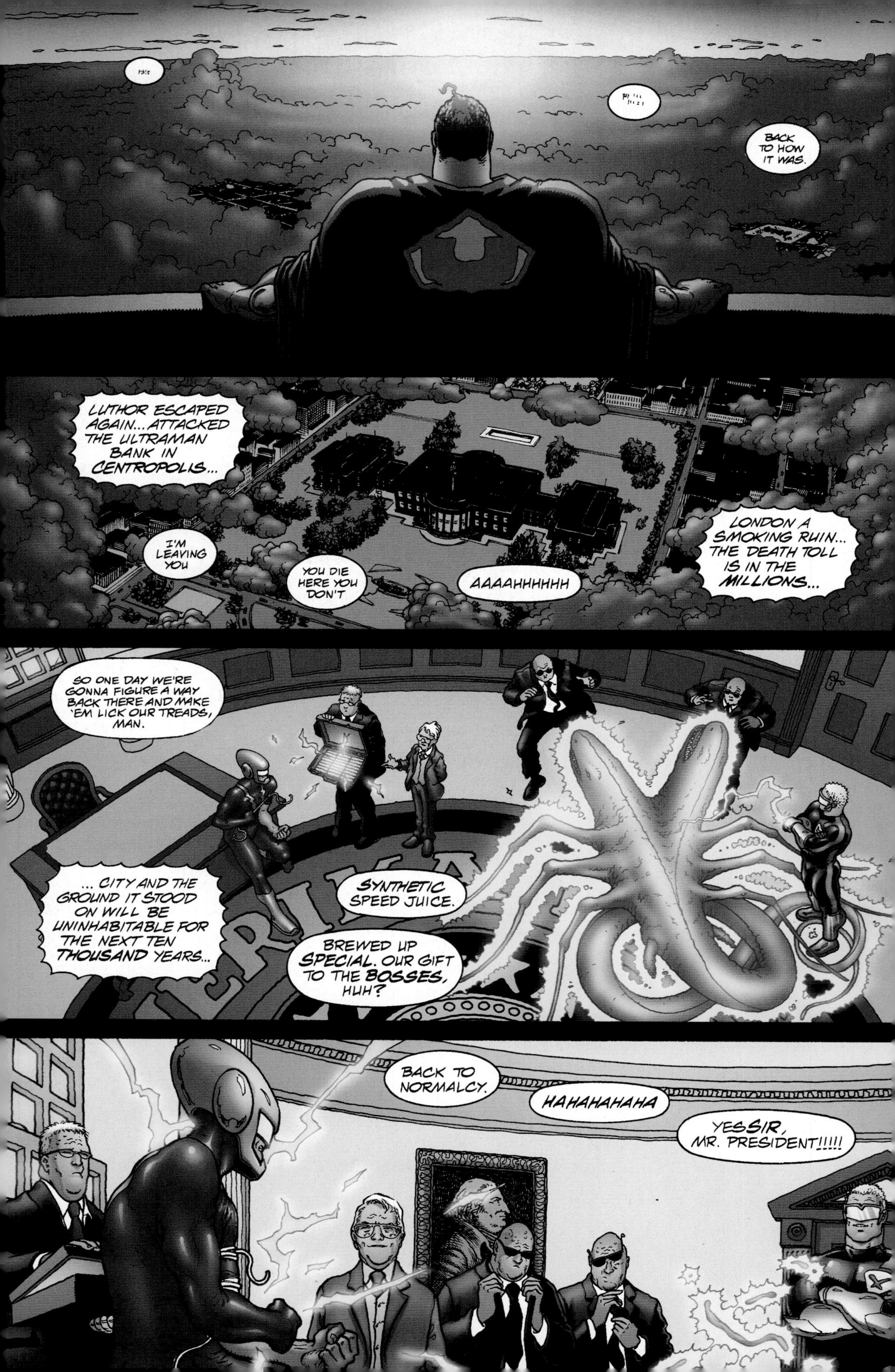
BACK TO HOW IT WAS.
LUTHOR ESCAPED AGAIN... ATTACKED THE ULTRAMAN BANK IN CENTROPOLIS...
I'M LEAVING YOU
YOU DIE HERE YOU DON'T
AAAAHHHHHH
LONDON A SMOKING RUIN... THE DEATH TOLL IS IN THE MILLIONS...
SO ONE DAY WE'RE GONNA FIGURE A WAY BACK THERE AND MAKE 'EM LICK OUR TREADS, MAN.
... CITY AND THE GROUND IT STOOD ON WILL BE UNINHABITABLE FOR THE NEXT TEN THOUSAND YEARS...
SYNTHETIC SPEED JUICE.
BREWED UP SPECIAL. OUR GIFT TO THE BOSSES, HUH?
BACK TO NORMALCY.
HAHAHAHAHA
YESSIR, MR. PRESIDENT!!!!!

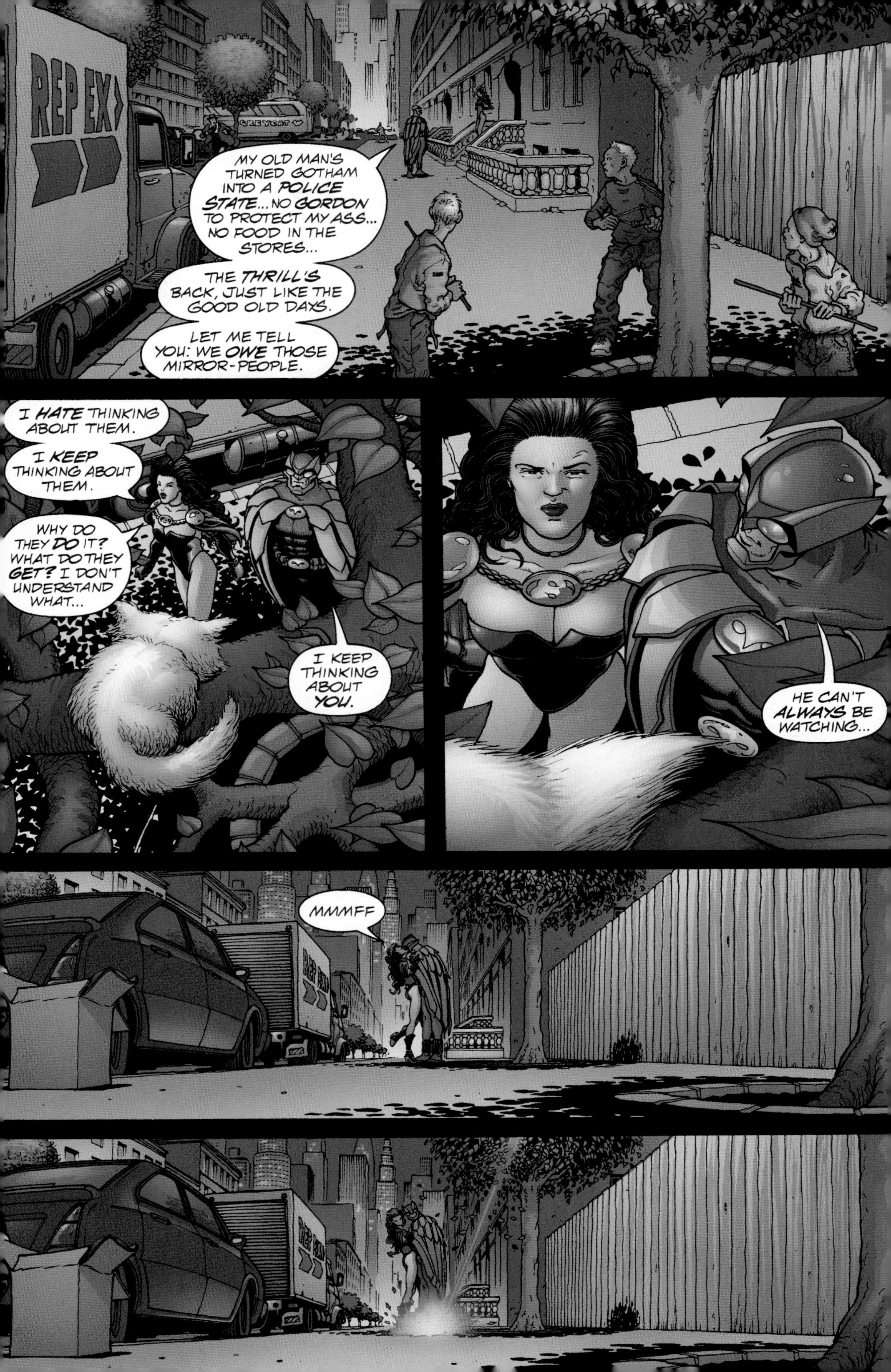
REP EX
GREYCAT
MY OLD MAN'S TURNED GOTHAM INTO A POLICE STATE... NO GORDON TO PROTECT MY ASS... NO FOOD IN THE STORES...
THE THRILL'S BACK, JUST LIKE THE GOOD OLD DAYS.
LET ME TELL YOU: WE OWE THOSE MIRROR-PEOPLE.
I HATE THINKING ABOUT THEM.
I KEEP THINKING ABOUT THEM.
WHY DO THEY DO IT? WHAT DO THEY GET? I DON'T UNDERSTAND WHAT...
I KEEP THINKING ABOUT YOU.
HE CAN'T ALWAYS BE WATCHING...
MMMFF

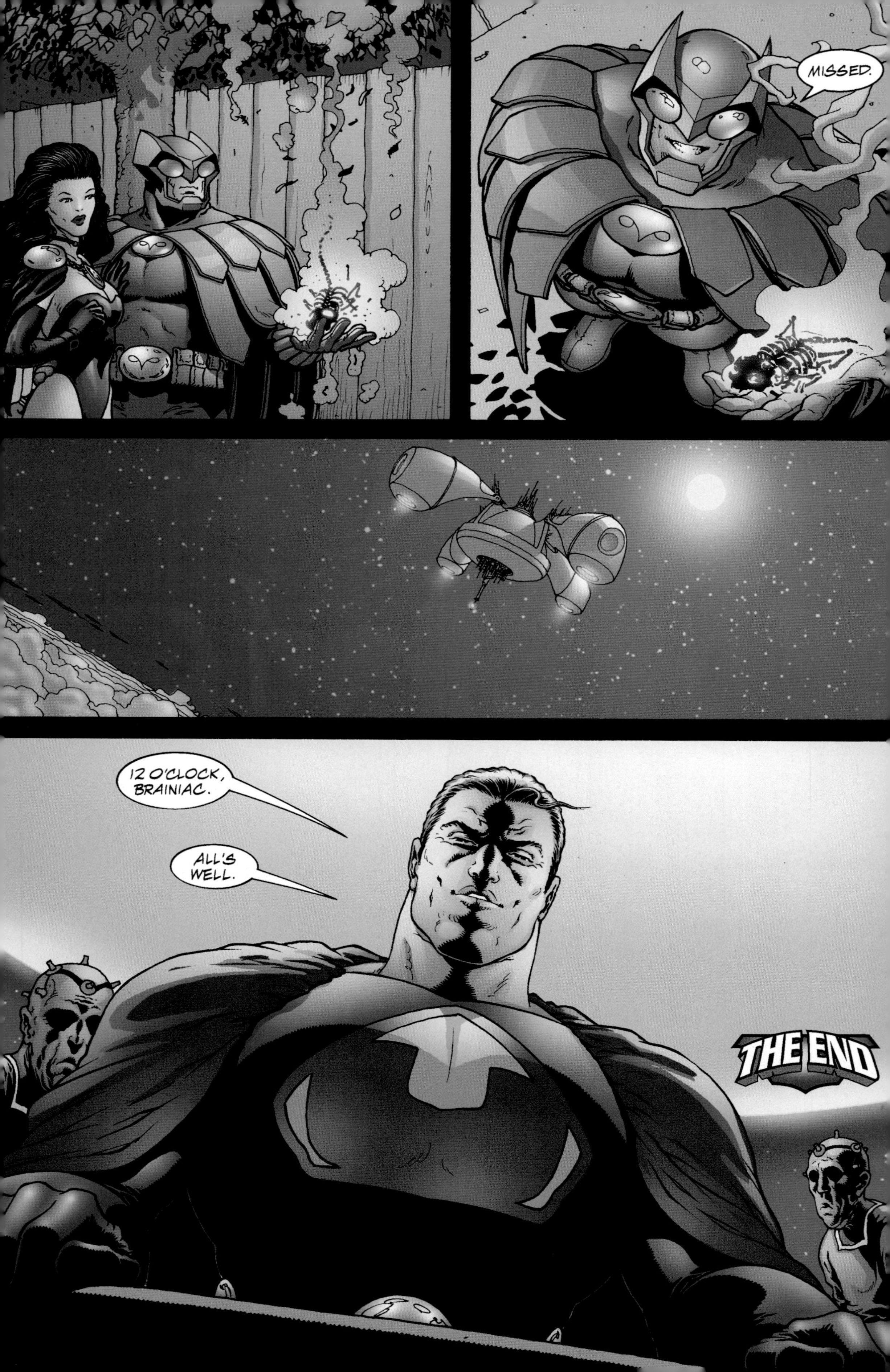
MISSED.
12 O'CLOCK, BRAINIAC.
ALL'S WELL.
THE END

Evolution of **EARTH 2**

Development sketches and script from

Grant Morrison and **Frank Quitely**

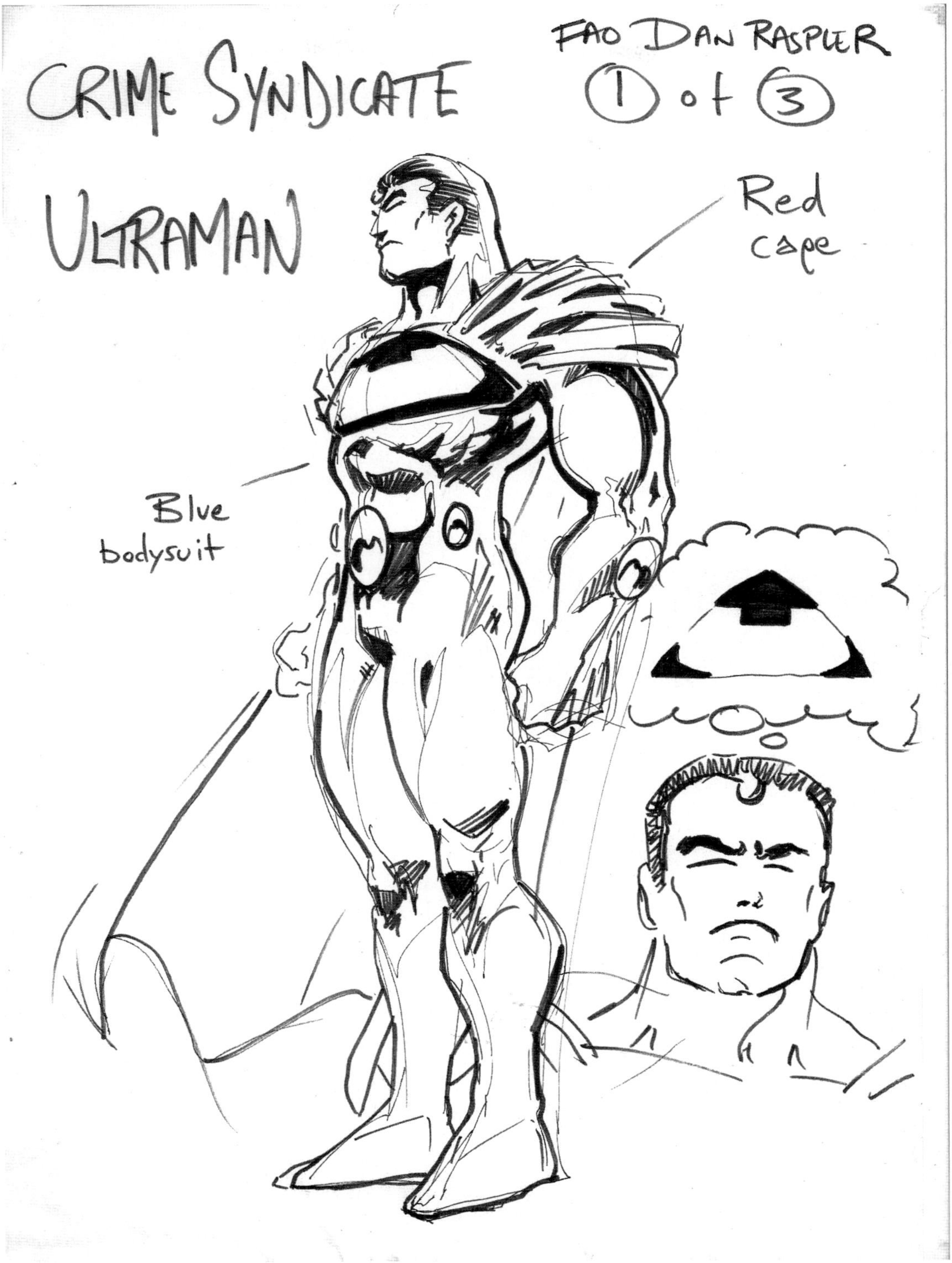
FAO DAN RASPLER
CRIME SYNDICATE
1 of 3
ULTRAMAN
Red cape
Blue bodysuit

character designs and concepts by **Grant Morrison**

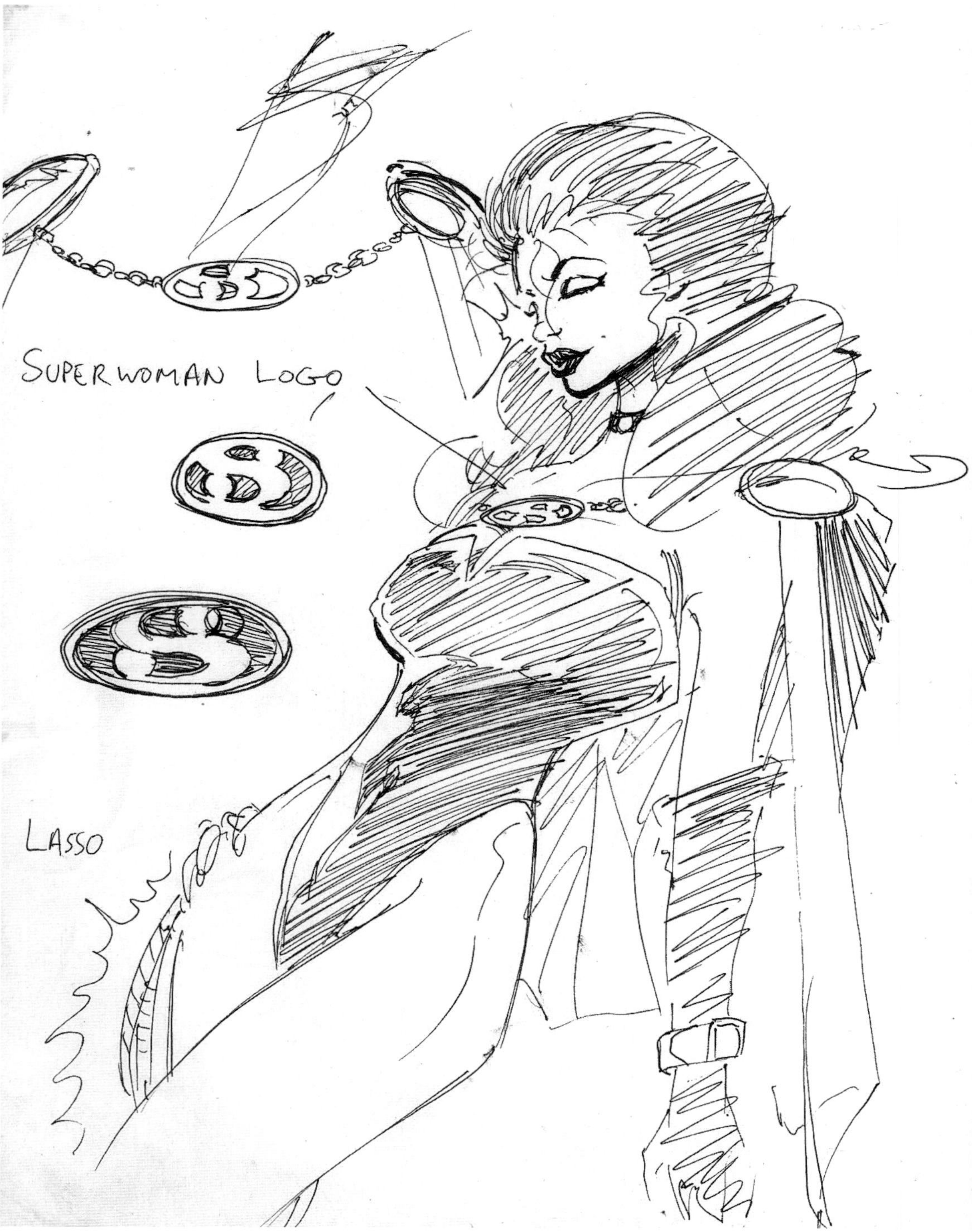
SUPERWOMAN LOGO
LASSO

POWER RING

INSIGNIA
(I don't know what
it is either)

Green stripe

'KYLE-STYLE'
GAUNTLETS (WHITE)

+ BOOTS - GREEN

RING ON
LEFT HAND

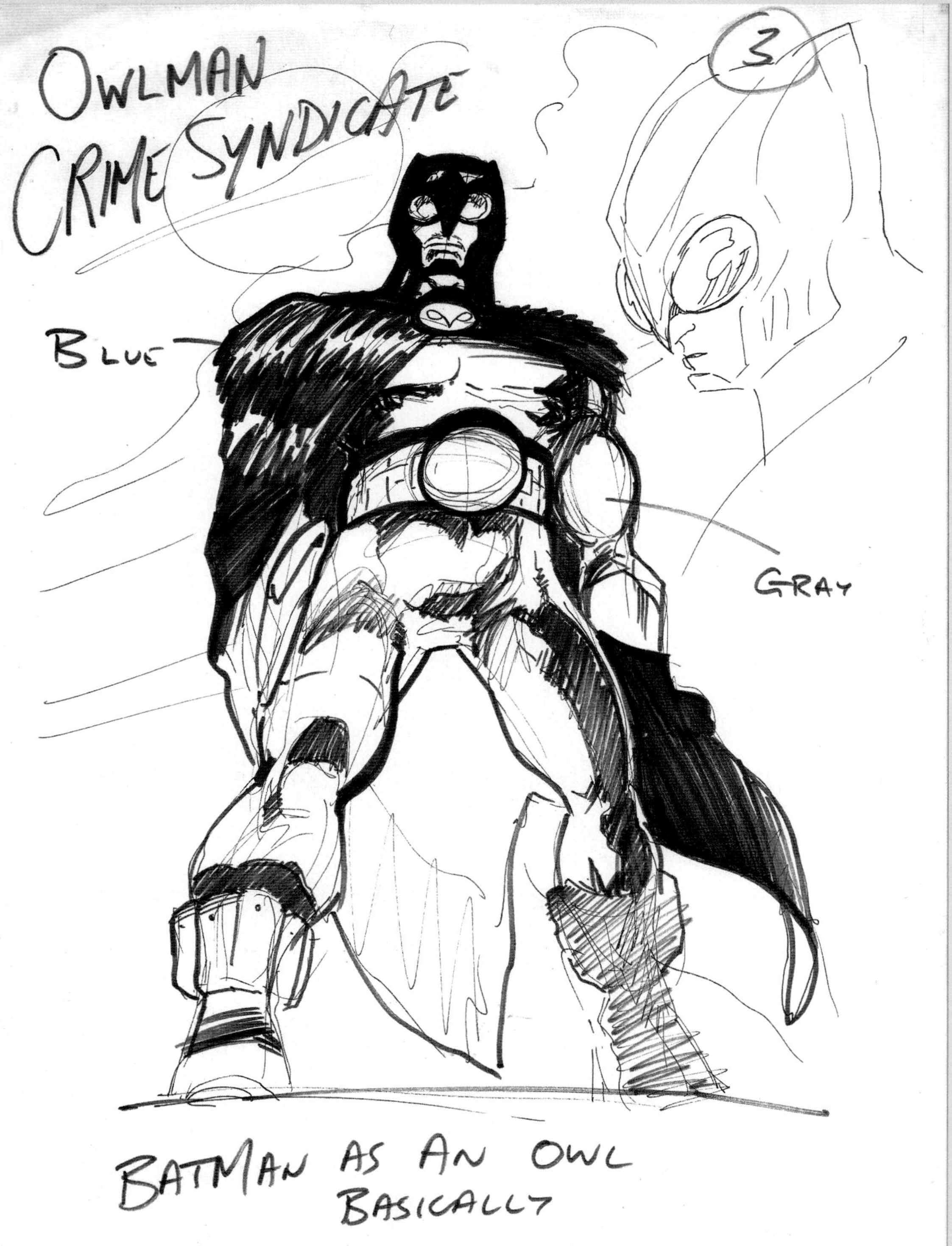

OWLMAN
CRIME SYNDICATE
3
BLUE
GRAY
BATMAN AS AN OWL
BASICALLY

CRIME SYNDICATE ②

JOHNNY QUICK

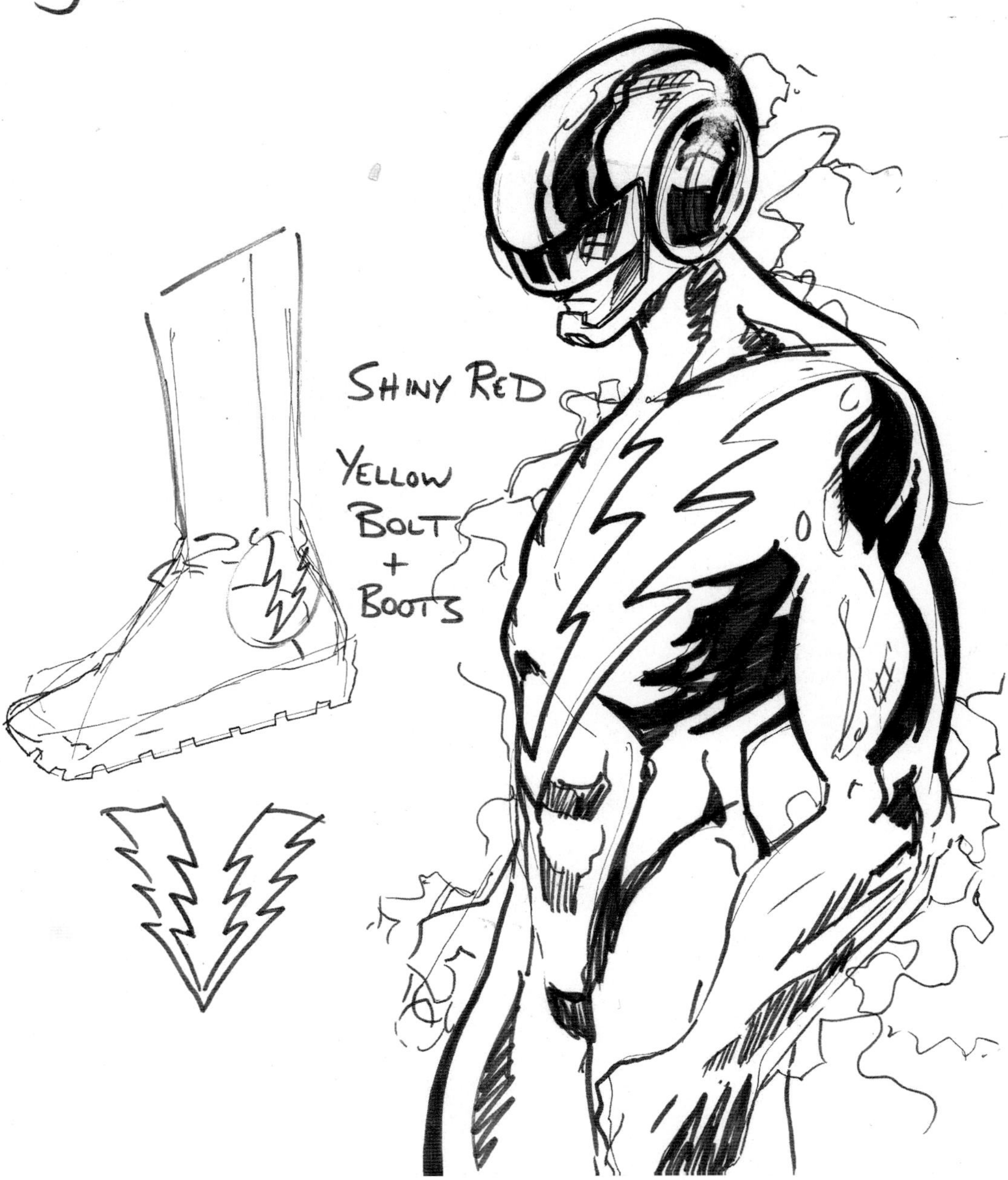
SHINY RED
YELLOW BOLT + BOOTS

original script by **Grant Morrison**
and notes and sketches by **Frank Quitely**

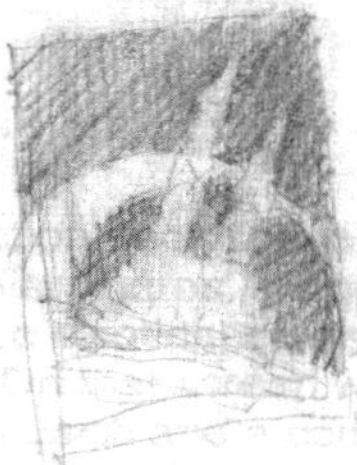

Grant Morrison

Company: DC Comics
Title: JLA: EARTH 2 (96 pages) FIRST DRAFT

Writer: Grant Morrison
Artist: Frank Quitely

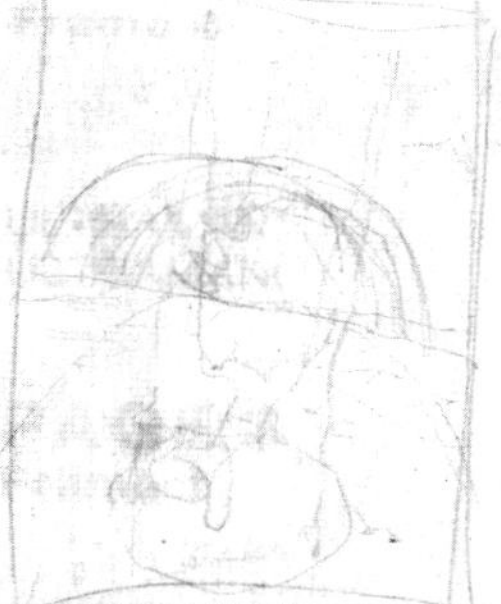

Frame 1

Full page splash to open on. This is an ominous shot of the Crime Syndicate's own version of the Watchtower - the Panopticon - rising up from the lunar surface and backlit by a dark, mostly-shadowed planet earth. Where the Watchtower soars in gleaming Utopian fashion, this building looks more like an oil refinery - flame jets burn in the rigging and scaffolding. Instead of one central tower, there are two chimneylike structures, like horns against the crescent of the Earth. Looming and sinister, we are clearly not in Kansas as we look at this oppressive shadowed edifice. The sky is jet black (no stars are ever seen in the lunar sky due to Earthlight). Imagine this as the pre-credits sequence of the JLA IV: The Movie Sequel...

ULTRAMAN: BAD NEWS.
ULTRAMAN: HE'S ESCAPED.

PAGE 2

Frame 1

Track in towards the Panopticon. A flame jet licks up past us as we move in through the dark girders, hanging cables, spotlights.

Frame 2

Keep moving in. Up ahead, through a curving, elliptical window we see a mysteriously-lit observation room.

Frame 3

We move in through the window so that we're standing

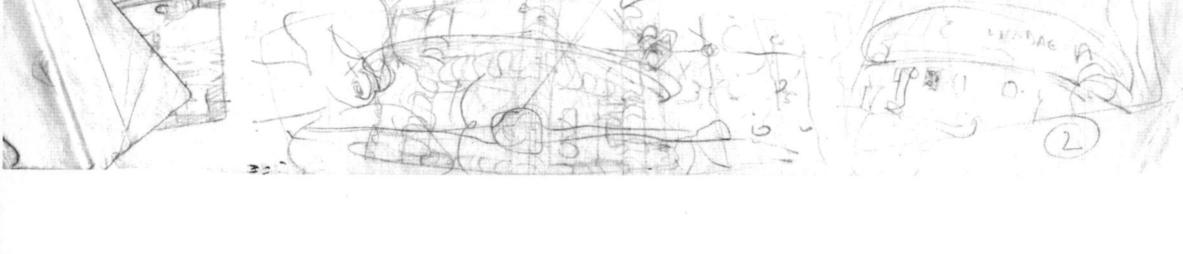

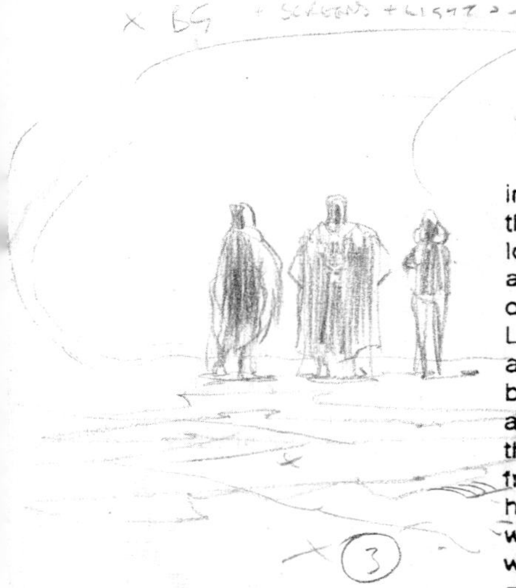

in a huge observation deck space. Up ahead stand three almost-familiar figures, facing away from us and looking at the huge elliptical screen which occupies all of the far wall. On that screen we can see graphics of the sun and the Earth and a computer schematic of Luthor's flight path - looping around Earth and slingshotting around the sun.The three figures are largely silhouetted by the huge screen graphic but there are two men and a woman - the man in centre could be Superman - he has the cape and the build. Ditto for the other man who looks from here, like Batman...except that there are little hardly-noticeable differences. The third figure is a woman *who could be Wonder Woman except that she is also* wearing a cape. They look at the screen. Something has gone wrong and they seem grave. The lighting is subdued, moody.

ULTRAMAN: HE USED SOME OF THE ALIEN MACHINERY FROM MY FORTRESS.

ULTRAMAN: WE LOST THE TRAIL. SOME KIND OF GRAVITATIONAL DISTORTION.

OWLMAN: SO WHAT DO YOU WANT TO DO ?

Frame 4 Move right on the big man's back, closing until the dark red and black of his cape fills the panel. And right there, shadowy on his back, we discern not an 'S' symbol but a 'U'.

ULTRAMAN: WHAT DO <u>YOU</u> THINK ?
ULTRAMAN: MAKE THE MOST OF IT.

PAGE 3

Frame 1 Cut to Luthor's spaceship hurtling towards us on a trail that curves around behind the sun. The sun is big in background and the ship trails flame and glows white hot at the nose. It should look reminiscent of Superman's old escape rocket.

Frame 2 Special effects shot as the ship blasts through the matter/anti-matter barrier and changes state as it goes.

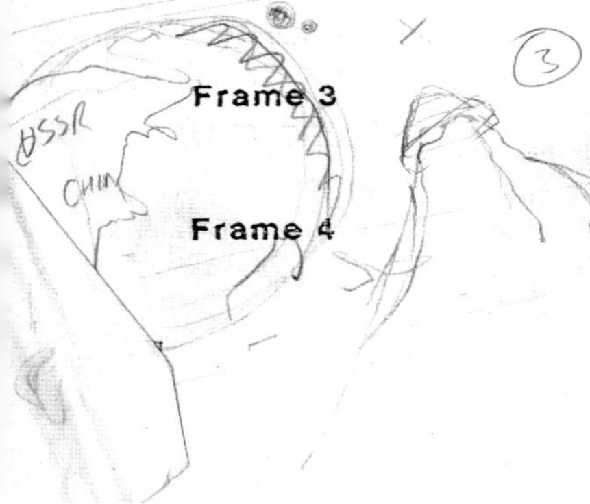

Frame 3 Ordinary space again and we're following Luthor's ship as it streaks away towards the Earth which appears in background with a little moon beyond.

Frame 4 Cut to Earth. Kansas. A big moon over the cornfields.

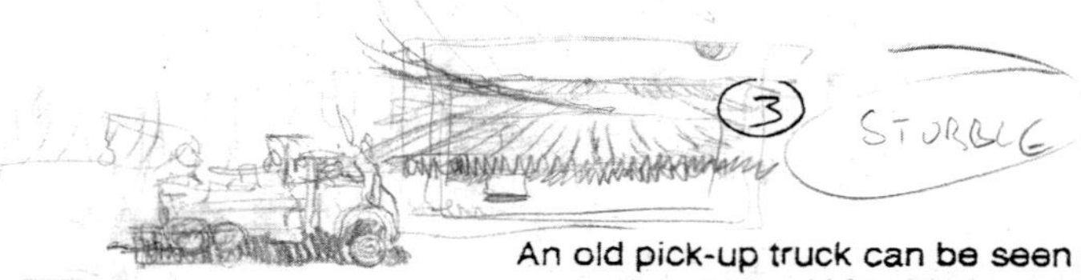
STUBBLE

An old pick-up truck can be seen stalled by the road. A young farmer and his girl. A meteor trail arcs down out of the sky at a fast, shallow angle.

MAN: ...BATTERY JUST WENT DEAD ON ME LIKE THAT. SAME AS THE RADIO...

WOMAN: OH MY GOSH, ETHAN.

WOMAN: LOOK AT

Frame 5

We're with the young farm couple in the truck as they shield their eyes from the light of impact as the ship hits the cornfield and ploughs a five hundred yard trench.

WOMAN: (BLANK)

PAGE 4

Frame 1

In foreground, part of the ship is sticking up out of the earth, smoldering but cooling rapidly. In background, the young man and the girl approach the crater cautiously He's falling back and she's more eager and curious.

MAN: HONEY, WAIT!

MAN: WE DON'T KNOW WHAT THAT IS! IT COULD BE AN ALIEN SPACESHIP OR IT MIGHT GIVE US WEIRD POWERS...

GIRL: OR SOMEBODY COULD BE HURT, JONATHAN.

GIRL: IT'S NOT ALL LIKE IN...

Frame 2

A hatch opens. Something rises up and the young couple freeze. It looks like a figure in a suit. (It's Lex Luthor of the Mirror Earth).

WOMAN: OH.

WOMAN: IS HE HUMAN ?

Frame 3

We're behind Luthor as he reaches up and disengages the collar of his suit. Pressurised hiss and puff of air as *he begins to remove his helmet.*

LUTHOR: HOW VERY CHARMING. (From off)

Frame 4

The couple fall back, gasping. The guy moves to protect the girl but his gaze is fixed off panel. Artificial light falls on their faces.

LUTHOR: I'VE JUST REVERSED ACROSS THE MATTER/ANTI/MATTER MEMBRANE IN A HOMEMADE SHIP AND THIS IS THE RECEPTION I FACE ?

LUTHOR: MY DEAR COUNTRY COUSIN, YOU ARE HUMAN...

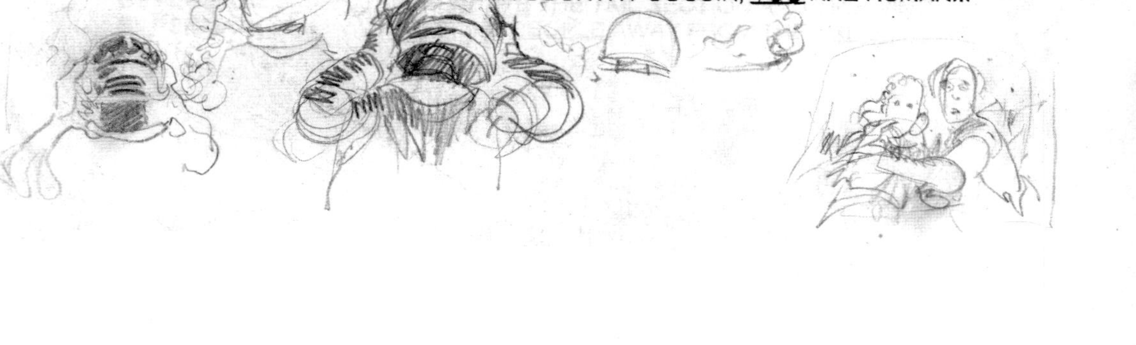

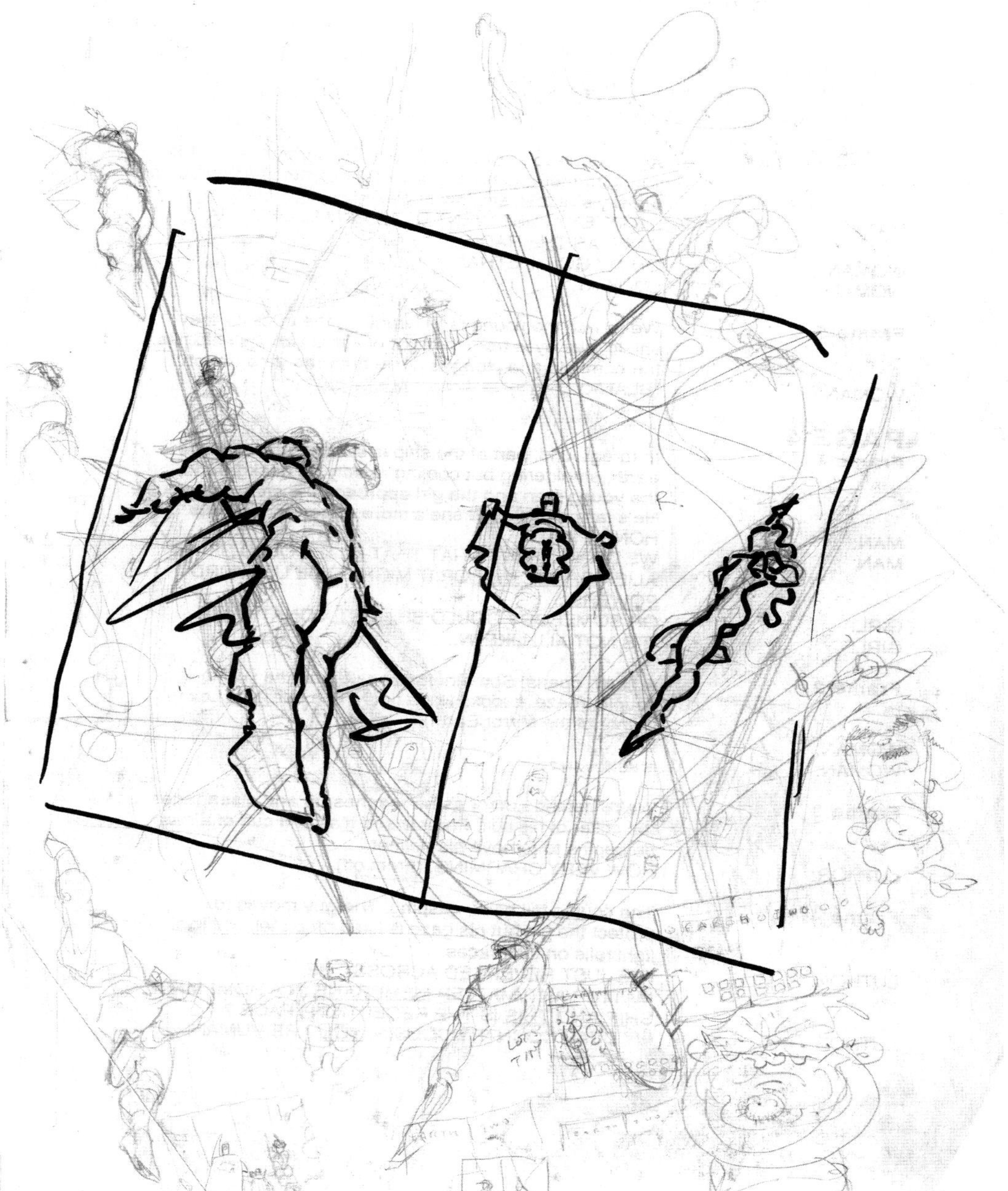

PAGE 5
Frame 1

Full page shot of Lex Luthor, bald as you like and with an undeniably self-assured and - the cruel might say - superior expression on his calm, clever face. He stands in his green and purple spacesuit (which looks pretty much like the famous Luthor battlesuit from the 70s and 80s) with steam rising up around him, lit by the instrument and cabin lights of his little ship. He's standing up on the hull with his helmet in one hand simply looking past us as if expecting to be taken to our leader right now. The sky beyond is starry and moonlit.

LUTHOR: I AM <u>LUTHOR</u>.

LUTHOR: NOW...WHERE CAN I FIND THE <u>SUPER-PEOPLE</u> AROUND HERE?

PAGE 6/7
Frame 1

Double page title splash with the JLA in widescreen action. Dominating the splash is a 747 Jumbo jet in bad trouble. One of the engines on the wing is already burning and tearing itself apart with little explosions. The other engine is belching smoke as is the one under the tail. Bad news for travellers in this or any other world we know but in the DC Universe it's just one more routine job for the Justice League. Superman is coming in from the left hand side. J'onn J'onnz the Martian Manhunter hangs in the air, rapidly appraising the situation and the potential danger. Wonder Woman is balancing on the wing of her Invisible Robot Plane, sailing in towards the stricken jet.

TITLE/CREDITS: <u>EARTH 2</u>

ROLL CALL: SUPERMAN*BATMAN*WONDER WOMAN*FLASH* GREEN LANTERN*AQUAMAN*J'ONN J'ONNZ - MANHUNTER FROM MARS

ROLL CALL: ULTRAMAN*OWLMAN*SUPERWOMAN* JOHNNY QUICK*POWER RING*

PAGE 8
Frame 1

Superman, determined and without a moment's idle thought, is flying towards us. His eyes light up red as he stares off panel.

SUPERMAN: SEPARATE THE TAIL SECTION AND THE WING.

SUPERMAN: GET THE <u>PEOPLE</u> AWAY FROM THE <u>EXPLOSIONS</u>.

Frame 2

Long shot. Superman shears the whole wing off with a laser vision blast. Precision heat rays remove the wing with surgical skill even as the engines really start to explode. Wonder Woman dives from her plane towards the Jumbo.

J'ONN BALLOON: TELEPATHIC LINK ENGAGED.
SUPERMAN: LOUD AND CLEAR, J'ONN.
SUPERMAN: EVERYONE KNOWS WHAT TO DO.

Frame 3

Wonder Woman's flying through the exploding engines surrounded by flames and molten metal. She is completely focussed.

WONDER WOMAN: AND IF NOT WE'LL SOON LEARN.
WONDER WOMAN: I'LL TAKE THE FRONT SECTION, IF J'ONN HANDLES THE BACK.

Frame 4

Longshot. Green Lantern swoops around and creates a giant fan or something cooler to put out the engine fires as J'onn moves in to rescue the back part of the plane sans tail section.

GREEN LANTERN: FLAMES ARE OUT, J'ONN.
GREEN LANTERN: YOU ARE GREEN TO GO.

Frame 5

Close on J'onn. He frowns, sensing something wrong as he catches the huge piece of spinning shearing metal. His finger dig into the hull as though metal were wax.

MARTIAN MANHUNTER: ...STRANGE...
MARTIAN MANHUNTER: I CAN DETECT NO...UNNH...NO BRAIN ACTIVITY WITHIN...

PAGE 9

Frame 1

Vertical plummeting shot. We're inside the doomed aircraft looking down the aisle past unconscious, seatbelted passengers. It's total chaos here - things are falling past us down the aisle. Drinks and meals are up-ended in people's faces and we realise that we're looking down, with gravity, and that there's no back to this plane, just a huge ragged hole through which we can see clouds and the lights of a city. Thousands of feet below! Oxygen masks bob wildly, having sprung from under the luggage racks. And running up the centre of the aisle towards us, muscles straining because she's actually running upwards, against gravity, is the indomitable Wonder Woman. Strangely, the still conscious people in the plane stare at her with horror and fear.

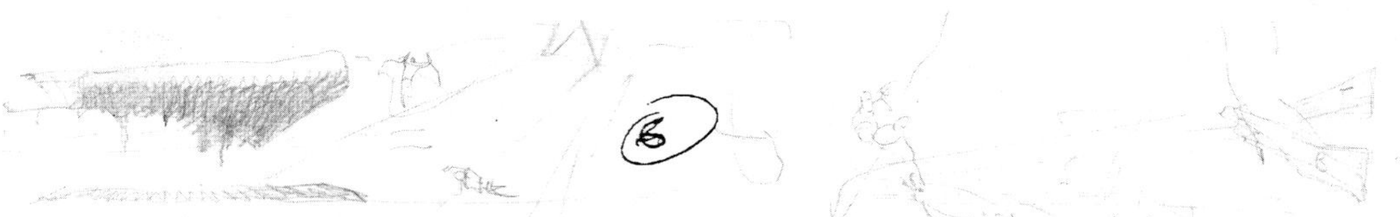

WONDER WOMAN: NNN

WONDER WOMAN: NO-ONE'S CONSCIOUS HERE. THE WHOLE CABIN'S ROLLING AND DEPRESSURISED!

WONDER WOMAN: I MAY NEED SOME HELP HERE!

Frame 2 Longshot. Superman is lowering the wing to the ground.

SUPERMAN: ONE MOMENT, WONDER WOMAN...

Frame 3 Cut back to Wonder Woman - as the plane falls she's bracing herself with her lasso as she rips out seat after seat and throws them out the back. She looks at the child she's saving but the kid's not conscious (is, in fact, dead but Wonder Woman is not aware of anything other than her duty as the plane continues to fall and things fly from the luggage racks and smoke and flames lick through the wreck). A woman sits, head lolling, fingers still crossed.

Frame 4 Seats with people strapped in them falling and tumbling at 120 miles an hour through the skies. It's surreal. They're falling out of the sky like leaves. And we're with Superman as he leaps up towards them.

SUPERMAN: I'M ON MY WAY.

PAGE 10

Frame 1 Long shot. In foreground, Green Lantern twists in the air and aims his ring at the falling seats - he's creating an army of winged luminous green monkeys to catch the falling seats that Superman can't carry.

GREEN LANTERN: I GOT 'EM ALL! WE GOT 'EM, SUPERMAN!

GREEN LANTERN: SO WHERE D'YOU WANT US TO PUT 'EM ?

SUPERMAN: THE FLASH IS GENERATING A CUSHION OF PRESSURISED AIR BELOW US. LOWER THEM GENTLY.

SUPERMAN: I DON'T HEAR HEARTBEATS...

3-40 - 5-10

Frame 2 Now we're on the ground looking at an uncanny scarlet tornado that whirls in front of us - a huge circular wall of pressurised air acting as a cushion.

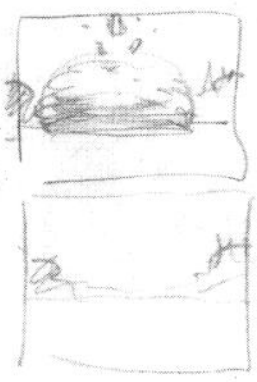

FLASH: OKAY

FLASH: LET'S GET

FLASH: THESE

FLASH: PEOPLE ON THE

FLASH: GROUND AND

FLASH: I'LL SLOW DOWN

FLASH: A LITTLE. (Lots of overlapping balloons)

Frame 3

Same POV. Suddenly in an eyeblink, the Flash is
standing in front of us. Very still, arms folded, but
crackling with runners of speed force energy. Behind
him are rows of dead people lined up neatly in
their seats. The Flash has a wallet in his hands.

FLASH: UH...BAD NEWS.
FLASH: THEY'RE ALL <u>DEAD</u>.
FLASH: AND LISTEN, GUYS...

Frame 4

Flash pauses for a moment to look up at the sky, grim.
He's holding a dollar bill in his hand and it's one of those
weird Earth 2 bills with 'IN SATAN WE TRUST' on one
side and the face of Benedict Arnold on the other.

FLASH: I JUST CHECKED EVERYBODY FOR <u>ID</u>.
FLASH: STARTERS: A DOLLAR BILL WITH THE FACE OF
<u>BENEDICT ARNOLD</u> WHERE GEORGE <u>WASHINGTON</u>
SHOULD BE.
FLASH: ANYBODY *ELSE* HEARING THAT LITTLE '<u>X FILES</u>'
WHISTLE ON THIS ONE ?

PAGE 11
Frame 1

Superman and J'onn are crushing and compacting
tons of metal into a huge ball. Their muscles bulge as
they flatten the plane down to manageable size.
Crushing it down.

SUPERMAN: IF WHAT FLASH IS SAYING IS <u>TRUE</u>...
SUPERMAN: ANOTHER DIMENSION, J'ONN ? WHERE HAVE THESE
PEOPLE <u>COME</u> FROM ?
MARTIAN MANHUNTER: WE CAN ONLY SPECULATE AT THIS STAGE,
SUPERMAN.
MARTIAN MANHUNTER: AQUAMAN ?

Frame 2

Aquaman's looking up at something as he bobs
in the sea...something juts up from the water and what
it is is the tailfin on the 747, so we don't really see all
of it yet, we only see Aquaman looking up at this vague,
looming presence. The sense of some on enormous
scale as the sea creatures lift the great fin up out of the
water and seawater drains off it in gallons.

AQUAMAN: RIGHT HERE ON THE ATLANTIC SEABOARD.
AQUAMAN: HOW COME THE ONE PIECE OF WRECKAGE YOU
<u>MISSED</u> LANDED ON <u>MY</u> ROOF ?

Frame 3

GL lowering seats filled with dead people down to the
ground Wonder Woman shepherds them down. The
Flash

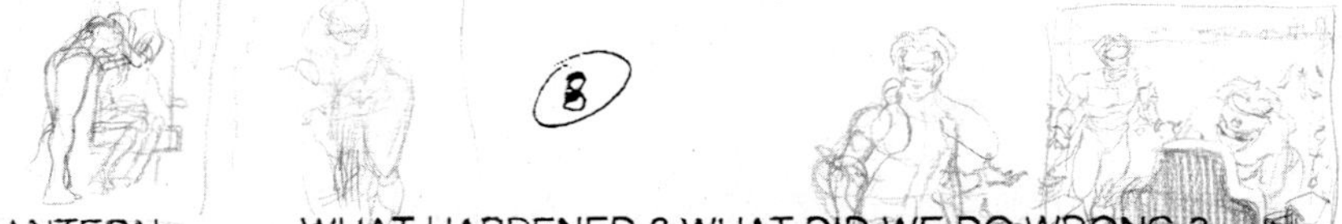

GREEN LANTERN: WHAT HAPPENED ? WHAT DID WE DO WRONG ?
WONDER WOMAN: THEY WERE ALREADY DEAD, KYLE. WHEN THEY ARRIVED HERE THEY WERE DEAD.

Frame 4 Green Lantern puzzled descends towards us out of the sky to join Wonder Woman as she checks the bodies. She shows surprise.
GREEN LANTERN: YEAH BUT WHAT KILLED 'EM ?
GREEN LANTERN: AND WHERE DID THEY ARRIVE FROM...
WONDER WOMAN: WE'LL SOON...
WONDER WOMAN: OH

Frame 5 *Close up on Wonder Woman looking back over her shoulders at us.*
WONDER WOMAN: THEIR HEARTS ARE ON THE RIGHT SIDE OF THEIR BODIES.

PAGE 12

Frame 1 The plane is just a little four inch cube of impossibly compacted metal in J'onn's hands as he gives a final gigatonne squeeze. He looks at the lump with a curious expression. Something strange about this one.
S/Fx: KKRUMPP
MARTIAN MANHUNTER: THE WRECKAGE IS SAFELY DISPOSED OF BUT IT APPEARS WE HAVE A MYSTERY ON OUR HANDS, SUPERMAN.
MARTIAN MANHUNTER: ARE THERE ANY CLUES ON THE FLIGHT RECORDER ?

Frame 2 Superman scans the flight recorder grimly.
SUPERMAN: I'M READING SOMETHING ABOUT....A CALL FOR HELP...AND...
SUPERMAN: WAIT A MINUTE.

Frame 3 Close up as Superman's eyes narrow.
SUPERMAN: LUTHOR ?
BALLOON: THIS IS AQUAMAN.

Frame 4 Cut away to a close up of Aquaman looking up at something off panel. His eyes narrow too.
AQUAMAN: I THINK YOU SHOULD SEE THIS.

Frame 5 Big one. We're just behind Aquaman as he floats in the water and looks at the huge tailfin lifted up out of the water - it has a *curious logo design - a flaming cross* against a black ground and the words KKK SOUTHERN

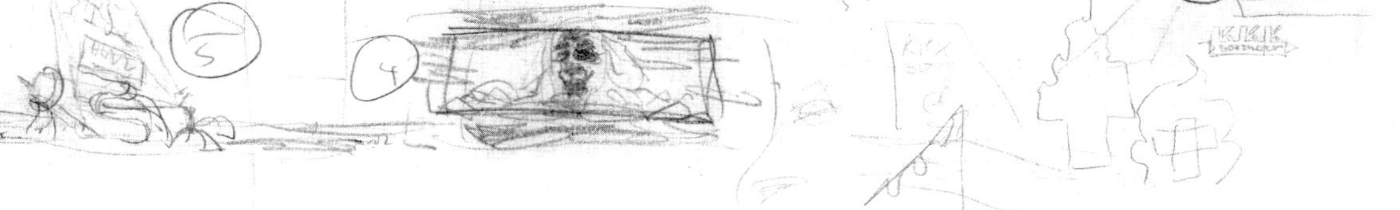

CRESENT EARTH - N & S AMERICA IN REVERSE
PANOPTICON - MORE LIKE EMPIRE STATE SHAPE, TAPERING AT TOP
MORE LIKE FUTURISTIC PRISON AT BOTTOM - MORE SQUARE,
LESS "STALAGMITAL"

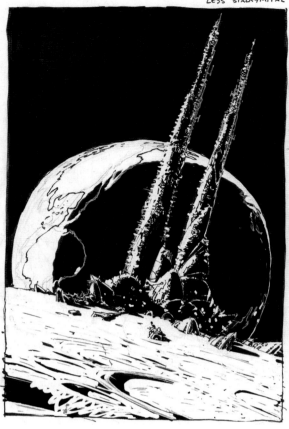

F.A.O. DAN RASPLER   PAGE ②
① FIRE + SMOKE LIKE THIS   DUE TO THINNER ATMOS.
② FROM STEPPED EMPIRE STATE SHAPE, TOWER TAPERS INTO
CYLINDRICAL "COMMUNICATIONS - TOWER" - STYLE AT TOP WITH
ARIELS, SAT. DISHES DOORS + LADDERS. CURVED WINDOW REVEALS
COLOR-SCHEME FOR ③. LURID GREEN (FOR eg.) AGAINST RUSTY
EXTERIOR.

N+S
AMERICA
REVERSED

③ & ④ OUTLINE OF FIGURES BURNT-OUT FROM BRIGHTNESS
OF SCREEN.

F.A.O. DAN RASPLER. PAGE ③
① NOSE AGLOW. OUTLINE BURNT-OUT AGAINST NEAR-WHITE SUN.
② SPFX. MAYBE SHIP & TRAIL OUT-OF-FOCUS, SPARKS ETC IN FOCUS?
③ EUROPE, ASIA, AFRICA, AUSTRALIA → SO USA AT NIGHT. (ROUND THE BACK)
DARK, MOONLIT. FIELD LOCALLY LIT BY TRAIL.
④ ⑤ SAME TRAIL-COLOUR BUT BRIGHTER.

FADING
DOWN

F.A.O. DAN RASPLER (4)

(1) MOONLIT. (2) UPLIT FROM CRAFT INTERIOR. UMBILICAL/LIFE SUPPORT-STYLE TUBES FALLING OFF

(3) COUPLE LIT BY SAME CRAFT LIGHT.

(4) UPLIT NOT DOWNLIT. SAME LIGHT. REFLECTION OF COUPLE-HUDDLED.

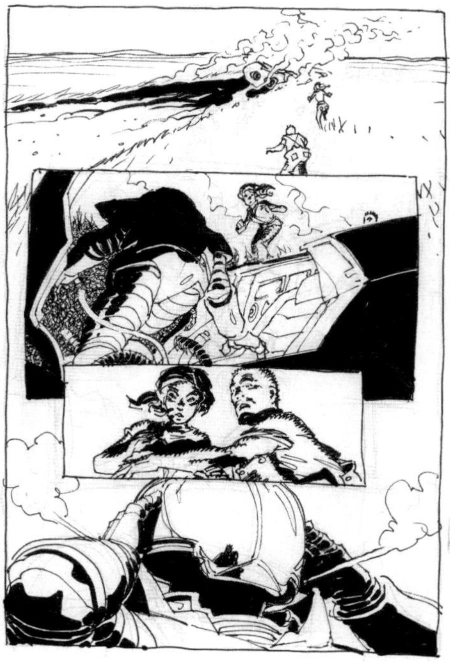

F.A.O. DAN RASPLER. PAGE (5)

UPLIT BY SHIP INTERIOR. SLIGHTLY BACK-LIT (JUST ON HEAD & SHOULDERS) BY MOONLIGHT.
NIGHT SKY AS BACKGROUND.
REFLECTED COUPLE NOW PASSIVE.

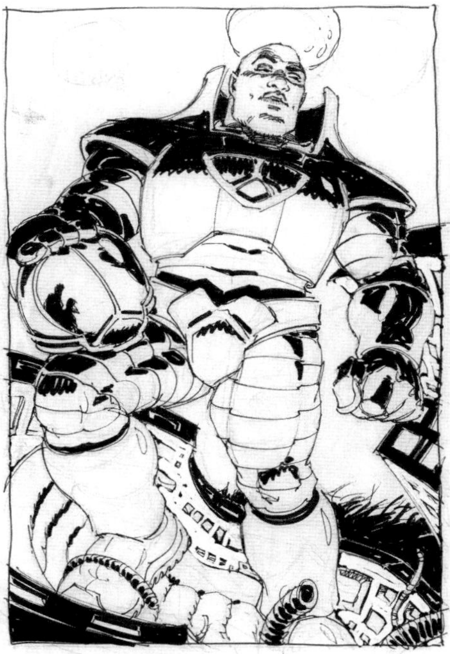

F.A.O. DAN RASPLER PAGE (6)

NIGHT SKY.

THIS ENGINE BLOWING UP - LOTS SMALL EXPOSIONS.

THIS ENGINE SMOKING (MAYBE SOME SPARKS)

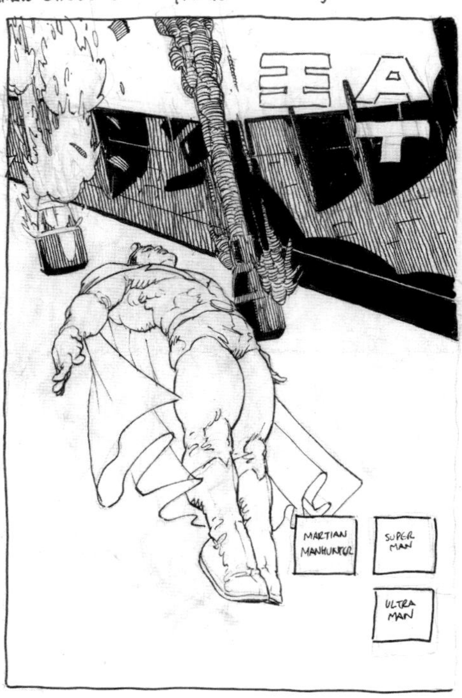

MARTIAN MANHUNTER
SUPER MAN
ULTRA MAN

F.A.O. DAN RASPLER PAGE (7)

NIGHT SKY.

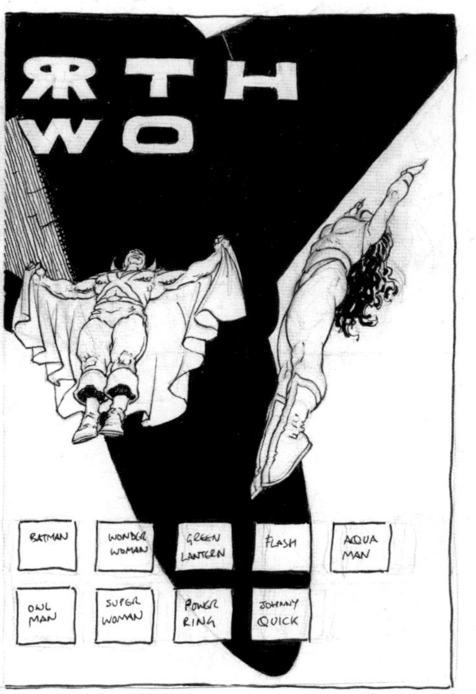

BATMAN
WONDER WOMAN
GREEN LANTERN
FLASH
AQUA MAN
OWL MAN
SUPER WOMAN
POWER RING
JOHNNY QUICK

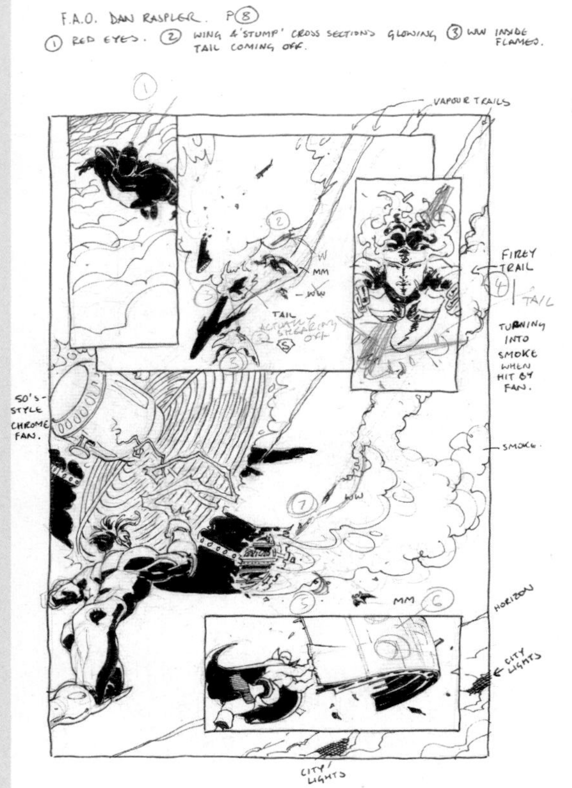
F.A.O. DAN RASPLER P 8
1 RED EYES. 2 WING & 'STUMP' CROSS SECTIONS GLOWING TAIL COMING OFF. 3 WW INSIDE FLAMES.
VAPOUR TRAILS
FIREY TRAIL
TAIL
TURNING INTO SMOKE WHEN HIT BY FAN.
50's-STYLE CHROME FAN.
SMOKE.
HORIZON
CITY LIGHTS
CITY LIGHTS

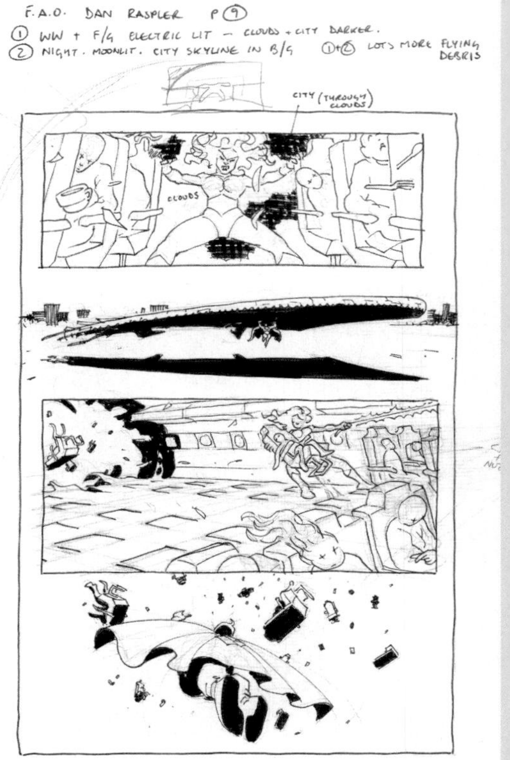
F.A.O. DAN RASPLER P 9
1 WW + F/G ELECTRIC LIT — CLOUDS + CITY DARKER.
2 NIGHT. MOONLIT. CITY SKYLINE IN B/G 1+2 LOTS MORE FLYING DEBRIS
CITY (THROUGH CLOUDS)
CLOUDS

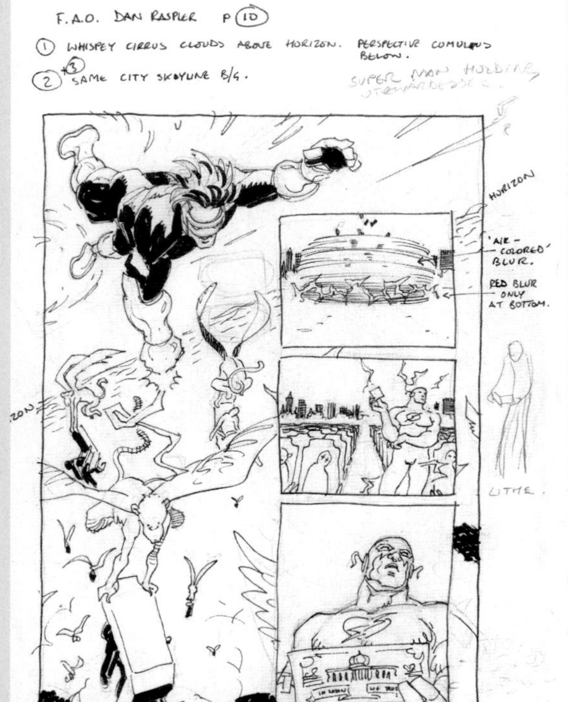
F.A.O. DAN RASPLER P 10
1 WHISPEY CIRRUS CLOUDS ABOVE HORIZON. PERSPECTIVE COMULOUS BELOW.
2 +3 SAME CITY SKYLINE B/G.
HORIZON
'AIR-COLORED' BLUR.
RED BLUR ONLY AT BOTTOM.
LITHE.
CITY STREETS CLEARER NOW.
4 WHITEHOUSE SIMILAR BUT WITH COMMUNIST / ARABIC POINTY DOME + WINDOWS.

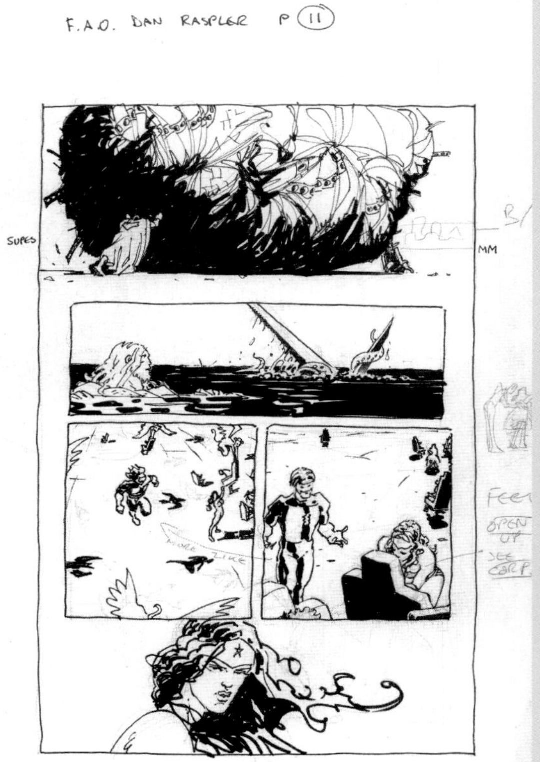
F.A.O. DAN RASPLER P 11
SUPES
MM

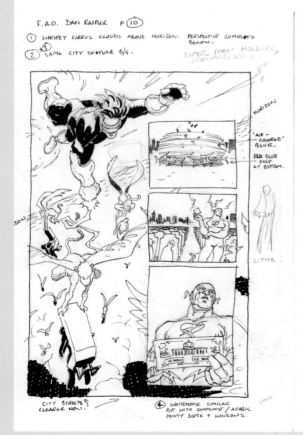

F.A.O. DAN RASPLER P (12)

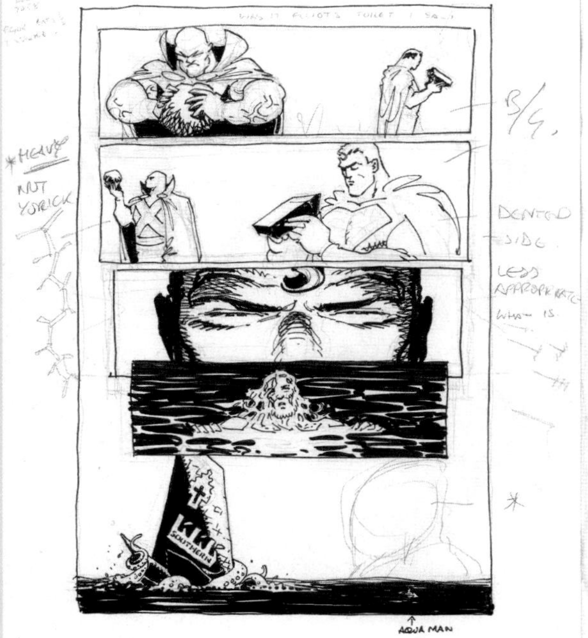
*HEAVY
NOT YORICK
B/4.
DENTED SIDE
LESS APPROPRIATE
WHAT IS
AQUA MAN

F.A.O. DAN RASPLER P (13)

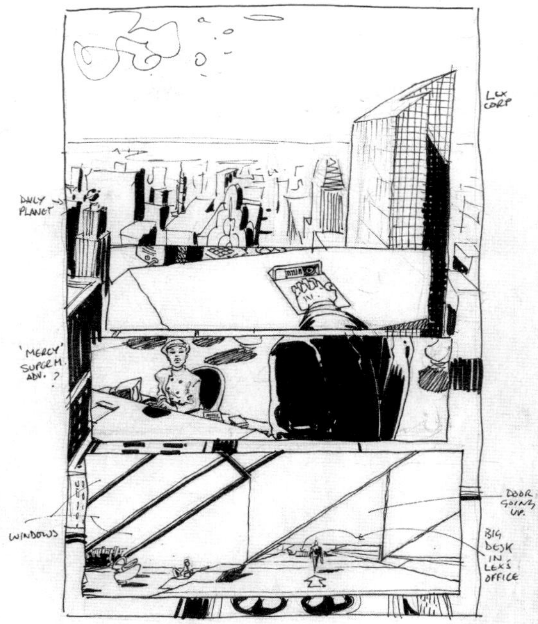
LEX CORP
DAILY PLANET
'MERCY' SUPERM. ADV. ?
WINDOWS
DOOR GOING UP.
BIG DESK IN LEX'S OFFICE

F.A.O. DAN RASPLER P (14)

DESK. CROSS-SECTION-STYLE SLICE OF BASE OF RARE EQUATORIAL RAINFOREST TREE.

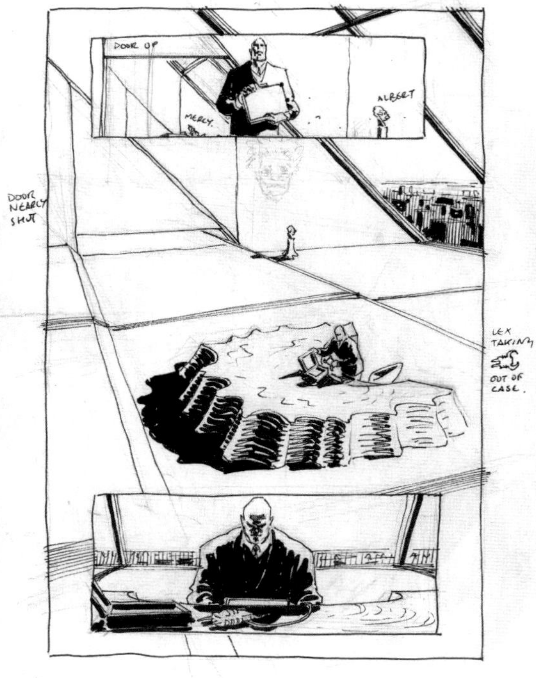
DOOR UP
MERCY.
ALBERT
DOOR NEARLY SHUT
LEX TAKING
OUT OF CASE.

F.A.O. DAN RASPLER P (15)

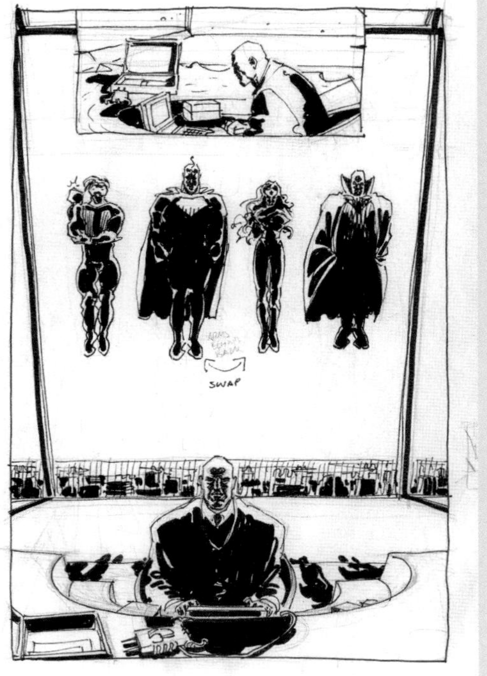
SWAP

F.A.O. DAN RASPLER P (16)

(1)+(2) MIRRORED GLASS
(3) SMOKED GLASS.

BETTER COMPOSITION FOR (1). MAYBE LEX SEEN ONLY IN GAP.

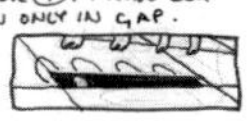

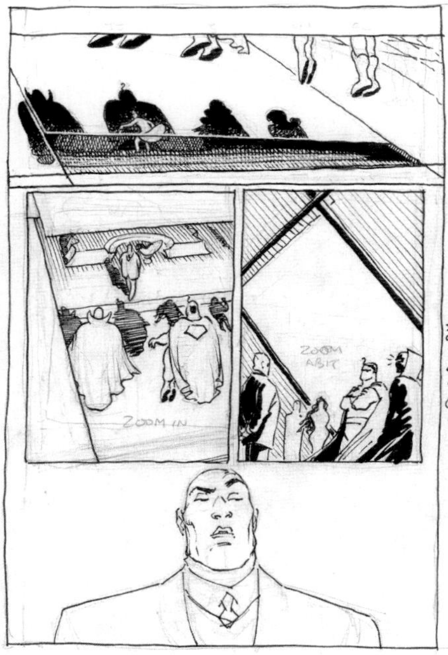
ZOOM A BIT
ZOOM IN

JON GIVING LEX THE GLAD EYE (SHUT THAT DOOR!)

F.A.O. DAN RASPLER P (17)

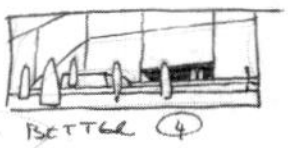

BETTER (4)

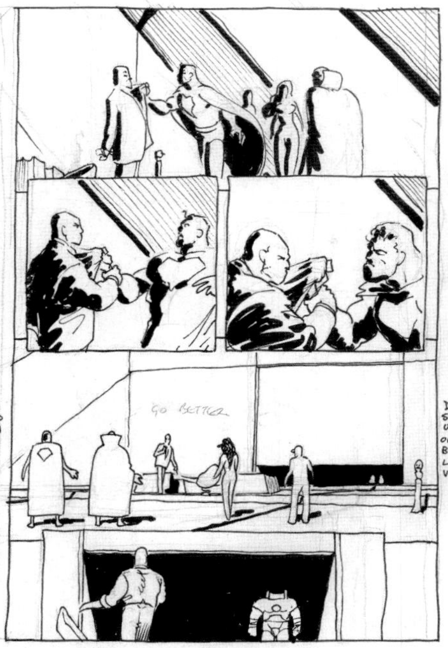
GO BETTER

LEX FIXES LAPEL + PRESSES BUTTON

DOOR SLIDES UP - ONLY BOOTS/LEGS VISIBLE

JACKET

F.A.O. DAN RASPLER P (18)

NIGHT.

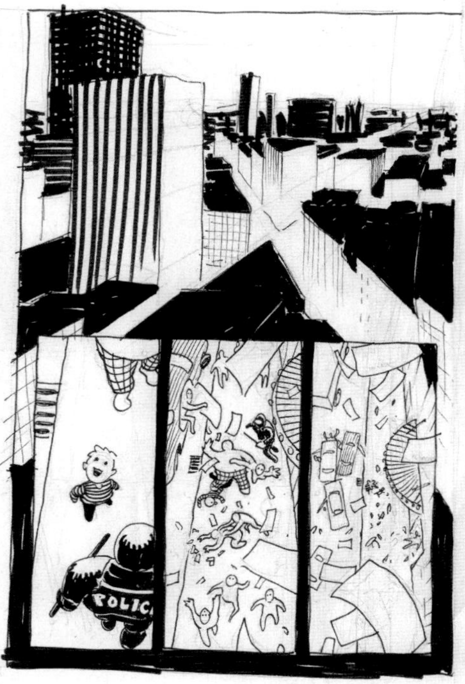
POLIC

DAN RASPLER P (19)

BLUE + GREEN PERSPEX GLOBE (LIT UP FROM WITHIN) WITH RED NEON 'DAILY PLANET'

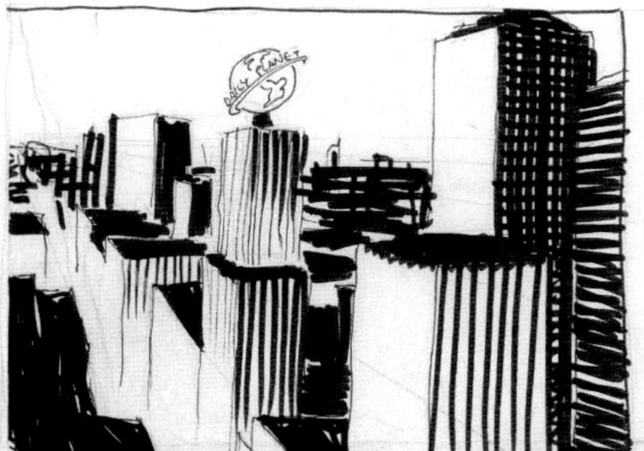
DAILY PLANET

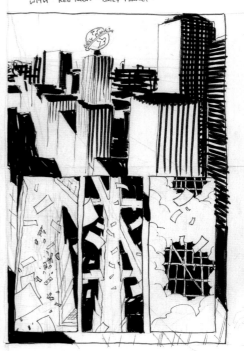

F.A.O. DAN RASPLER P (20)

NIGHT.

SKY. DARKEST BLUE (JUST COLOR- NO INKS) ↓ FADING DOWN TO "HIGH ALTITUDE BLUE" ↓ FADING DOWN TO "DAYLIGHT BLUE" AT HORIZON.

WHISPEY CIRRUS CLOUDS FAIRLY BRIGHT.

CUMULUS CLOUDS BRIGHT AT HORIZON ↓ FADING DOWN TO BLACK.

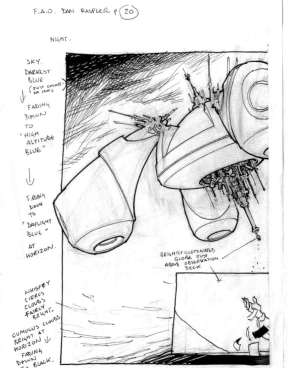

BRIGHTLY ILLUMINATED GLOBE JUST ABOVE OBSERVATION DECK

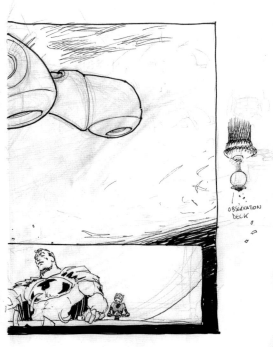

F.A.O. DAN RASPLER P (21)

OBSERVATION DECK

F.A.O. DAN RASPLER P (22)

F.A.O. DAN RASPLER P (23)

BIGGER PANEL(S) ?

CONCENTRIC CIRCLES OVERLAY?

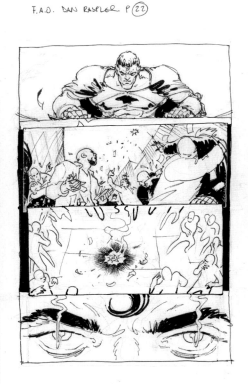

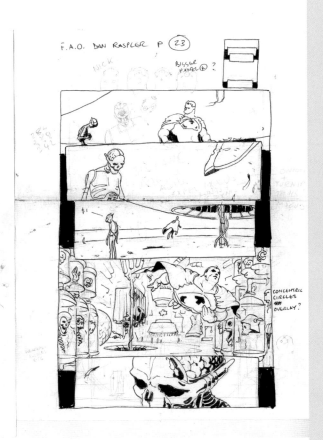

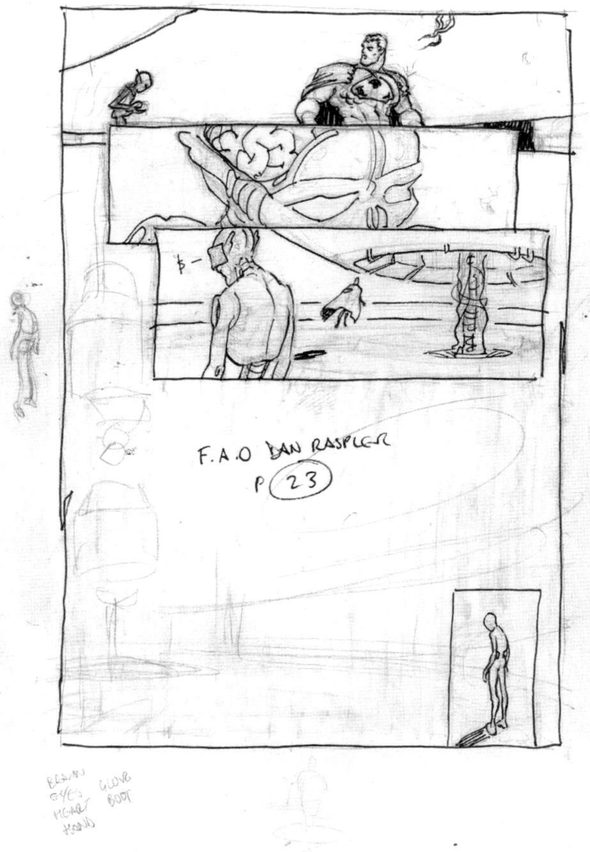
F.A.O DAN RASPLER
P 23
GLOVE
BOOT

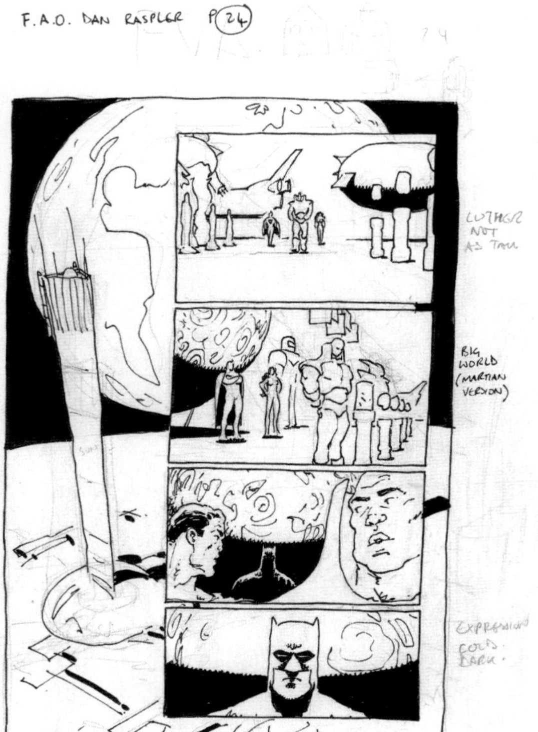
F.A.O. DAN RASPLER P 24
LUTHER NOT AS TALL
BIG WORLD (MARTIAN VERSION)
EXPRESSION COLD. DARK.

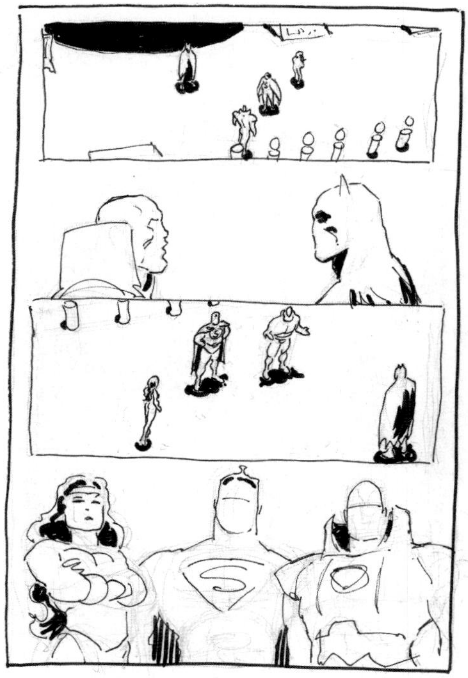
F.A.O. DAN RASPLER P 25

F.A.O. DAN RASPLER P (26)

V. DARK B/G. V. BRIGHT TABLE + FIGURES.
HAZY - LIKE V. BRIGHT LIGHTS IN DARK ROOM - NOT QUITE AS HAZY AS SMOKEY ROOM.

FLOOR BRIGHT NEAR TABLE.

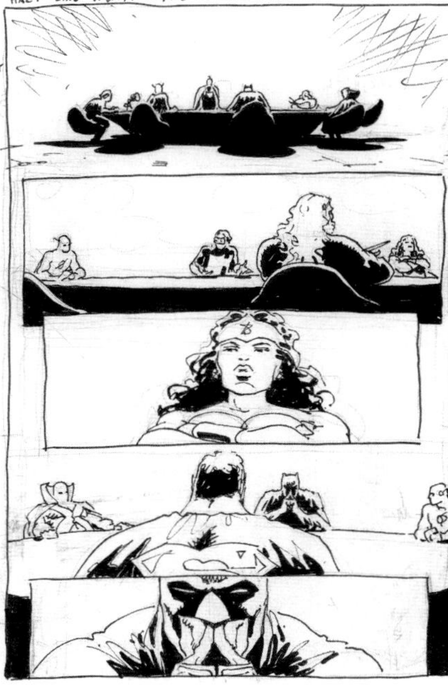

F.A.O. DAN RASPLER (27)

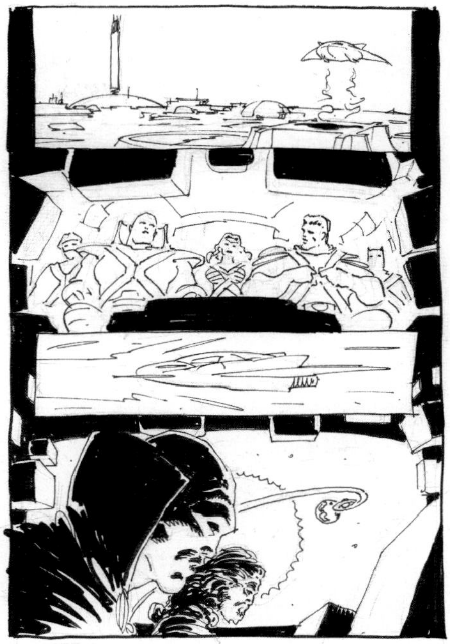

F.A.O. DAN RASPLER P (28)

RAINY.

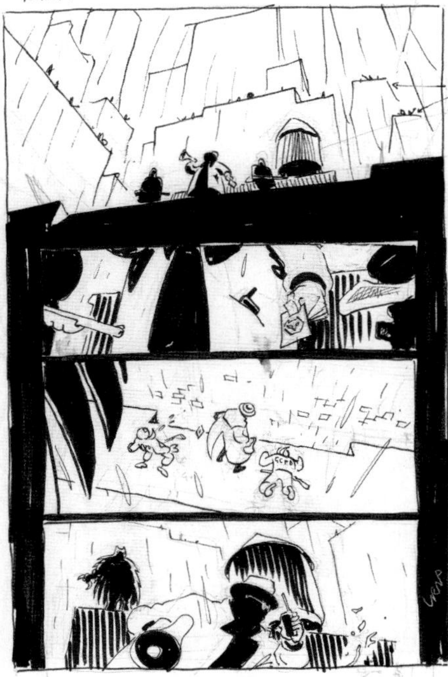

POLIS

CLEAN DECO. GOTHIC

CLOSER ON CARD.

F.A.O. DAN RASPLER P (29)

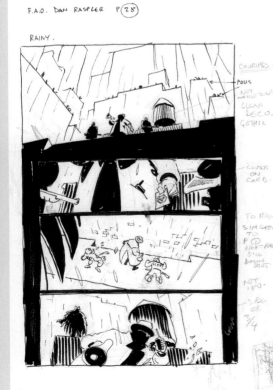

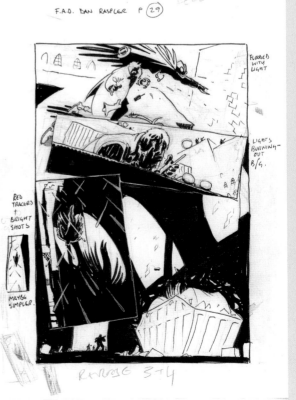

FLOODED WITH LIGHT

LIGHTS BURNING-OUT B/G.

RED TRACERS + BRIGHT SHOTS

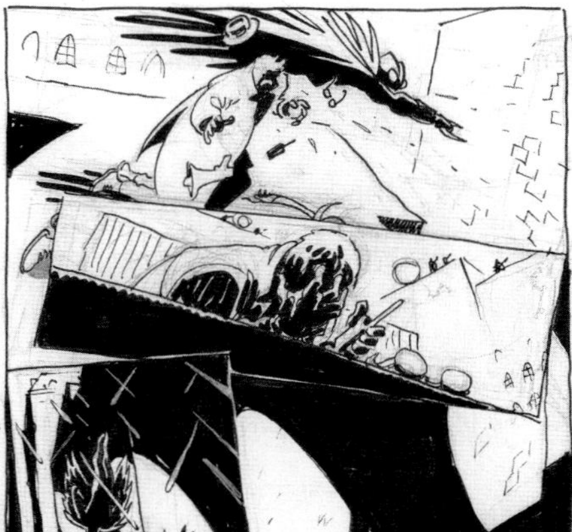

MAYBE SIMPLER.

F.A.O. DAN RASPLER. P 30

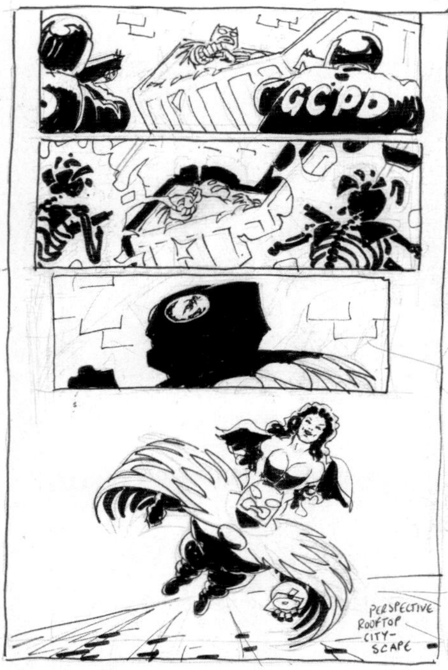
GCPD
PERSPECTIVE ROOFTOP CITY-SCAPE

TOUCHING RIGHT ARM WITH LEFT HAND

LOOKING UP. MAYBE STILL WITH L HAND ON GAUNTLET (LESS STARTLED)

SAME

F.A.O. DAN RASPLER PAGE 31

MORE GOTHIC.

2–5 BIGGER

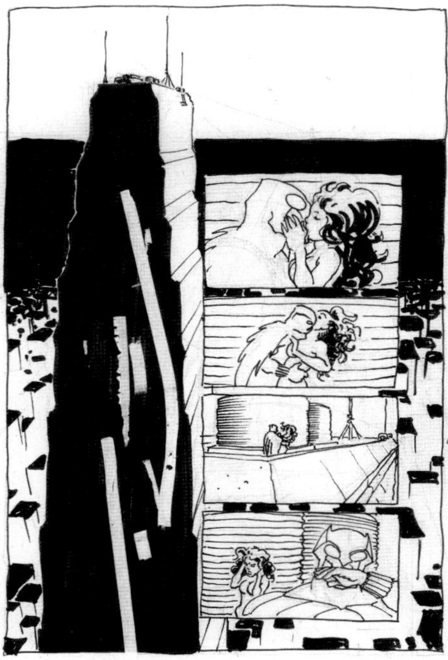

4 IN CLOSER.

FAO DAN RASPLER PAGE 32

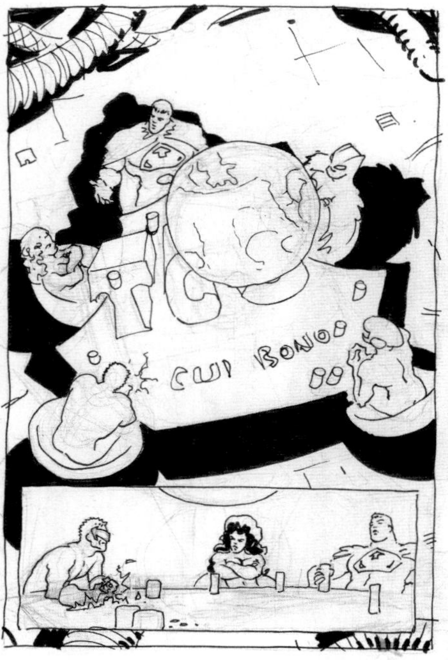
CUI BONO?

F.A.O. DAN RASPLER PAGE 33

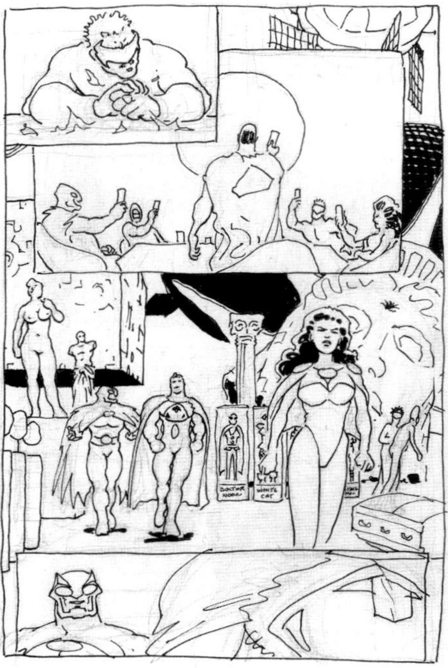

MOVE IN + DOWN

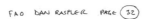

F.A.O. DAN RASPLER P 34

URINALS IN B/G.

SINKS ROUND PILLAR.

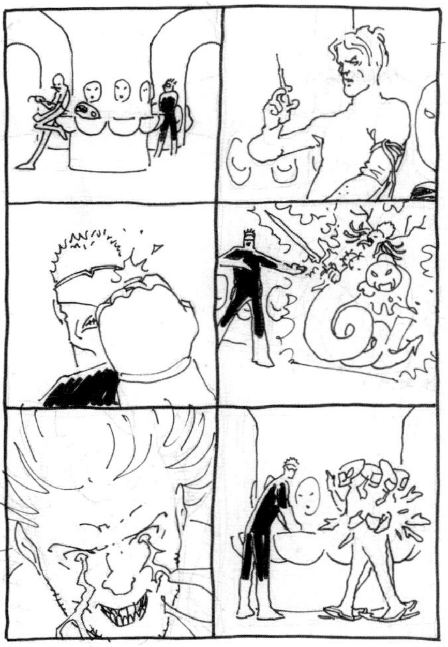

SHITTIER.

FAO DAN RASPLER PAGE 35

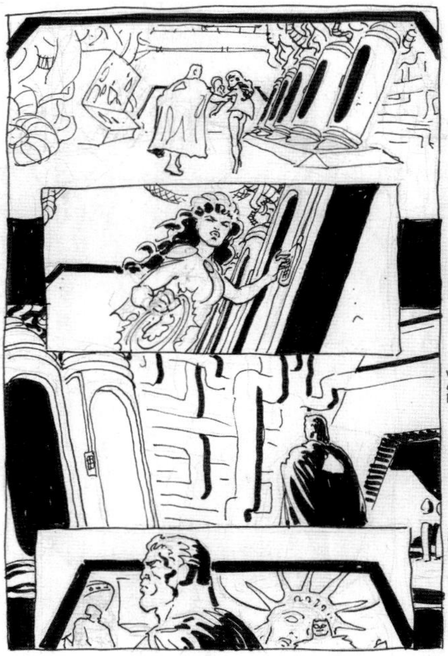

V. BRIGHT COLOURED FLASH

SAME COLOURED LIGHT FADED NOW

F.A.O DAN RASPLER 36

WW S LEX.

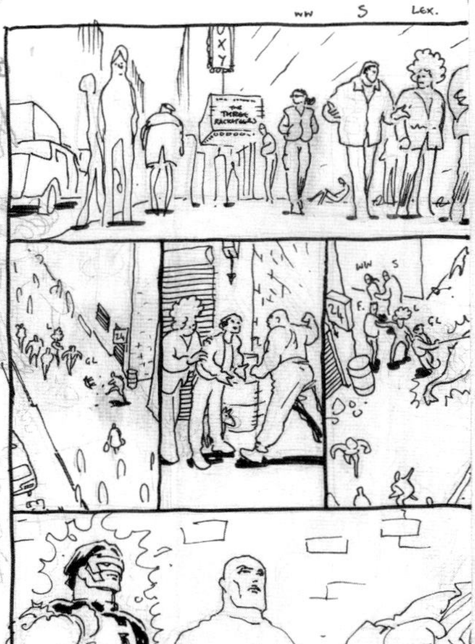

OXY
WW
S
GL

F.A.O. DAN RASPLER 37

PAN RIGHT.

BADDIE.

F. GL.

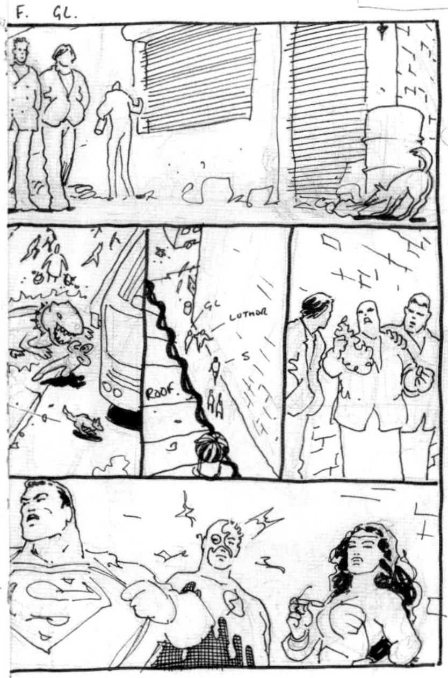

GL
LUTHOR
S
ROOF.

(2) MOVE IN!

(3). BLOCKING OR PARRYING. BADDIE COMING OUT LANG.

(4) SMALLER UPRIGHT DOG BADDY NEARER.

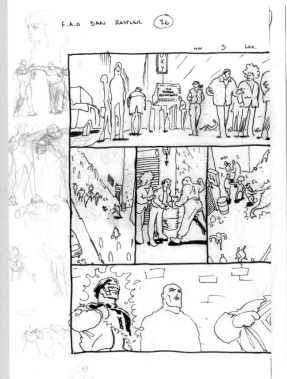

F.A.O. DAN RASPLER (38)

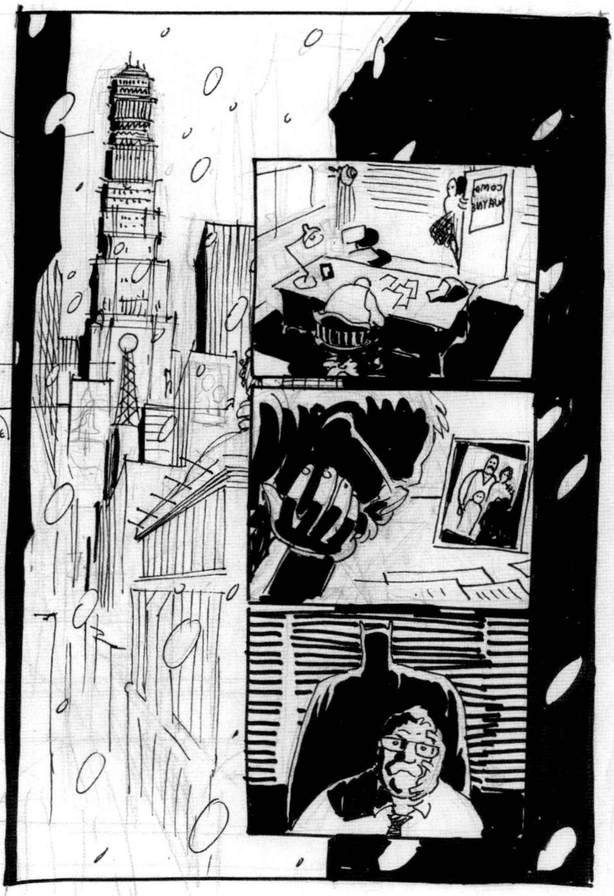
TOWER FROM P 31
"OUR" GOTHAM TOWER
WAYNE
STATUE OF VIGILANCE

F.A.O DAN RASPLER (40)

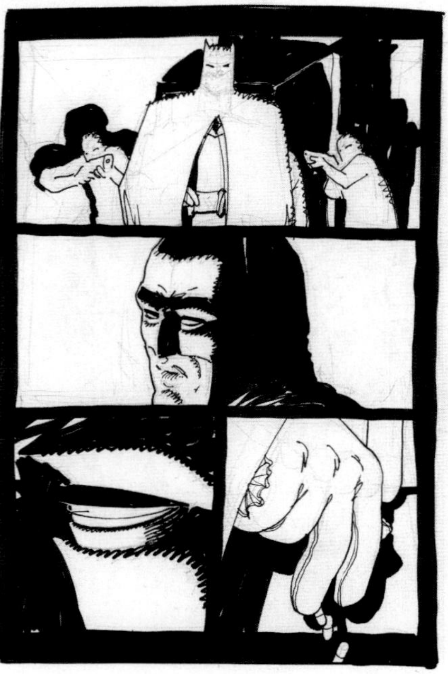
COLOUR-TINTED EYE-SHIELD

F.A.O. DAN RASPLER (41)

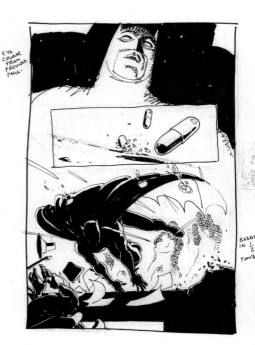

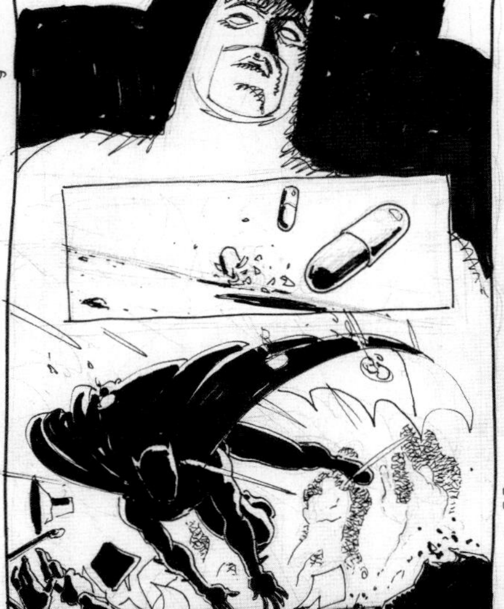
EYE COLOUR FROM PREVIOUS PAGE.
BADDIES IN 1/2-TONE

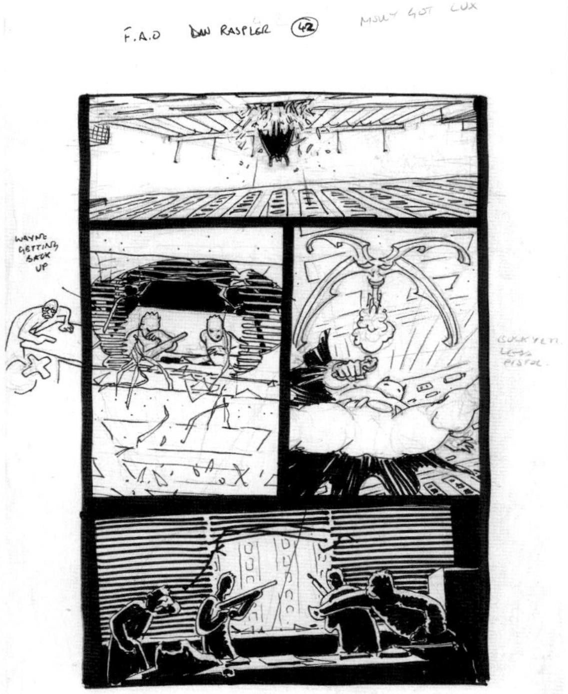

F.A.O DAN RASPLER 42
MSUY GOT LUX
WAYNE GETTING BACK UP
BULKYER. LESS PISTOL.

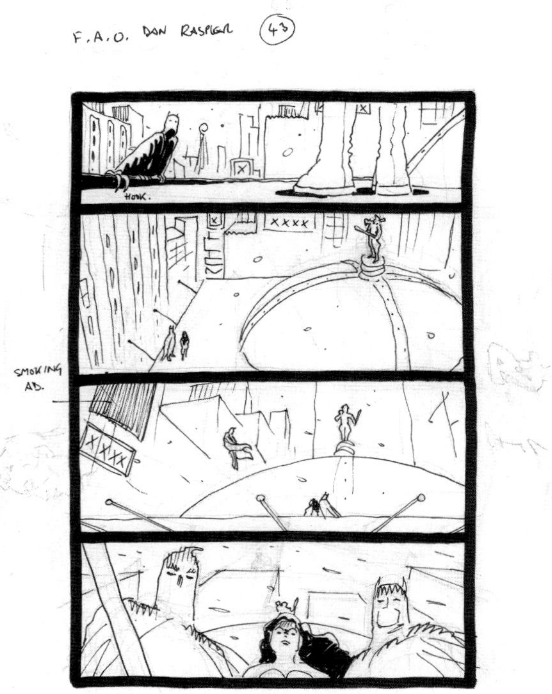

F.A.O. DAN RASPLER 43
HOOK.
XXXX
SMOKING AD.
XXXX

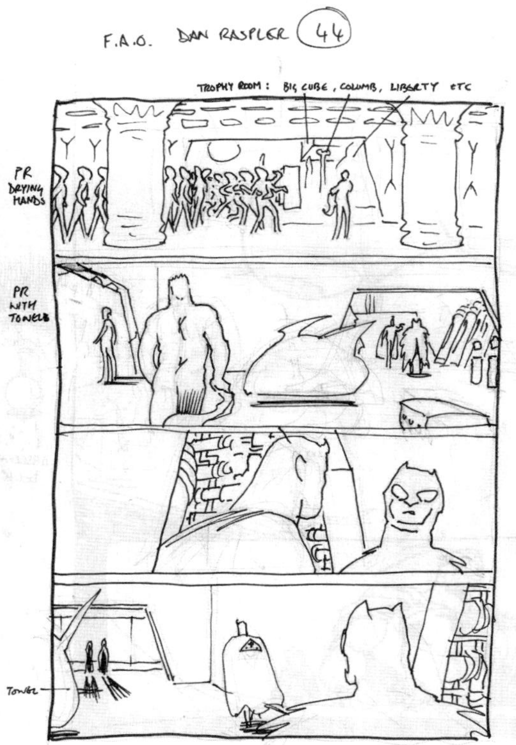

F.A.O. DAN RASPLER 44
TROPHY ROOM: BIG CUBE, COLUMB, LIBERTY ETC
PR DRYING HANDS
PR WITH TOWELS
TOWEL

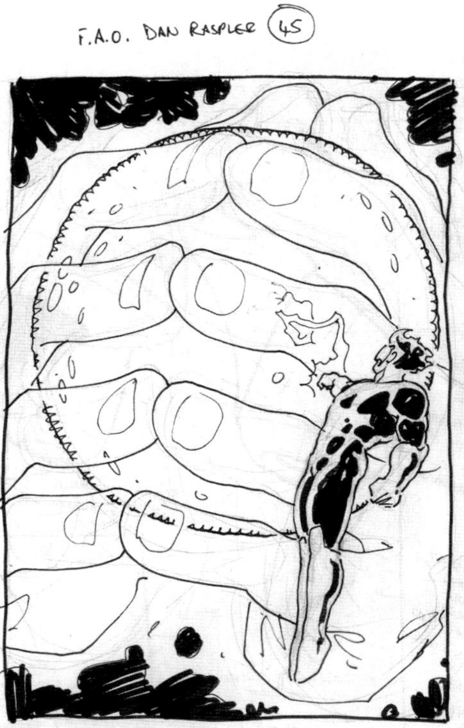

F.A.O. DAN RASPLER 45

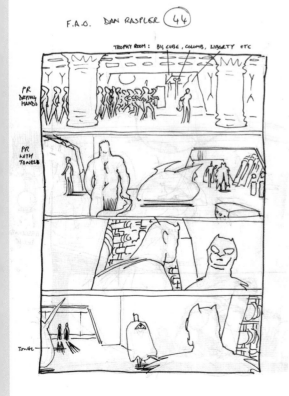

F.A.O. TONY BEDARD P ~~14~~ 46

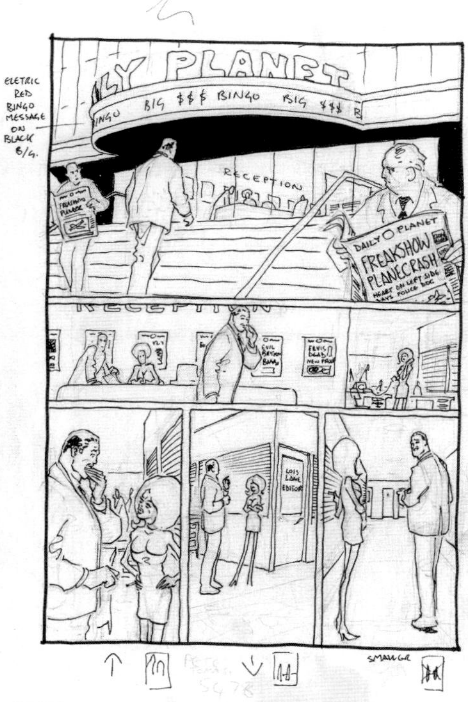
ELETRIC RED BINGO MESSAGE ON BLACK B/G.
LY PLANET
BIG $$$ BINGO BIG $$$
RECEPTION
DAILY PLANET
FREAKSHOW PLANECRASH
HEART ON LEFT SIDE SAYS POLICE DOC
LOIS LANE EDITOR

F.A.O. TONY BEDARD P ~~45~~ 47

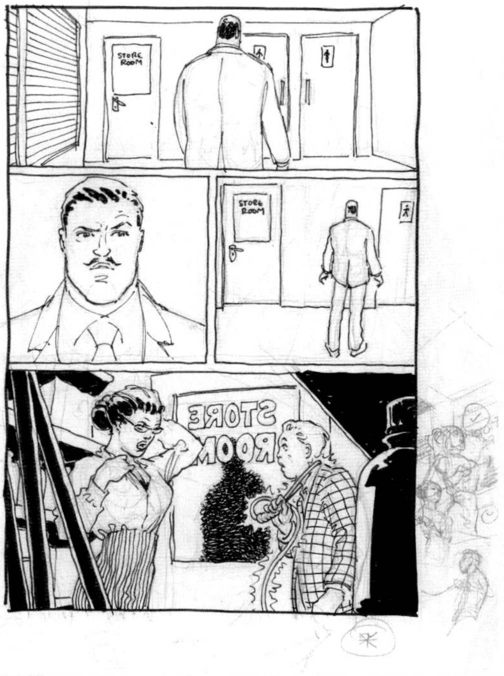
STORE ROOM
STORE ROOM
STORE ROOM

F.A.O. DAN RASPLER ~~46~~ 48

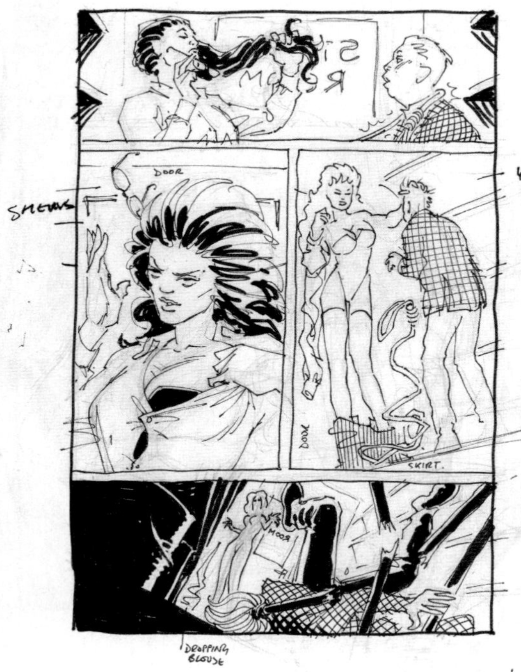
DOOR
SKIRT.
DROPPING BLOUSE

F.A.O DAN RASPLER ~~47~~ 49

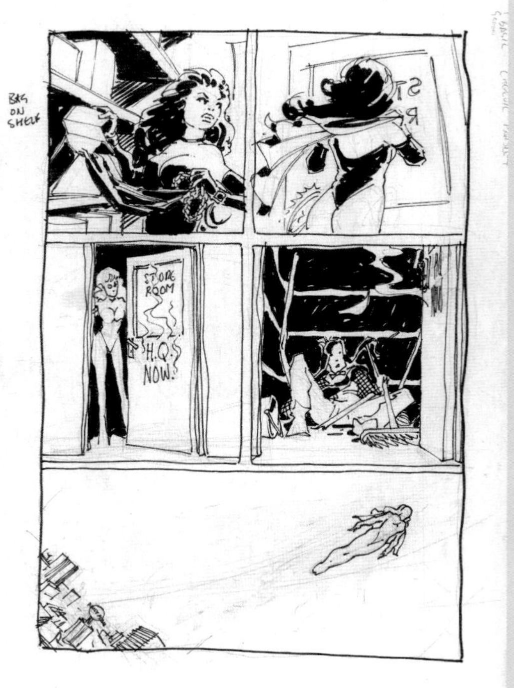
BAG ON SHELF
STORE ROOM
H.Q.'S NOW!

F.A.O DAN RASPLER (50)

REV. ANGLE ON TROPHY-ROOM STUFF P23

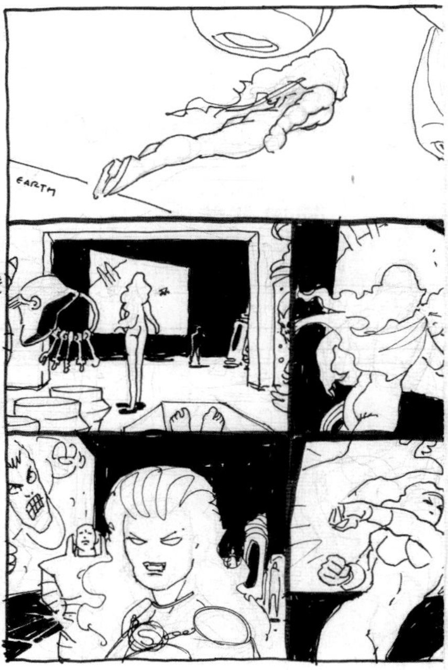

EARTH

F.A.O. DAN RASPLER (51)

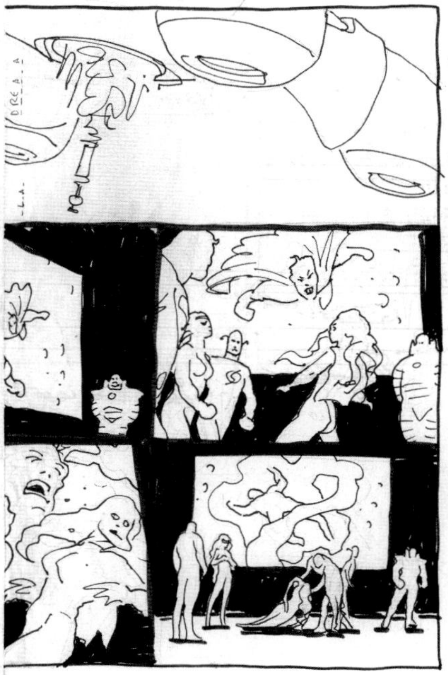

FORTRESS LIT BY SETTING SUN. AUTUMN COLOURS.

SKY V. DARK SLIGHTLY LIGHTER AT LEFT. ← (OPP. PAGE)

F.A.O DAN RASPLER (52)

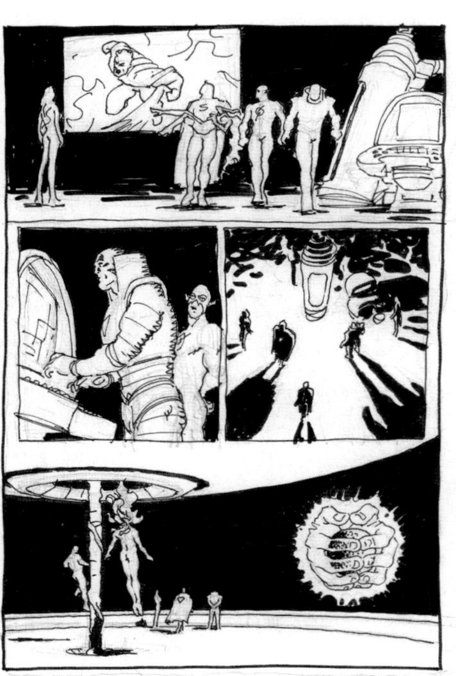

* TRANSPARENT HANDS

F.A.O. DAN RASPLER (53)

* MISSED THIS OUT LAST TIME *

LOTS OF JOHNNY QUICKS

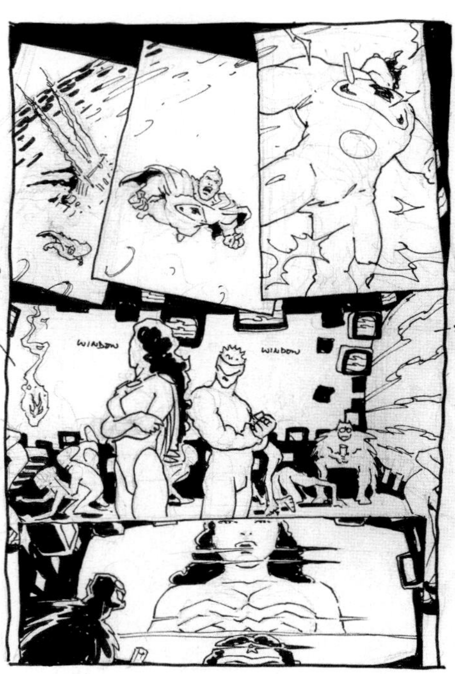

WINDOW
WINDOW

SCREEN

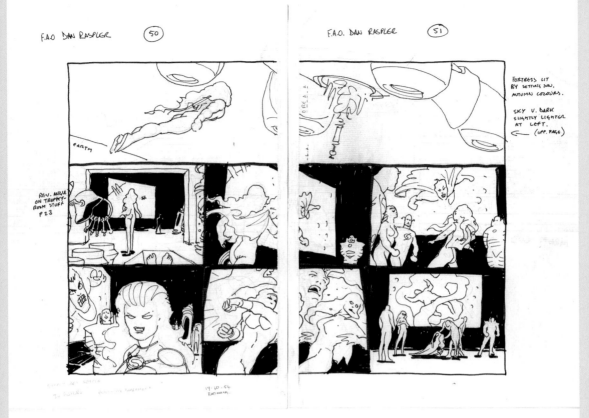

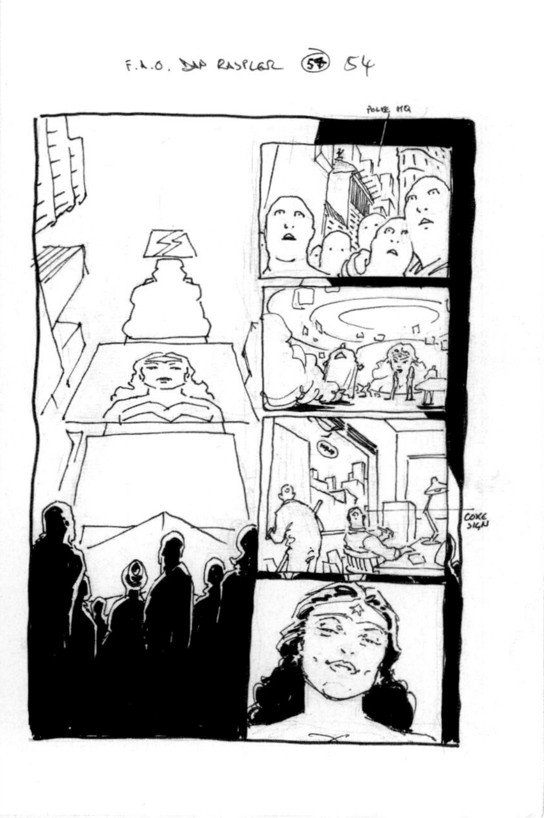
F.A.O. DAN RASPLER 58 54
POLICE HQ
COKE SIGN

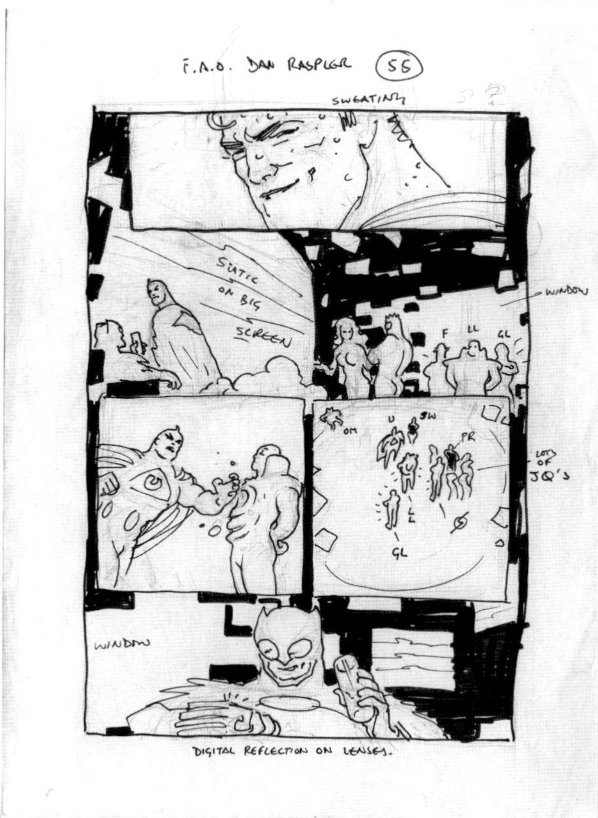
F.A.O. DAN RASPLER 55
SWEATING
STATIC ON BIG SCREEN
WINDOW
F
GL
OM
SW
PR
LOTS OF JQ'S
GL
WINDOW
DIGITAL REFLECTION ON LENSES.

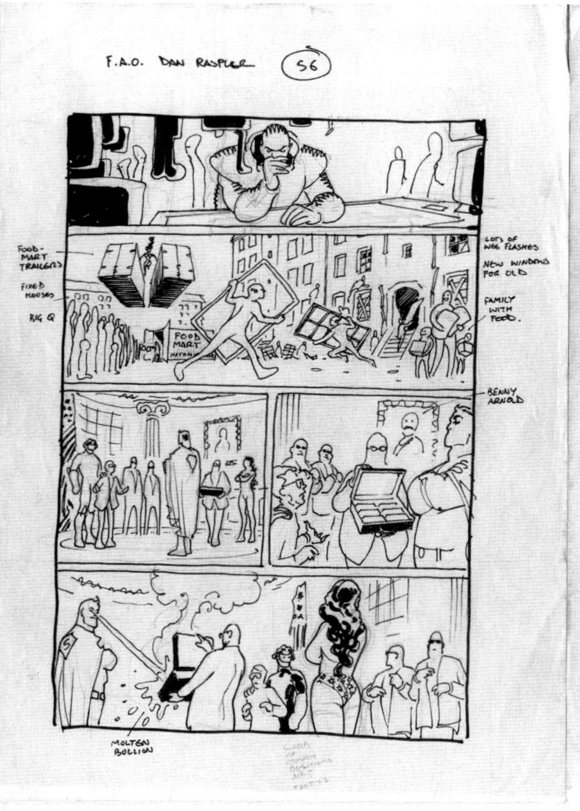
F.A.O. DAN RASPLER 56
FOOD-MART TRAILERS
FIXED HOUSES
BIG Q
LOTS OF NEG FLASHES
NEW WINDOWS FOR OLD
FAMILY WITH FOOD.
BENNY ARNOLD
FOOD MART
MOLTEN BULLION

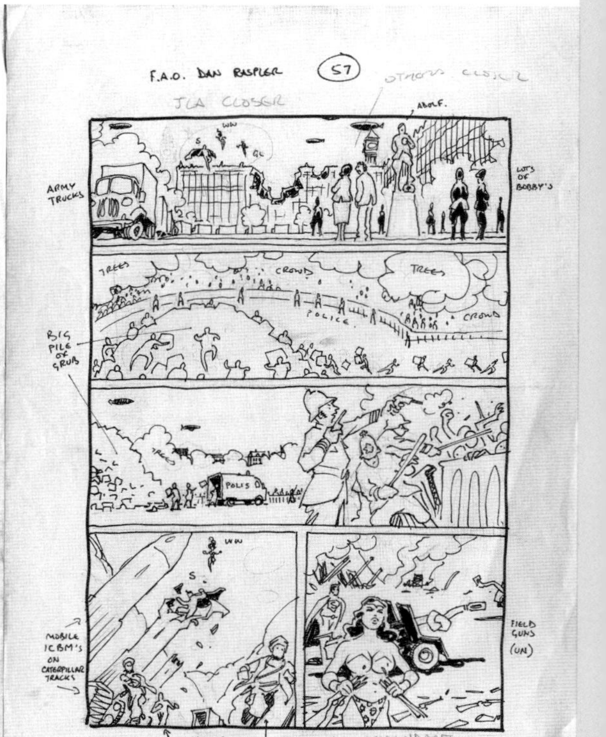
F.A.O. DAN RASPLER 57
OTHERS CLOSER
JLA CLOSER
ADOLF.
ARMY TRUCKS
LOTS OF BOBBY'S
TREES
CROWD
TREES
POLICE
CROWD
BIG PILE OF GRUB
POLICE
MOBILE ICBM'S ON CATERPILLAR TRACKS
FIELD GUNS (UN)
SHADY MIDDLE-EASTERN TYPES
TRANSCENDANT

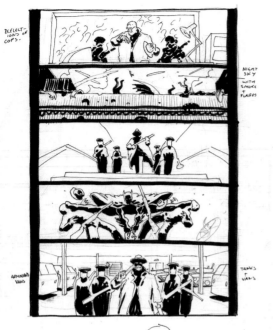

NIGHT
SKY
WITH
SMOKE
+
FLARES

ARMOURED
VANS

TANKS
+
VANS

F.A.O. DAN RASPLER 58

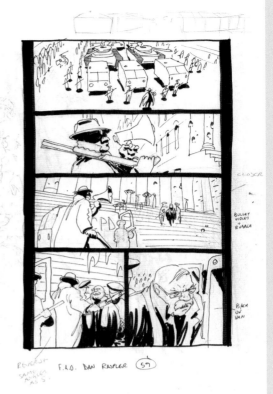

CLOSER

BULLET
HOLES
+
RUBBLE

BACK
OF
VAN

REVERSE
SAME AS
ANGLE AS 5.

F.A.O. DAN RASPLER 59

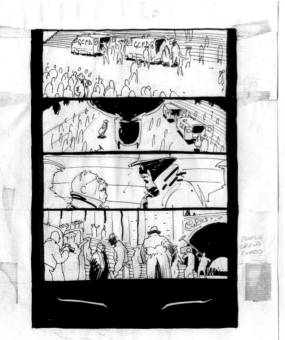

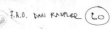

F.A.O. DAN RASPLER 60

PEOPLE
CROWD
CHAOS

SMOKE

FIRING

DAN RASPLER 61

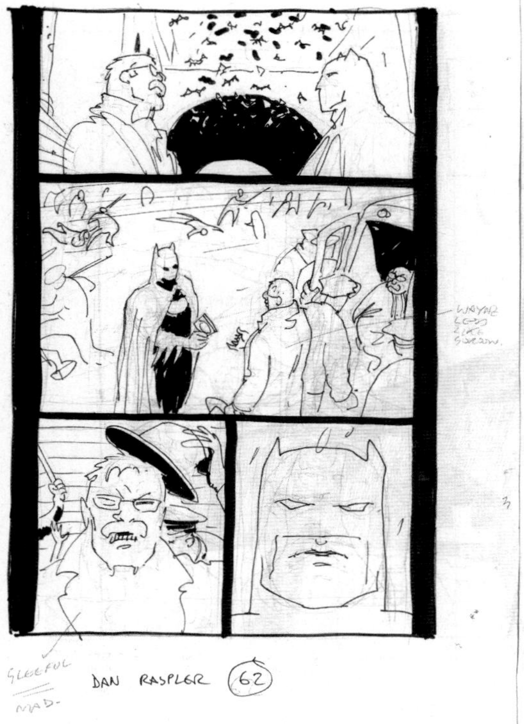
GLEEFUL
MAD-
DAN RASPLER 62

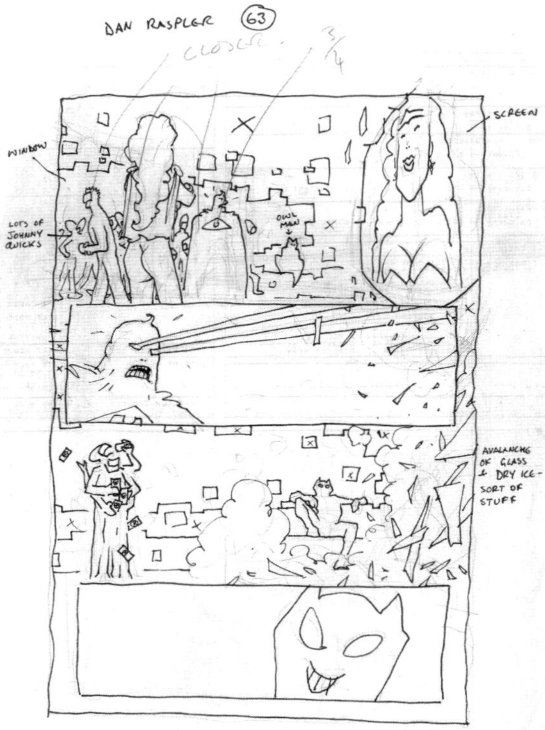
DAN RASPLER 63
CLOSER
3/4
WINDOW
LOTS OF JOHNNY QUICKS
OWL MAN
SCREEN
AVALANCHE OF GLASS + DRY ICE-SORT OF STUFF

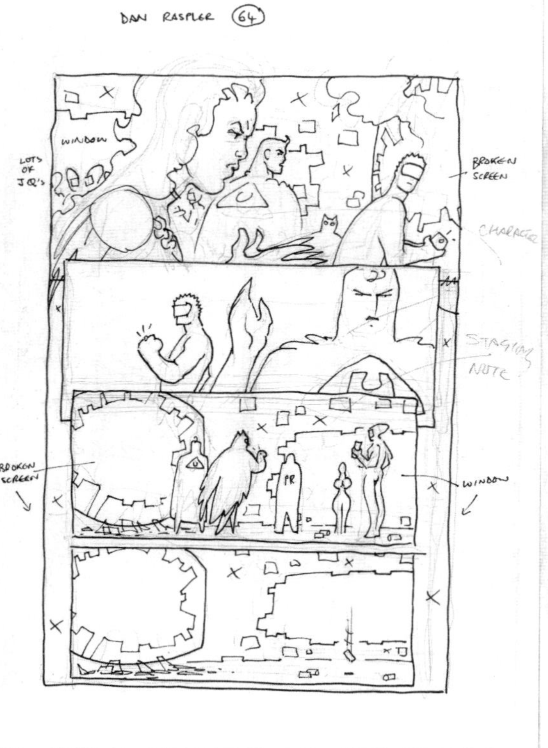
DAN RASPLER 64
WINDOW
LOTS OF JQ's
BROKEN SCREEN
CHARACTER
STAGING NOTE
PR
BROKEN SCREEN
WINDOW

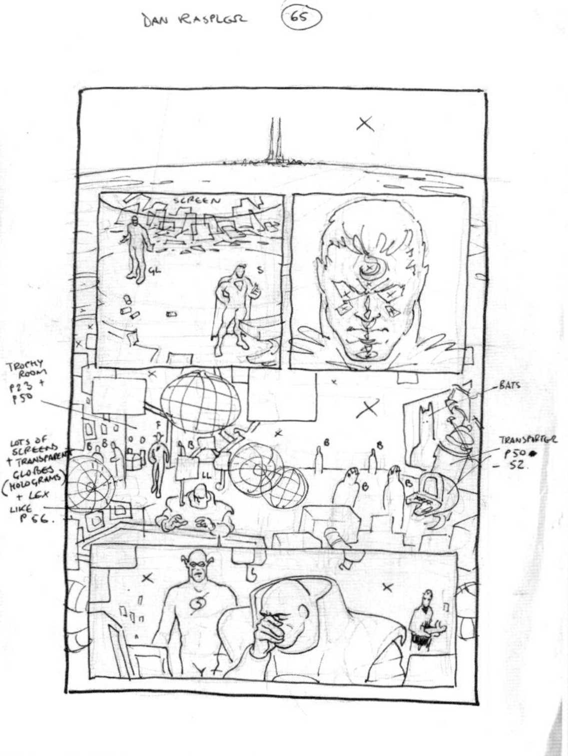
DAN RASPLER 65
SCREEN
GL
S
TROPHY ROOM P23 + P50
LOTS OF SCREENS + TRANSPARENT GLOBES (HOLOGRAMS) + LEX LIKE P56.
BATS
TRANSPORTER P50 - 52.

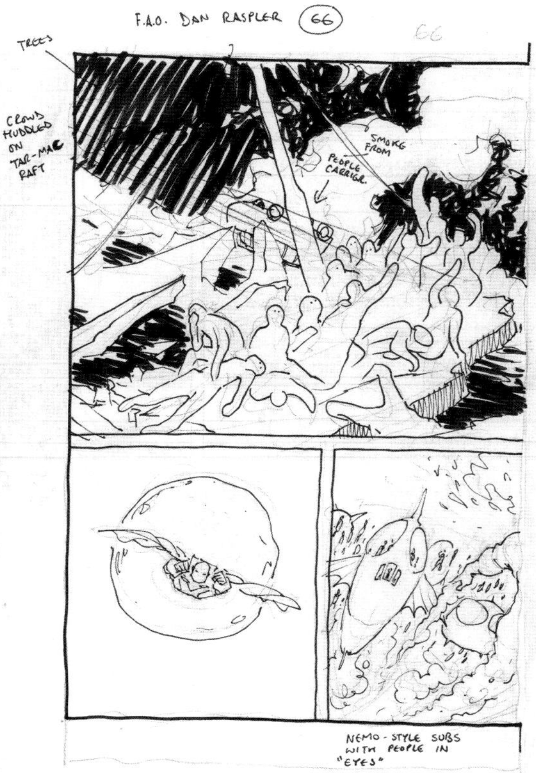
F.A.O. DAN RASPLER 66
TREES
CROWD HUDDLED ON TAR-MAC RAFT
SMOKE FROM
PEOPLE CARRIER
NEMO-STYLE SUBS WITH PEOPLE IN "EYES"

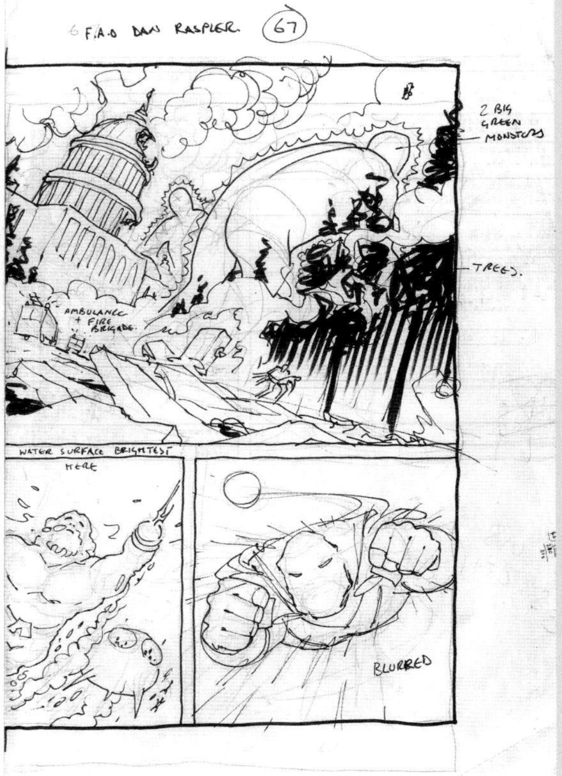
F.A.O DAN RASPLER 67
2 BIG GREEN MONSTERS
TREES.
AMBULANCE + FIRE BRIGADE.
WATER SURFACE BRIGHTEST HERE
BLURRED

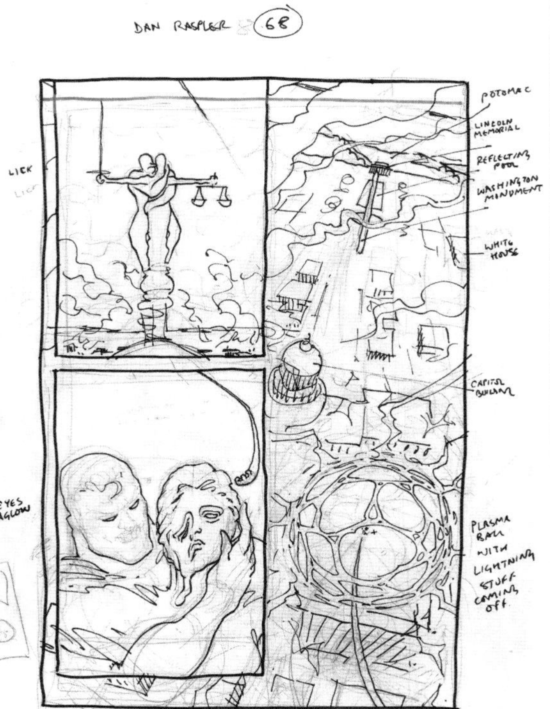
DAN RASPLER 68
POTOMAC
LINCOLN MEMORIAL
REFLECTING POOL
WASHINGTON MONUMENT
WHITE HOUSE
LICK
CAPITOL BUILDING
EYES AGLOW
PLASMA BALL WITH LIGHTNING STUFF COMING OFF.

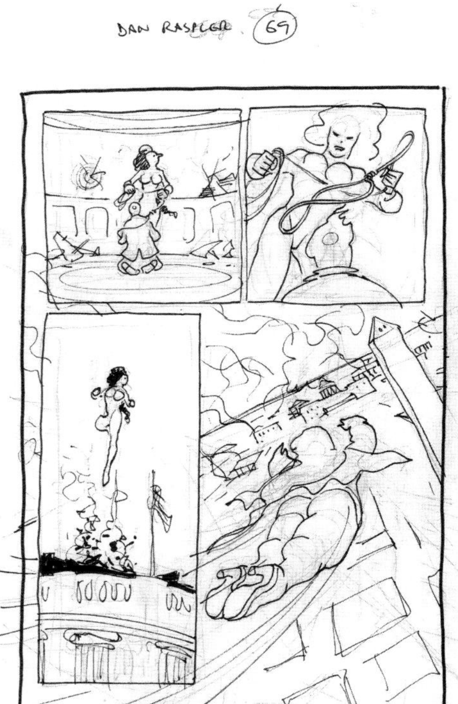
DAN RASPLER 69

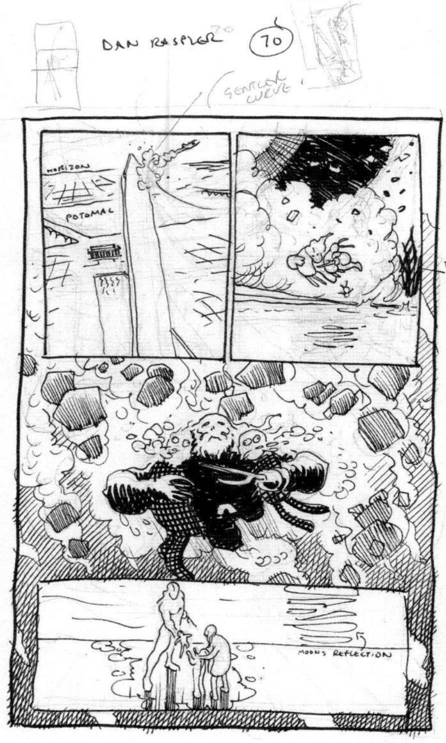
DAN RASPLER 70
HORIZON
POTOMAC
TREES
MOONS REFLECTION

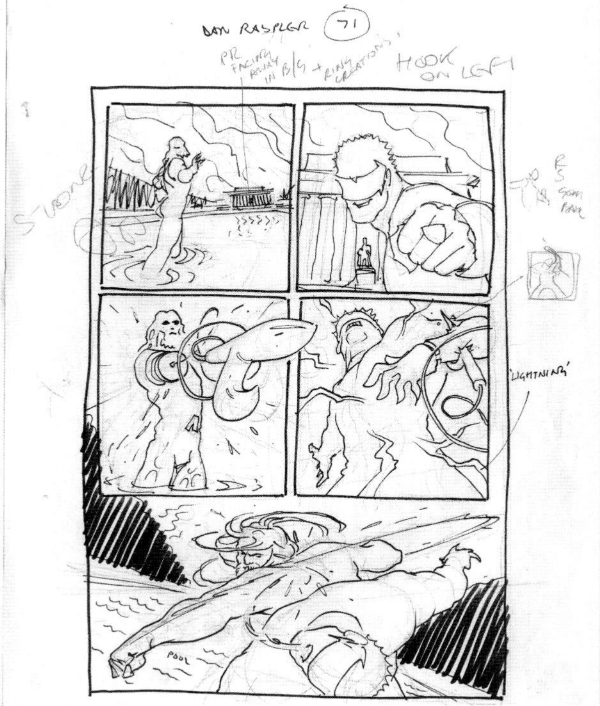
DAN RASPLER 71
HOOK ON LEFT
'LIGHTNING'
POOL

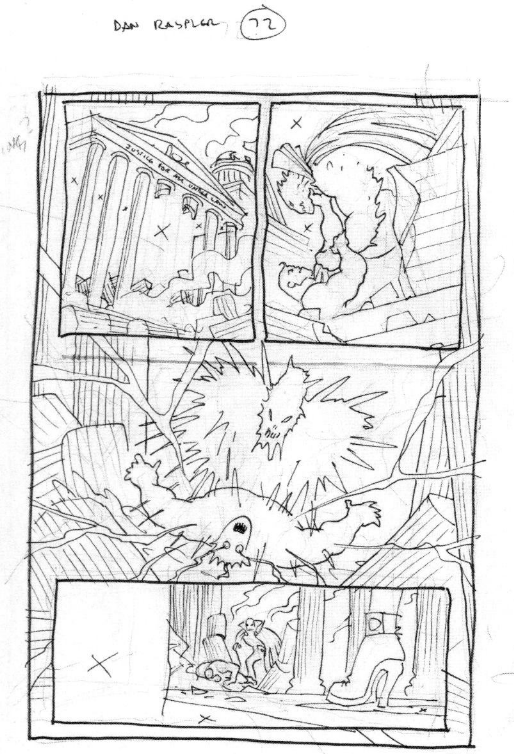
DAN RASPLER 72

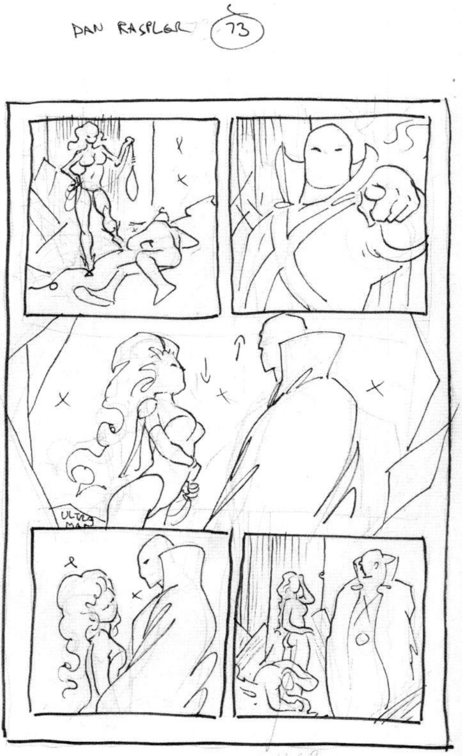
DAN RASPLER 73
ULTRA MAN
ANGER

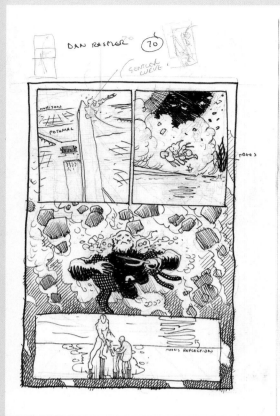

567
0309
0403

DAN RASPLER (74)

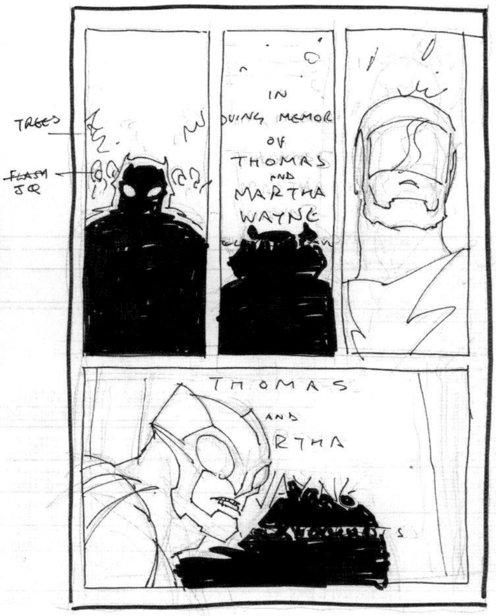
TREES
FLASH JQ
IN
UING MEMOR
OF
THOMAS
AND
MARTHA
WAYNE
THOMAS
AND
RTHA

DAN RASPLER (75)

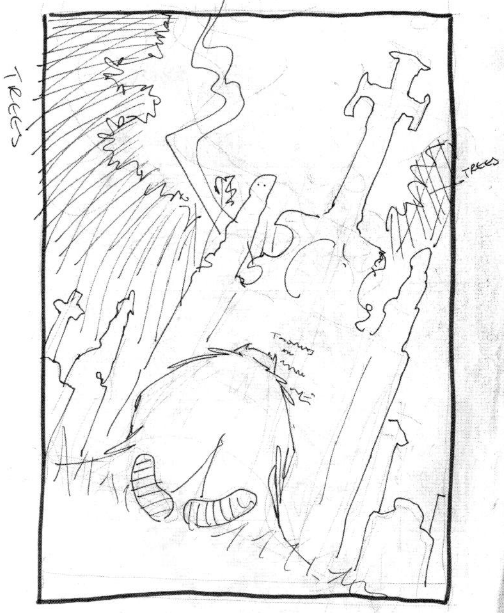
TREES
TREES.

DAN RASPLER (76)

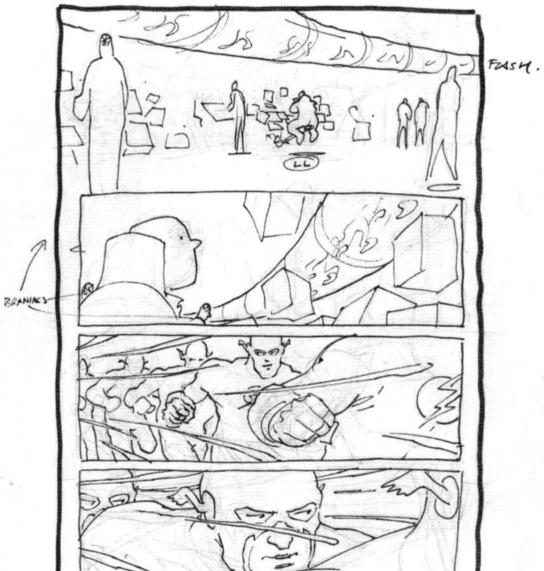
FLASH.
LL
BRAINIACS

DAN RASPLER (77)

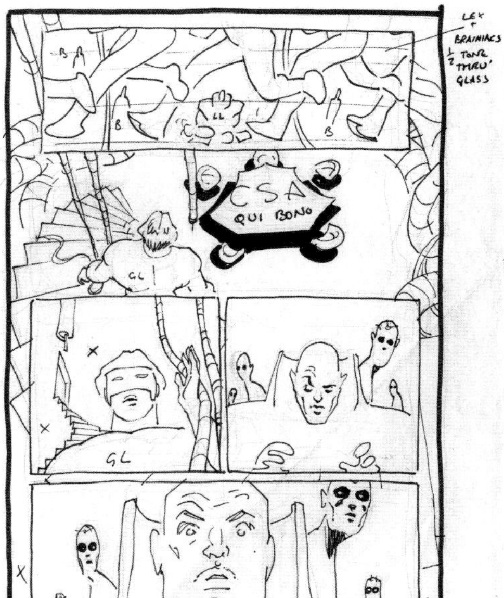
LEX + BRAINIACS
1/2 TONE THRU' GLASS
B
LL
CSA
QUI BONO
GL
GL

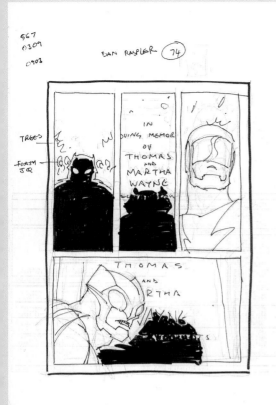

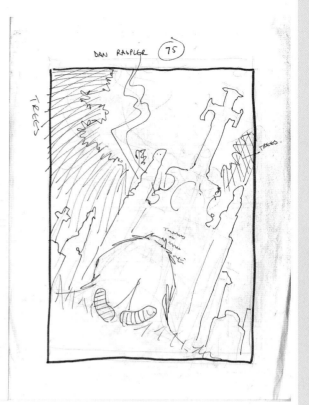

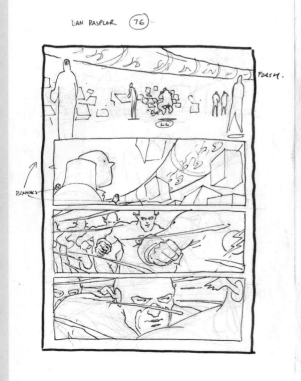

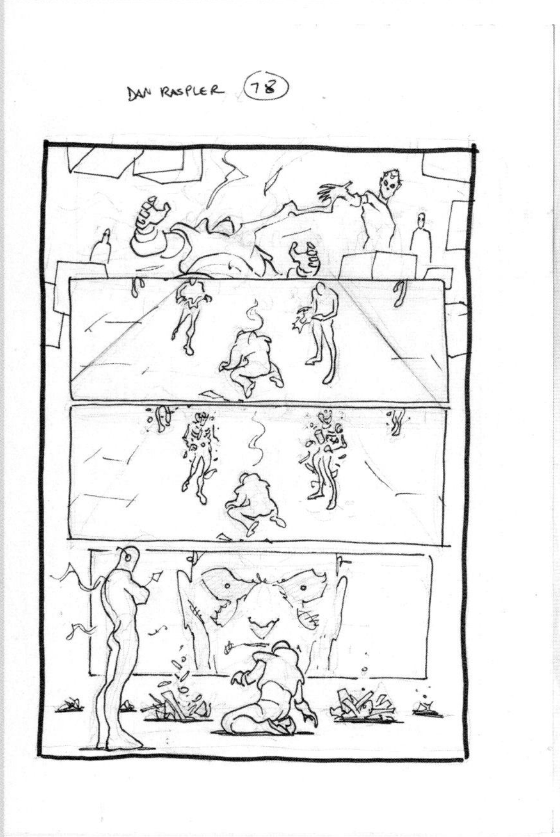
DAN RASPLER 78

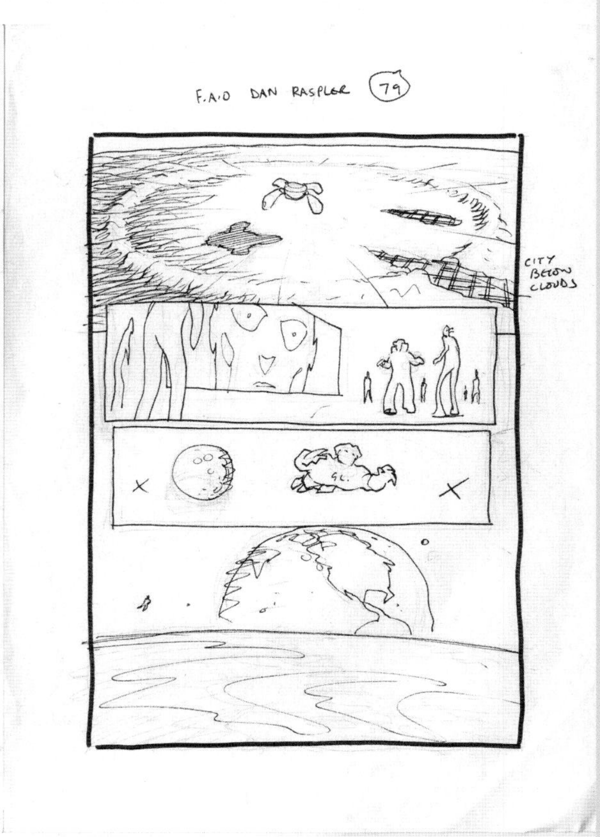
F.A.O DAN RASPLER 79
CITY BELOW CLOUDS
GL

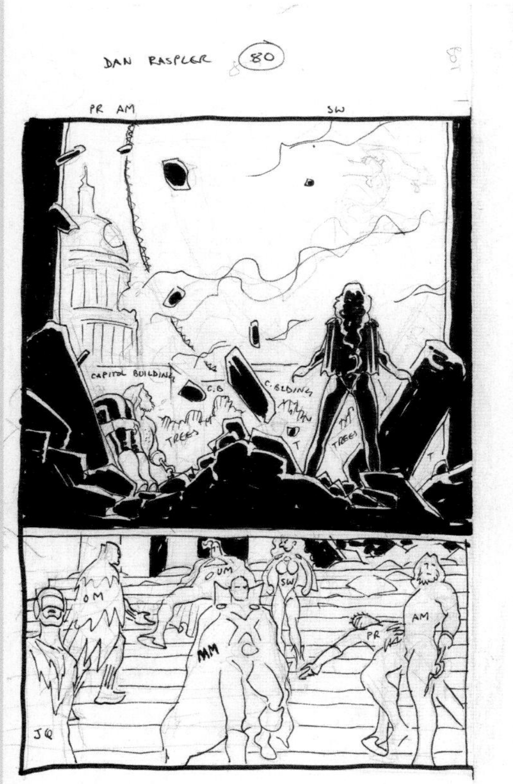
DAN RASPLER 80
PR AM
SW
CAPITOL BUILDING
C.B
C. BLDING
TREES
T
TREES
OM
UM
SW
MM
PR
AM
JQ

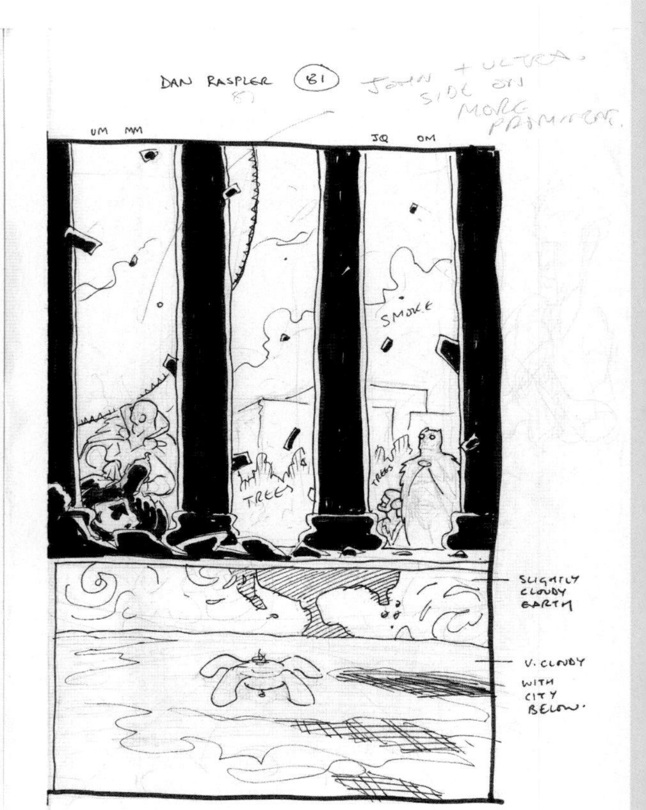
DAN RASPLER 81
JOHN + ULTRA. SIDE ON MORE PROMINENT.
UM MM
JQ OM
SMOKE
TREES
TREES
SLIGHTLY CLOUDY EARTH
V. CLOUDY
WITH CITY BELOW.

DAN RASPLER 82
DAN RASPLER 83
DOWN WITH THE JUSTICE LEAGUE
DAN RASPLER 84.
SAME POSITION AS LAST PAGE.
HI-STRATOSPHERIC BLUE FADING DOWN INTO SKY BLUE
SCREEN
CYCLOTRON.
FLASH'S SOLES.
LEX PULLING ~~A BRAINIAC HEAD OFF.~~ CONTROLS APART
ROTATE TO RIGHT
DAN RASPLER. 85
SMOKE
CAPE
SHOULDER
CYCLOTRON. - FLASH NOW JUST A RED BLUR.
SCREEN.
MOVE IN

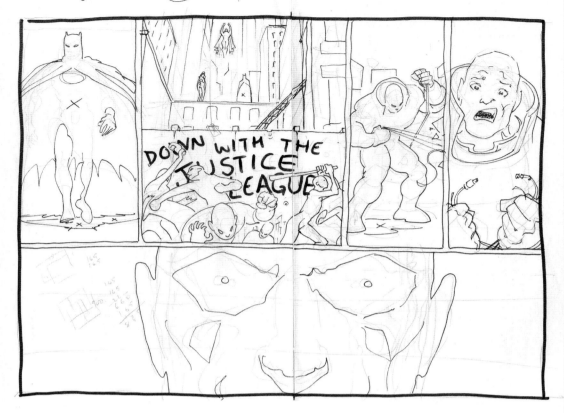

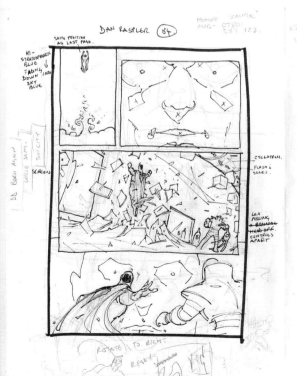

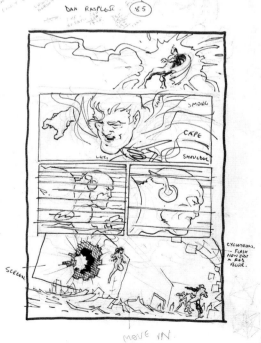

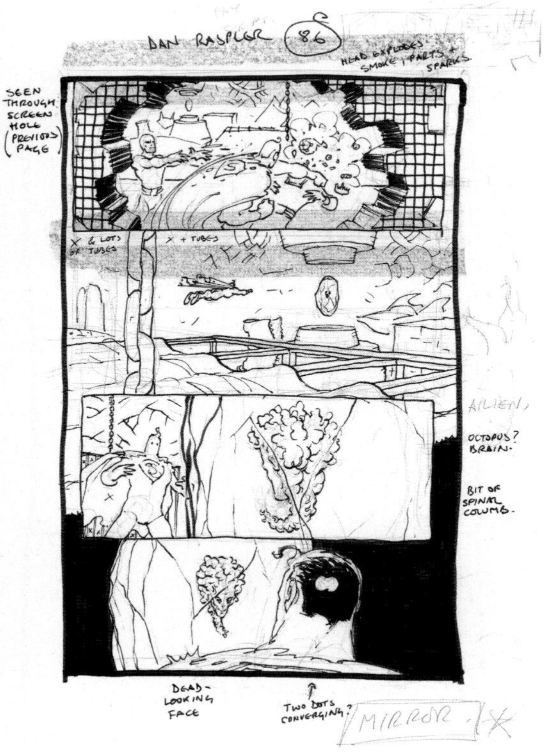
DAN RASPLER
86
HEAD EXPLODES SMOKE, PARTS + SPARKS
SEEN THROUGH SCREEN HOLE (PREVIOUS PAGE)
X & LOTS OF TUBES
X + TUBES
ALIEN,
OCTOPUS? BRAIN.
BIT OF SPINAL COLUMB.
DEAD-LOOKING FACE
TWO DOTS CONVERGING?
MIRROR.

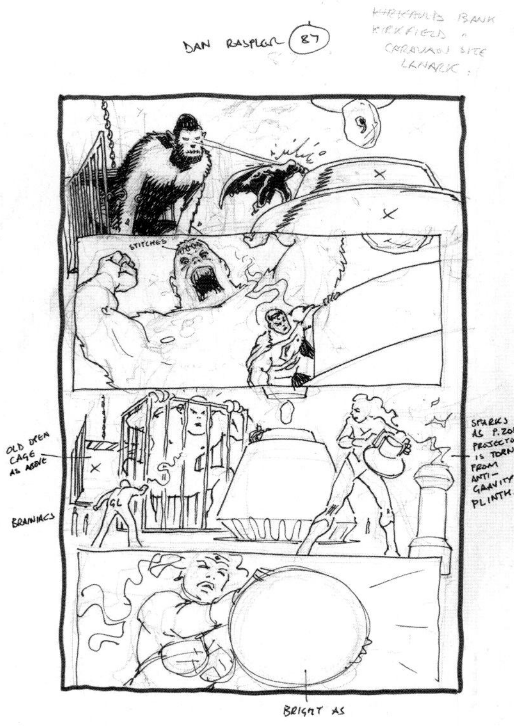
DAN RASPLER
87
STITCHES
OLD OPEN CAGE AS ABOVE
BRAINIACS
SPARKS AS P.ZONE PROJECTOR IS TORN FROM ANTI GRAVITY PLINTH.
BRIGHT AS

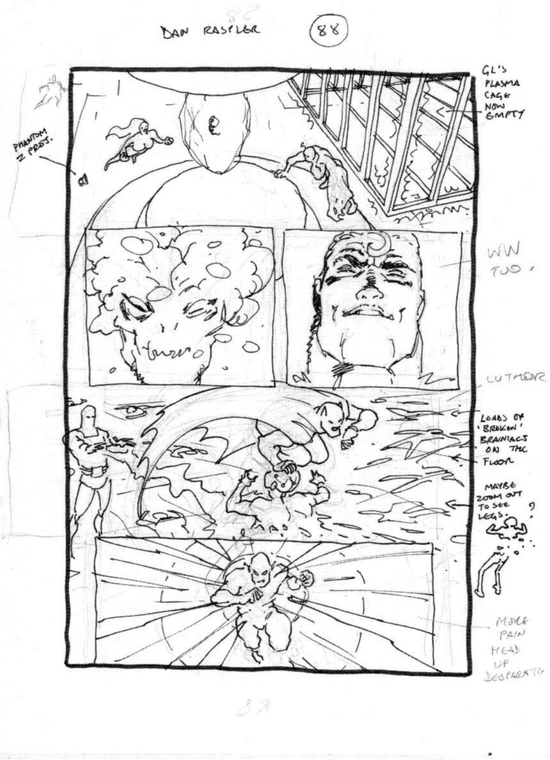
DAN RASPLER
88
GL'S PLASMA CAGE NOW EMPTY
PHANTOM Z PRES.
WW TOO.
LUTHOR
LOADS OF 'BROKEN' BRAINIACS ON THE FLOOR
MAYBE ZOOM OUT TO SEE LEGS.
MORE PAIN HEAD UP DESPERATE

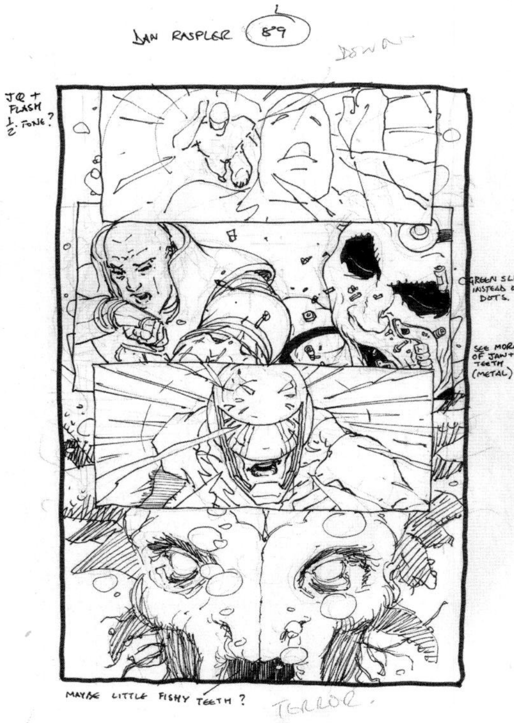
DAN RASPLER
89
DOWN
JQ + FLASH 1. 2. TONE?
GREEN SLITS INSTEAD OF DOTS.
SEE MORE OF JAW + TEETH (METAL)
MAYBE LITTLE FISHY TEETH?
TERROR.

DAN RASPLER (90)

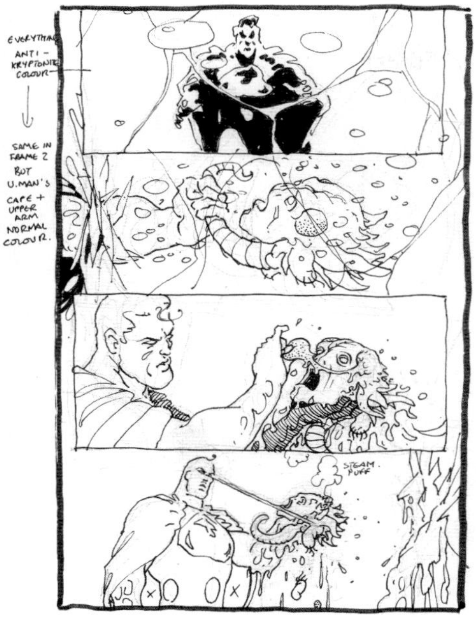
EVERYTHING ANTI-KRYPTONITE COLOUR
SAME IN FRAME 2 BUT U.MAN'S CAPE + UPPER ARM NORMAL COLOUR.
STEAM PUFF

DAN RASPLER (91)

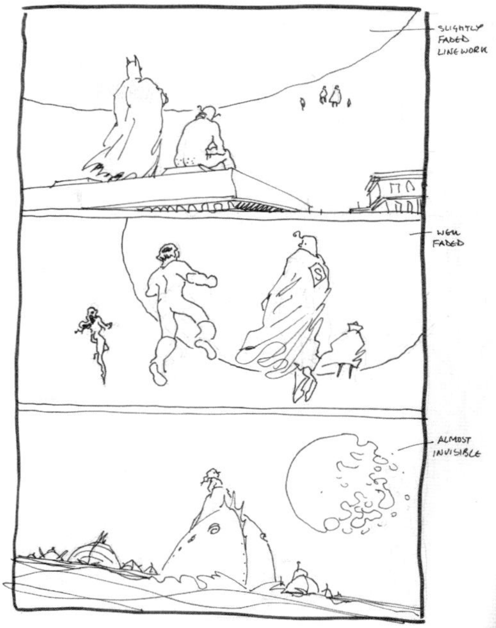
SLIGHTLY FADED LINEWORK
WELL FADED
ALMOST INVISIBLE

DAN RASPLER (92)

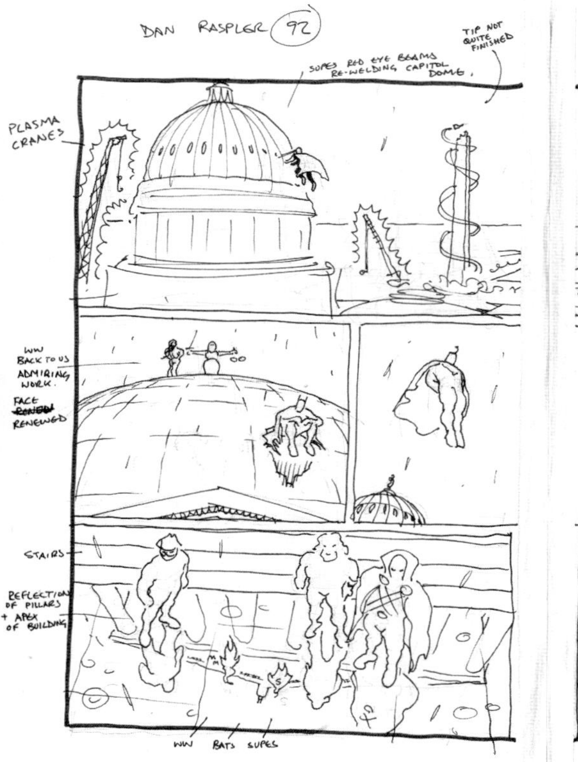
SUPES RED EYE BEAMS RE-WELDING CAPITOL DOME.
TIP NOT QUITE FINISHED
PLASMA CRANES
WW BACK TO US ADMIRING WORK.
FACE ~~RENEW~~ RENEWED
STAIRS
REFLECTION OF PILLARS + APEX OF BUILDING
WW BATS SUPES

DAN RASPLER (93)

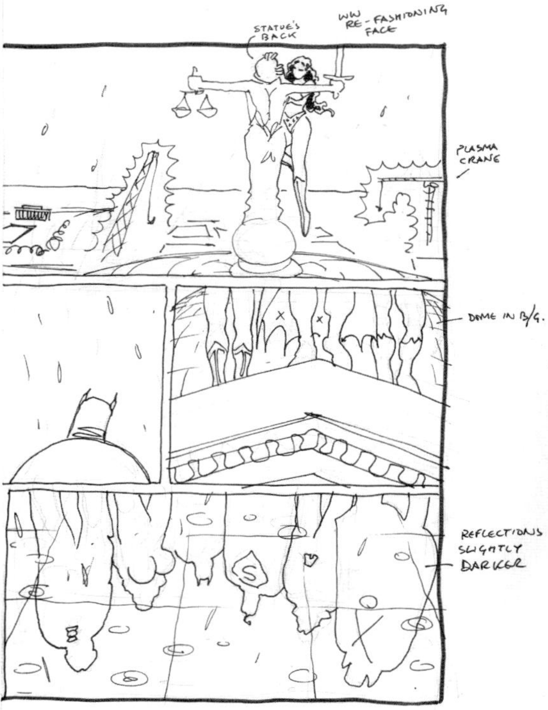
STATUE'S BACK
WW RE-FASHIONING FACE
PLASMA CRANE
DOME IN B/G.
REFLECTIONS SLIGHTLY DARKER

DAN RASPLER. 94

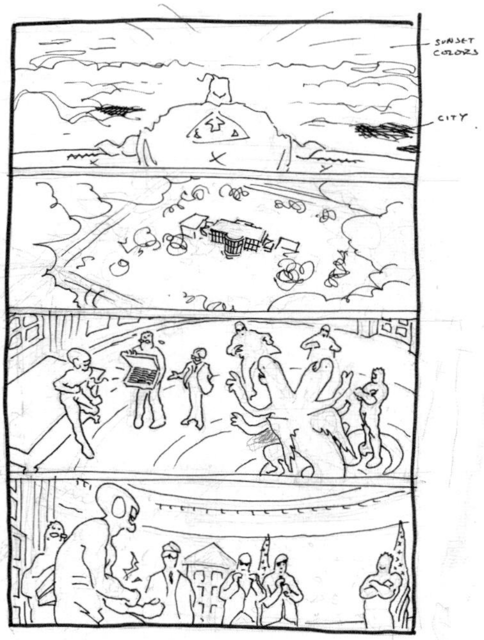
SUNSET COLORS
CITY

DAN RASPLER. 95

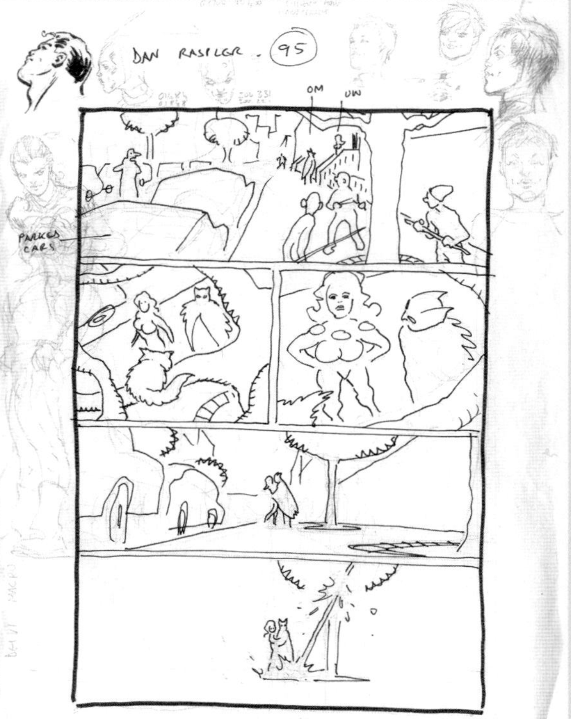
OM
UW
PARKED CARS

DAN RASPLER 96

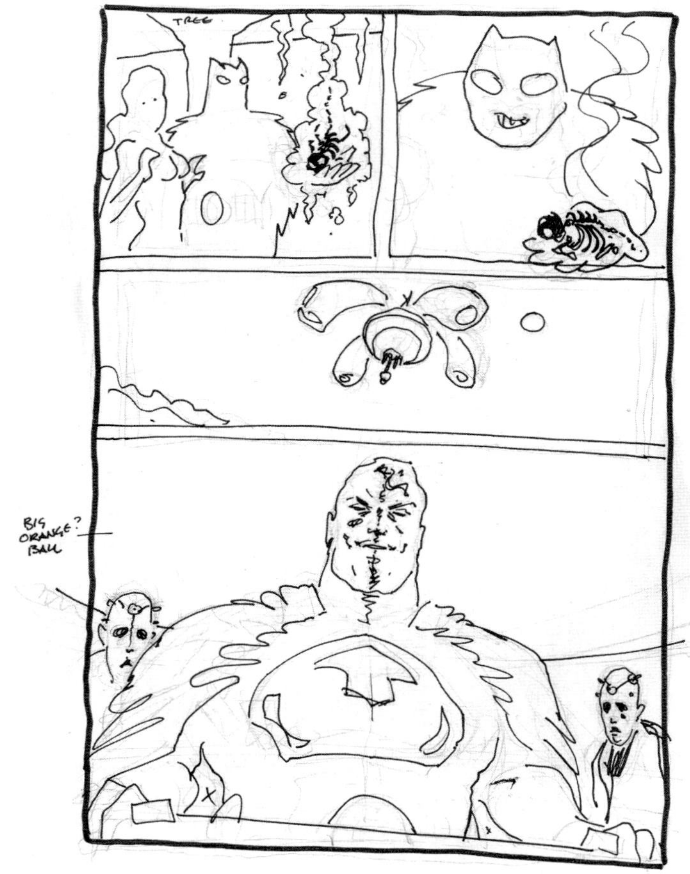
TREE
BIG ORANGE? BALL

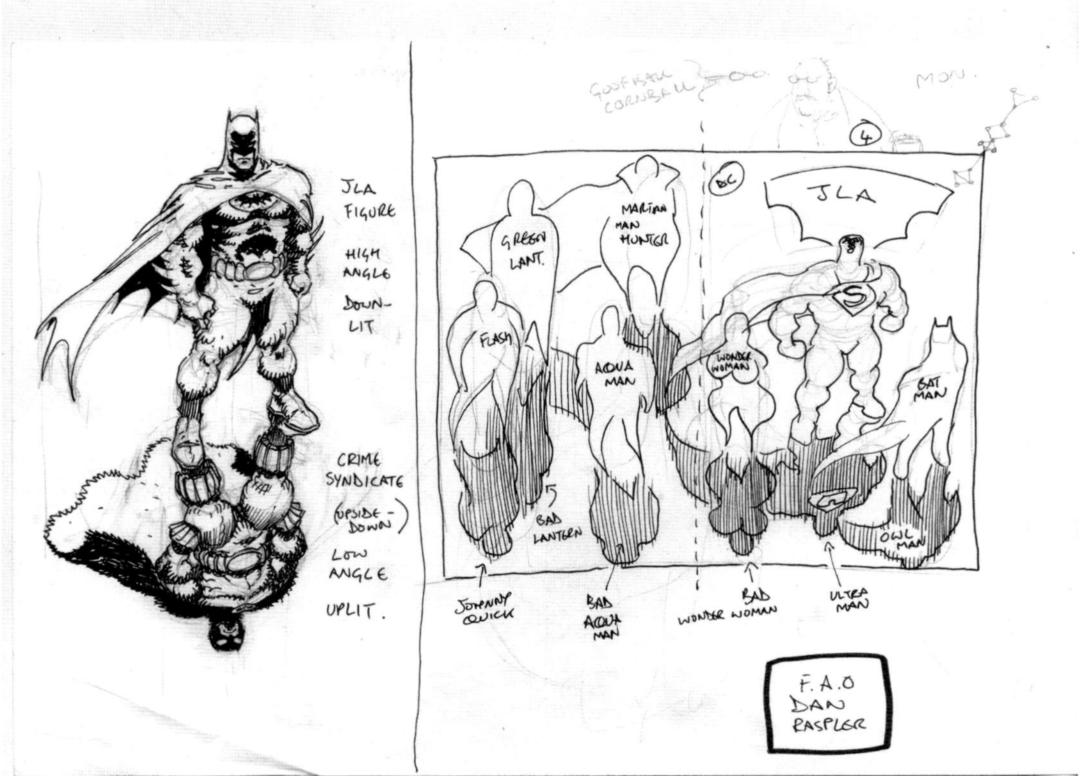
JLA
FIGURE
HIGH
ANGLE
DOWN-
LIT
CRIME
SYNDICATE
(UPSIDE-
DOWN)
LOW
ANGLE
UPLIT.
GOOFBALL
CORNBALL
MON.
4
DC
JLA
GREEN
LANT.
MARTIAN
MAN
HUNTER
FLASH
AQUA
MAN
WONDER
WOMAN
BAT
MAN
BAD
LANTERN
OWL
MAN
JOHNNY
QUICK
BAD
AQUA
MAN
BAD
WONDER WOMAN
ULTRA
MAN
F.A.O
DAN
RASPLER

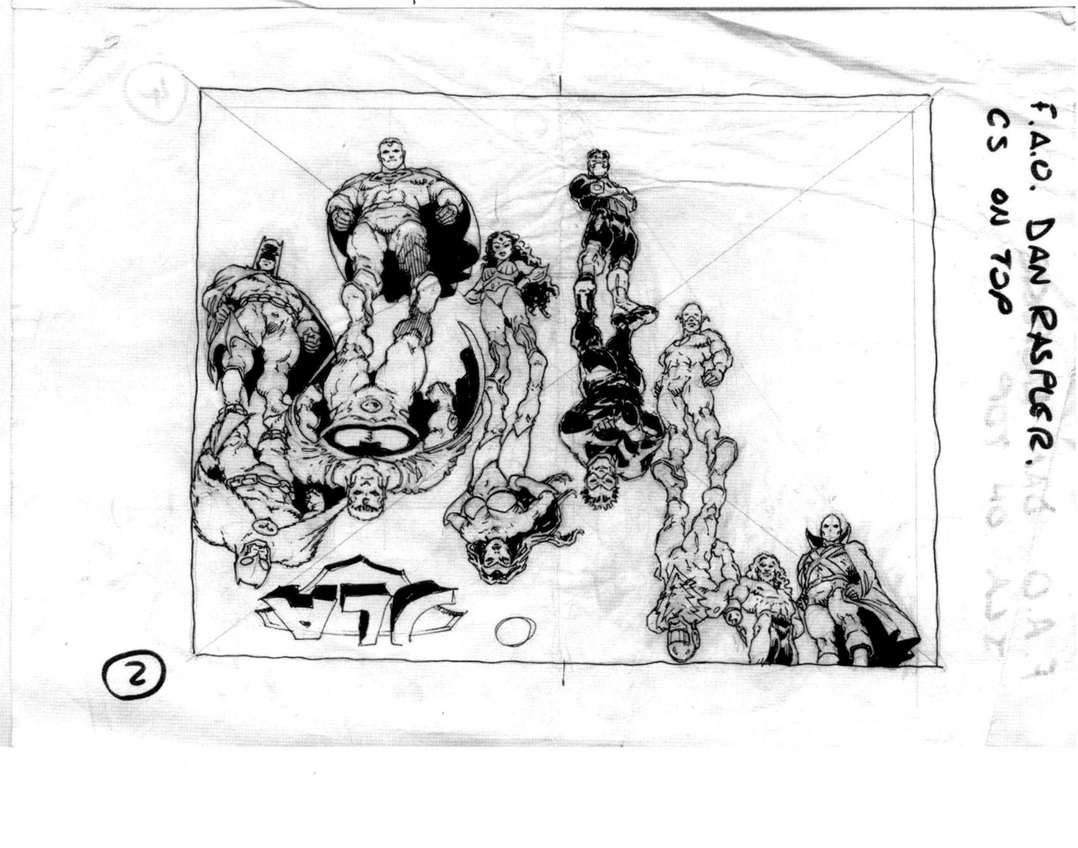
F.A.O. DAN RASPLER.
CS ON TOP
JLA
2

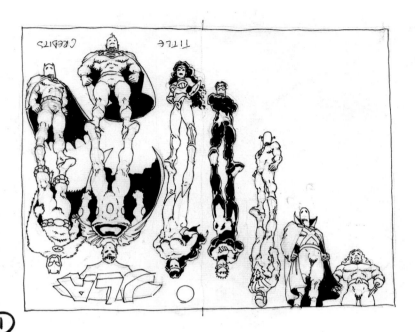

F.A.O. DAN RASPLER
CS ON TOP

CREDITS
TITLE
JLA

1

JLA

7

LADY JUSTICE ON DOME (OF HIGH COURT?)
ULTRAMAN SLEAZY EMBRACE
CITY (WHOLE WORLD) BURNING IN B/G
COULD BE SUPERMAN AT FIRST GLANCE -
'BAD SUPERMAN' STORIES ARE ALWAYS
ATTRACTIVE.

8

SLIGHT UPSHOT.
ULTRAMAN - BETTER
VIEW OF OUTFIT.
LOOKING AT US WITH
EVIL SMILE • HOLDING
THE SNAPPED - OFF
JUSTICE IN AN
ARCHETYPAL EMBRACE

THIS ONE'S BETTER.

F.A.O DAN
RASPLER

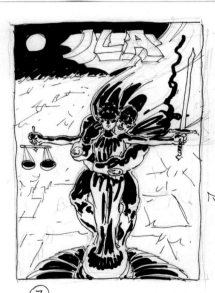

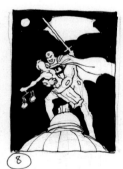

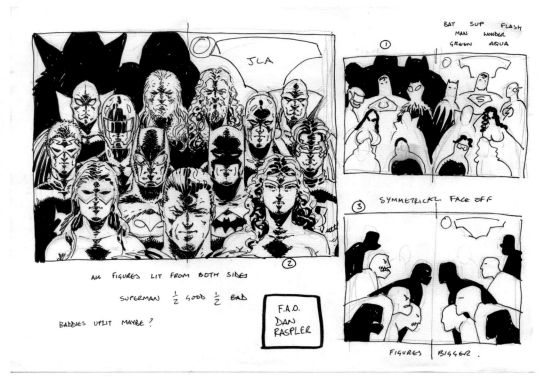

JLA

BAT SUP FLASH
MAN WONDER
GREEN AQUA

①

②

SYMMETRICAL FACE OFF

③

ALL FIGURES LIT FROM BOTH SIDES

SUPERMAN ½ GOOD ½ BAD

BADDIES UPLIT MAYBE?

F.A.O.
DAN
RASPLER

FIGURES BIGGER.

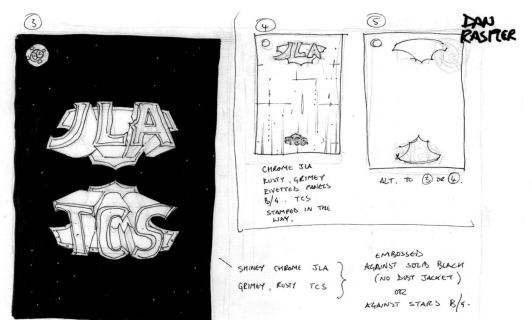

③

④

⑤

DAN
RASPLER

CHROME JLA
RUSTY, GRIMEY
RIVETTED PANELS
B/G. TCS
STAMPED IN THE
WAY.

ALT. TO ③ OR ④.

SHINEY CHROME JLA
GRIMEY, RUSTY TCS

EMBOSSED
AGAINST SOLID BLACK
(NO DUST JACKET)
OR
AGAINST STARS B/G.

grant **MORRISON**

has been working with DC Comics for twenty-five years, beginning his American comics career with acclaimed runs on ANIMAL MAN and DOOM PATROL. Since then he has written such best-selling series as JLA, BATMAN and *New X-Men*, as well as such creator-owned works as THE INVISIBLES, SEAGUY, THE FILTH, WE3 and JOE THE BARBARIAN. In addition to expanding the DC Universe through titles ranging from the Eisner Award-winning SEVEN SOLDIERS and ALL-STAR SUPERMAN to the reality-shattering epic of FINAL CRISIS, he has also reinvented the worlds of the Dark Knight Detective in BATMAN AND ROBIN and BATMAN, INCORPORATED and the Man of Steel for the all-new ACTION COMICS.

In his secret identity, Morrison is a "counterculture" spokes-person, a musician, an award-winning playwright and a chaos magician. He is also the author of the New York Times bestseller Supergods, a groundbreaking psycho-historic mapping of the superhero as a cultural organism. He divides his time between his homes in Los Angeles and Scotland.

frank **QUITELY**

was born in Glasgow in 1968. Since 1988 he's drawn *The Greens* (self-published), *Blackheart*, *Missionary Man*, *Shimura*, *Inaba*, ten shorts for Paradox Press, six shorts for Vertigo, FLEX MENTALLO, 20/20 VISIONS, BATMAN: THE SCOTTISH CONNECTION, THE KINGDOM: OFFSPRING, JLA: EARTH 2, THE INVISIBLES, TRANSMETROPOLITAN, THE AUTHORITY, *Captain America*, *New X-Men*, THE SANDMAN: ENDLESS NIGHTS, WE3, ALL-STAR SUPERMAN and BATMAN AND ROBIN. He has also created covers for *Negative Burn*, *Judge Dredd Megazine*, *Classic 2000 AD*, JONAH HEX, BOOKS OF MAGICK: LIFE DURING WARTIME, BITE CLUB, AMERICAN VIRGIN and ALL-STAR BATMAN. He lives in Glasgow with his wife and three children. He used to design his own hats and clothing. Currently his favorite hobby is cooking.